Faith and Culture

african christian studies series (africs)

This series will make available significant works in the field of African Christian studies, taking into account the many forms of Christianity across the whole continent of Africa. African Christian studies is defined here as any scholarship that relates to themes and issues on the history, nature, identity, character, and place of African Christianity in world Christianity. It also refers to topics that address the continuing search for abundant life for Africans through multiple appeals to African religions and African Christianity in a challenging social context. The books in this series are expected to make significant contributions in historicizing trends in African Christian studies, while shifting the contemporary discourse in these areas from narrow theological concerns to a broader inter-disciplinary engagement with African religio-cultural traditions and Africa's challenging social context.

The series will cater to scholarly and educational texts in the areas of religious studies, theology, mission studies, biblical studies, philosophy, social justice, and other diverse issues current in African Christianity. We define these studies broadly and specifically as primarily focused on new voices, fresh perspectives, new approaches, and historical and cultural analyses that are emerging because of the significant place of African Christianity and African religio-cultural traditions in world Christianity. The series intends to continually fill a gap in African scholarship, especially in the areas of social analysis in African Christian studies, African philosophies, new biblical and narrative hermeneutical approaches to African theologies, and the challenges facing African women in today's Africa and within African Christianity. Other diverse themes in African Traditional Religions; African ecology; African ecclesiology; inter-cultural, inter-ethnic, and inter-religious dialogue; ecumenism; creative inculturation; African theologies of development, reconciliation, globalization, and poverty reduction will also be covered in this series.

SERIES EDITORS

Dr. Stan Chu Ilo (DePaul University, Chicago, USA)
Dr. Esther Acolatse (University of Toronto, Canada)
Dr. Mwenda Ntarangwi (Calvin College, Grand Rapids, MI, USA)

Faith and Culture

Elochukwu Uzukwu and the Making of
an African Sacramental Theology

EMMANUEL OSIGWE

FOREWORD BY
GEORGE WORGUL

PICKWICK Publications · Eugene, Oregon

FAITH AND CULTURE
Elochukwu Uzukwu and the Making of an African Sacramental Theology

African Christian Studies Series 20

Copyright © 2022 Emmanuel Osigwe. All rights reserved. Except for brief quotations in critical publications or reviews, no part of this book may be reproduced in any manner without prior written permission from the publisher. Write: Permissions, Wipf and Stock Publishers, 199 W. 8th Ave., Suite 3, Eugene, OR 97401.

Pickwick Publications
An Imprint of Wipf and Stock Publishers
199 W. 8th Ave., Suite 3
Eugene, OR 97401

www.wipfandstock.com

PAPERBACK ISBN: 978-1-6667-1000-7
HARDCOVER ISBN: 978-1-6667-1001-4
EBOOK ISBN: 978-1-6667-1002-1

Cataloguing-in-Publication data:

Names: Osigwe, Emmanuel, author. | Worgul, George, foreword.

Title: Faith and culture : Elochukwu Uzukwu and the making of an African sacramental theology / by Emmanuel Osigwe ; foreword by George Worgul.

Description: Eugene, OR: Pickwick Publications, 2022 | African Christian Studies Series 20 | Includes bibliographical references and index.

Identifiers: ISBN 978-1-6667-1000-7 (paperback) | ISBN 978-1-6667-1001-4 (hardcover) | ISBN 978-1-6667-1002-1 (ebook)

Subjects: LCSH: Uzukwu, E. Elochukwu. | Catholic Church—Africa. | Theology, Doctrinal—Africa.

Classification: BR1430 O85 2022 (print) | BR1430 (ebook)

12/01/22

To the memory of my father, Sylvester Osigwe (1938–2000), an extraordinary gentleman and teacher.

Contents

Foreword by George Worgul | ix
Preface | xi
Acknowledgements | xv
List of Abbreviations | xvii

Chapter 1
The Question of African Theology | 1

Chapter 2
History and Theology of Christian Sacraments | 11

Chapter 3
Anthropology and Sociology of Sacraments | 47

Chapter 4
Encountering Elochukwu Uzukwu and His Theology | 58

Chapter 5
Rethinking Sacraments through African Values System | 95

Chapter 6
Implications of Reimagining Sacraments | 123

Chapter 7
Uzukwu's Contributions to African Theology and Christian Thinking | 168

Conclusion | 179

Appendix | 183
Bibliography | 203
Index | 215

Foreword

EMMANUEL OSIGWE HAS OFFERED an excellent entry point for understanding the plethora of important issues and challenges faced by the many Christian community around the globe in the arenas of church mission and life. He accomplishes this challenge by focusing on one of the most important trailblazers in recent African Theology circles, Elochukwu Uzukwu, CSSp. This focus brings both breadth and depth to his text.

Uzukwu investigates a wide range of theological areas e.g., liturgy, sacraments, ecclesiology, mission theology, Christian anthropology, and pneumatology throughout his substantial scholarly undertakings. Engaging with Uzukwu's enterprise is to embrace an effort at systematic theology i.e., an appreciation of the whole of the theological enterprise and how its desperate dimensions are in fact profoundly interrelated. Simultaneously, Uzukwu's research focuses on primary texts and experiences. He asks radical questions and challenges many former assumptions tacitly accepted as true. Uzukwu's theology is deeply rooted in the history, ritual, social lives, and living experience of concrete people.

Moreover, Osigwe chose well in concentrating on the ecclesial/sacramental nexus which is central to Uzukwu's enterprise. Such a centrality is not happenstance. Rather it appreciates the deep and crucial role that ritual plays in the life of all peoples and every culture. Ritual action, prayer, season, and materials disclose who a people are and how they make meaning of their shared lives. Ritual is the key hermeneutical tool in grasping the core convictions and the social practices and contours of any people. The health and power of a people's ritual is an excellent indicator of their cultural sustainability and a predictor of their future.

Osigwe does well to contextualize Uzukwu's theology in the dynamic theology emerging before and during the Second Vatican Council. Uzukwu is clearly a proponent of Vatican II and more. He understands and implements the council in his thought as an African who understands the history of western theology as well as the religiosity and dynamics of his African experiences and traditions. Osigwe carries on this enterprise as he illustrates how non-Africans can learn much from the African experience. In this way, Osigwe unfolds a very dynamic vision of inculturation, a vision continually underscored in the writings of Pope Francis.

Osigwe's work is courageous. He takes up the huge task of overcoming theological intellectual imperialism, whether unconscious or conscious. Until the intellectual imperialism of coloniality is rejected, it will be difficult if not impossible to create truly inculturated theology and truly inculturated worship. The privilege long afforded to western thought patterns and ideas must be relativized. Room must be made to listen to the authentic experience of lived faith present in African and all nonwestern cultural communities and their traditions. Osigwe's text help make room for the needed discussion and dialogue. There is much to learn by the west from other traditions. Osigwe's text helps us to understand better Africa's contributions and to move forward in open dialogue and mutual enrichment.

George Worgul Jr
Duquesne University

Preface

THIS TEXT IS PRODUCED from my doctoral dissertation in systematic theology at Duquesne University, Pittsburgh, Pennsylvania. Drawing upon the provisions of the Second Vatican Council and in dialogue with Elochukwu Uzukwu, the foremost African sacramental theologian, it reexamines sacraments through the lens of African culture, as a way of contextualizing and making the sacramental rituals more meaningful and relevant. The phenomenal growth of the church in Africa in post Vatican II era indicates the nexus.

A part of the work is being published as a chapter in the forthcoming book on the theology of Elochukwu Uzukwu. Another result of the research has been published in the *International Journal of African Catholicism*. The book employs interdisciplinary studies and focuses on the appropriation of African culture and anthropology to develop an African sacramental theology.

Recognition of the indispensable intersection of faith and culture has become an essential trend in contemporary theology. This renewed approach emphasizes various anthropologies and cultures as locations of divine activity. The Second Vatican Council's understanding of sacraments as pneumatological and ecclesiological, beyond the dominant Christological motif, and its call for profound adaptation give a wide latitude for rethinking the sacraments. This provision overcomes the danger of a monocultural model of sacramental celebration. Such a monolithic model submerges local voices and separate sacramentality from symbols and values that resonate with various anthropologies and cultures.

This book applies Vatican II's opening to non-Western cultures and how Uzukwu utilizes this provision in conjunction with resources from African traditional wisdom and culture to enhance a true border crossing of sacramental reasoning and celebrations. To think of sacraments from this perspective highlights African values of community life and views of the body, particularly its penchant for expressive worship, and its dominant philosophy of relationality. These virtues seek to bridge the disconnect, often experienced, between sacraments and ethics, thereby overcoming the danger of mere ritualism and make sacraments more relevant.

This approach finds a strong appeal to the long history of adapting anthropologies and sociological models to express the reality of the Christian experience. Reinterpreting sacraments in this way is a practical mission of the church, with implications that resonate with authentic Christian life. The centrality of the sacraments as rituals of encounter with God, resonating with cultural expression without negating the purely Christological dimension, makes the sacraments more meaningful and realistic.

Methodology and Chapter Overview

The methodology for this book encompasses historical, sociological, and anthropological dimensions, since an honest reflection on the sacraments involves these aspects in building a theology relevant to African contexts. Toward this end, chapter one answers the question of the reality and development of African theology. I consider this chapter a necessary starting point by engaging in historical excursus of theological exercise. Although Africa is a large content, we seek to decipher commonalities that allow us to speak of African theology. The second chapter discusses the history and theology of the Christian sacraments. It sets the historical foundation for a work that reimagines the sacramental thinking and establishes the meaning and development of the sacraments culminating in the work of the Scholastics and the Second Vatican Council's position on the sacraments. In the third chapter, I examine the anthropological and sociological dimensions that constitute sacraments, further providing the necessary foundation for rethinking the sacraments from other cultural perspectives. The chapter examines the reality of Christian sacraments

PREFACE

from their Jewish roots, highlighting the Greco-Roman influence, further demonstrating divine gratuity in his self-donation.

In the fourth chapter, I engage the theological methodology of Uzukwu and demonstrate why I have chosen him as a dialogue partner in this book. It delves into his basic worldview, which significantly informs his theological trajectory. As a post-Vatican II student and scholar, Uzukwu responds to the impact of the changes in Catholic theology, and I examine how this is exemplified in his graduate theological studies. This chapter develops Vatican II's rediscovery of the idea of local church by retrieving patristic theology. Indeed, this approach constitutes a major theological motif of Uzukwu, an essential foundation for the possibility of diverse and plurality of theology in response to the contemporary acknowledgement of theologies.

The fifth chapter rethinks sacraments through peculiar African cultural values and the interface of faith and culture. It retrieves and reinterprets sacramental liturgical expressions through the African value system. To arrive at this experience, it reexamines Vatican II's call for profound adaptation while engaging contemporary studies on rituals and symbols of sacraments. It also engages sacraments as passage rites. It explores Uzukwu's position and trajectory for inculturation. It gives expression to his role in the development of a liturgy that is truly Christian and truly African, engaging the African proclivity for expressive worship. Beyond this, his emphasis on eucharistic celebrations and other sacraments in a way that engages the sacred traditional ritual feature prominently. The chapter recalls his attempts at retrieving the Judeo-Christian foundations for the development of African Christian liturgical and sacramental theology. Finally, it demonstrates the connection he intends to create between the sacraments and Christian life.

The sixth chapter articulates implications of rethinking the sacraments in three significant areas of theology: liturgical and sacramental theology, ecclesiology, and pneumatology. These areas, which received ample attention at the Second Vatican Council, constitute the tripod on which Uzukwu's theology stands.

The seventh chapter undertakes an appraisal of Uzukwu's theological enterprise and highlights areas of further theological reflection and his contribution to African theology and global Christianity. It begins by stating the major areas of the previous chapters, leading to a general conclusion. Uzukwu's contributions to contemporary African theology significantly advance theological thinking.

Acknowledgments

TO THE TRINITARIAN GOD and the foundation of relationships, I am eternally grateful for the strength to accomplish this project.

I express my profound and respectful gratitude to my local ordinary, Most Reverend Camillus Etokudoh, for sending me to engage in advanced studies in systematic theology and for paternal support. I am particularly grateful to His Excellency Most Reverend Samuel J. Aquila, the Archbishop of Denver, and his excellent team of collaborators for welcoming me to his diocese and for the conducive atmosphere to enhance my spiritual and academic life. Indeed, the presbyterate of the archdiocese is the universal church in miniature.

My indebtedness goes particularly to professor George S. Worgul for his skillful academic guidance and directing my dissertation as chair of the dissertation committee. To the other members of my dissertation committee, professor Marinus Iwuchukwu, professor Radu Bordeianu, I remain grateful for shaping the work in a scholarly manner and ensuring timely completion of the dissertation. To other faculties who shaped my thinking in theology, especially professor Gerald Boodoo, professor William Wright IV, professor Anna Scheid, professor Maureen O'Brien, professor Marie Baird, and professor Elizabeth Cochran, I am deeply grateful for your expertise and generosity. In the same vein, I am incredibly grateful to professor Elochukwu Uzukwu for providing me with all his publications and granting numerous interviews as I was writing this work.

ACKNOWLEDGMENTS

I have enjoyed the support of numerous friends during my studies and the writing of the book. I want to mention a few of them: Rev. Walt Rydzon, Mike Jubick, Linda Boss, Elaine Beck, Larry Beardsley, Vicki and Fred Menzer, Nancy and Dudley Mitchell, Elizabeth Neela Okurut, and Rev. Rocco Porter.

Finally, I would like to extend my appreciation to my Mother, Florence Osigwe, my Father, Sylvester Osigwe, my siblings, and relatives for their immense warmth of love and encouragement.

Abbreviations

AA	*Apostolicam Actuositatem*
AG	*Ad Gentes*
AMECEA	Association of Member Episcopal Conferences of East Africa
CB/CBN	Catholic Bishops' Conference of Nigeria
ed./eds.	Editor/Editors
et al.	*et alii/et alia* (and other persons)
etc.	et cetera
GS	*Gaudium et spes*
LG	*Lumen Gentium*
NA	*Nostra Aetate*
PO	*Presbyterorum ordinis*
SC	*Sacrosanctum Concilium*
UR	*Unitatis redintegratio*

Chapter 1

The Question of African Theology

Introduction

THE INTERACTION OF FAITH and culture, the divine and the human, characterizes theological reflection. Faith in God's divine revelation requires the human response. To be a realistic interaction, the universal must engage the concrete historical realities and contexts of the faith. The Christ event—the incarnation, is determinative of what Christians think about Christ as a foundational question of every generation and the source of the ultimate answers to the human situation. Each generation must ask itself anew the question of the identity of Christ and its implications for the community of believers living at different historical and spatial locations. This constant reevaluation implies, as Pope Paul VI states in *Evangelii Nuntiandi*, that Christ and his kingdom must be the constant in Christian life.

Why African Theology

African theology represents the body of theological endeavors that, inspired by and in the light of the Christian faith, engage the realities of life in Africa. African theology engages the political, historical, economic, cultural, and religious experiences of the people in response to the Christian demand. Such contextual theology becomes possible with recognition of the diversity and the cultural plurality of the mid-twentieth century. Thus, the cultural and theological shifts of the 1950s and 60s, particularly the affirmation of identities beyond the earlier missionary and colonial definitions have given a strong encouragement to more realistic theological production in Sub Saharan Africa. In a sense, the formal recognition of voices from the southern hemisphere in response to their situations, often different from the experience of the North Atlantic as a valid theological response. Particularly for sub-Saharan Africa, negritude, the pan African movement that united Africans around a common cause to reaffirm their identities in the waning moments of colonial occupation defines a new beginning in theological reflection especially. African theology, therefore, engages the people's political, cultural, economic, and religious experience. Bolaji Idowu, a Nigerian religious scholar, gives a definition that captures the *raison d'e etre* of African theology: "We seek, in effect, to discover in what way the Christian faith could best be presented, interpreted, and inculcated in Africa so that Africans will hear God in Jesus Christ addressing himself immediately to them in their own native situation and particular circumstances."[1] One clearly understands Idowu's use of the "African native situation" as encompassing political, economics, cultures and the beginnings of a realistic African self-determination.

One must acknowledge that theology in Africa, broadly speaking, predates its academic dimension, which is a twentieth century reality. Just as for the early Christians, liturgy, hymns, and icons embody some theology in the same way that pre-academic African Christian theology existed long before the formal emergence of academic African Christian theology.[2] This pre-formal African theology can be found in the early hymns, carvings, and translations of Christian liturgical books into indigenous languages of Africa. The missionaries' interpreters and translators certainly had theology, and indeed, the daily struggles of African Christians in living the faith involves theology.[3] Beyond these, one must recognize that the theological and sociocultural shifts of the twentieth century have given theology in African a phenomenal boost.

The central challenge of African theology, within which Uzukwu's theology emerges, is the incarnation of the Gospel in Africa, in "such a way that it becomes the motivation for action."[4] With its strongly entrenched

---

1. Idowu, "Introduction," 8.
2. Odozor, *Morality*, 25–26.
3. Odozor, *Morality*, 26.
4. See Paul VI, *Evangelii Nuntiandi*, 22; John Paul II, *Ecclesia in Africa*, 3. This idea is also traceable to the position of the Second Vatican Council. See LG 11; NA 22; AG 9.

cultural and religious practices, theology in Africa becomes a way to engage the realities of African life through the light of the Christian faith. We can therefore safely locate Uzukwu's theological endeavor within the current theological and pastoral orientation of the church. Uzukwu, to this researcher's mind, represents an unfaltering fount of theological production from an African Roman Catholic theological perspective.

Methodologically therefore, African theology involves a different epistemological approach from the dominant Western theologies. It is precisely such a discontinuity that gives rise to the emergence and relevance of contextual theologies. A monocultural and monolithic theology will at best remain sterile outside the domains of its provenance, and at worse, will become oppressive and counterproductive. The local or contextual nature of every theology, though a novelty, calls for this break if theology is to become relevant and responsive to the multiplicity of contexts. Nevertheless, the epistemological break does not take away from the one faith which constitutes a basic provision of theology from outside the dominant tradition.

A dominant factor was the overwhelming influence of the prevailing political system, which found its way into the ecclesiology. Through historical analysis, the dominant European powers of the time, interested in expansionist agendas, acquired a papal mandate to evangelize the southern hemisphere.[5] Consequently two dissimilar, yet not necessarily opposing, interests converged in the colonization and evangelization of sub-Saharan Africa. The missionary drive of the second millennium closely followed the expansionist agenda of the empire, and local voices, cultures, and religions inevitably became displaced or under emphasized. Uzukwu has captured the ensuing ideology well,

> The colonial and missionary ideology had as [its] ultimate aim the changing of the identity of the colonized and evangelized. In those situations where nationalistic and evangelical interests were consciously merged, the deep-seated exploitative colonial program along with the then European prejudice against Africans failed to be lucidly examined by the missionaries.[6]

The theology of mission during that timeframe was clearly that of planting the Western church wherever the explorers went, closely following the

---

5. Richard Gray has documented the history of Christianity and the role of the Papacy in Africa. The papal bull ceding to Portugal and Spain areas south of the Sahara for exploration, colonization, and evangelization is a case in point. See Gray, *Christianity*.

6. Uzukwu, *A Listening Church*, 4.

conquest mentality of mere explorers and colonialists. Consequently, "the conquest paradigm for the church mission was still operative inasmuch as missionaries generally disparaged local cultures and sought to purge indigenous peoples of their cultural heritage as a precondition to receiving the Gospel."[7] In fact, Ikenga Metuh has argued that it was the intolerant stance of missionaries toward the new African converts, who wanted to introduce their indigenous traditional and cultural elements into Christianity that led to the proliferation of Afro-Christian indigenous churches.[8] Interestingly, the early church seems to have adopted indigenous practices to express the nascent faith. Elizabeth Isichei articulates this point clearly, "Wherever Christianity is professed, there is a constant dialectic arising in its relationship with the cultural presuppositions and practices of the cultures where it is located. Christianity came to sub-Saharan Africa in European cultural packaging, and contextualization."[9] This situation challenges the extent of border crossing that Christianity accommodates in its evangelization stride. In this narrative, we see the demise of local voices, and local churches, and the complete disavowal of the validity of indigenous traditions; however, Uzukwu notes the limited awareness of cultural differences as partly responsible for the missionary malpractice of the time.

The sixteenth through the nineteenth centuries were marked by massive discovery and expansion of European territories and missionary evangelization outside Europe. The historical developments within this period often left the church with an unclear missionary paradigm and equivocal responses to the Enlightenment and the ongoing changes in society. The emergence of modern science and the new forms of philosophy that were inconsistent with traditional Catholic thinking posed enormous challenges to theology. The result was a withdrawal from the world (no dialogue), with society and modernity exemplified by the budding of missionary outposts.

This was precisely the era of the missionary evangelization of West Africa. Historical facts that converged, mainly, colonialism and the slave trade, did not work for the good or proper incarnation of the Gospel. Philip Jenkins has argued that the twin evils of colonialism and imperialism were the vehicles for the presentation of the Gospel during that time.[10]

---

7. Gailladertz, *Ecclesiology for a Global Church*, 43.

8. Metuh, "Incarnating Christianity," 9. See also Uzukwu, *Worship as Body Language*, 28.

9. Isichei, *A History of Christianity in Africa*, 4.

10. Wickeri, "Mission from the Margins," 186.

The relationship between the Gospel and new areas of evangelization was marked by condemnation, derogation, and downright denial of any good human value. This situation coalesced with the other practices of the time, such as physical occupation and ideological manipulation.

Thus, the exclusivism that ensued characterized the Catholic position until modern times.[11] To say the least, this brand of missioning was largely inseparable from other historical indicators of its time. This interaction between evangelization and colonial mentality is often established by the fact that theology builds on prevailing philosophy. Hence, the irresistible drive to civilize and replicate itself in the missionaries led to the eclipse and loss of local churches. Consequently, in the view of Walter Mignolo, there was the collapse of the colonial difference.[12]

One must also consider the demographic shift of the center of Christianity from the industrial North to the global South. Several authors articulate reasons for this phenomenal rise and growth of the Christian faith in unfamiliar lands.[13] Interestingly, the former mission churches could now make contributions to enrich the church universal in a spirit of exchange of charity.

The Significance of Vatican II for the Church in Africa

The phenomenal growth of the church in Africa owes to a multiplicity of factors, as have been identified. But beyond the political and cultural shifts we must underscore the immense significance of the Second Vatican Council. The council's retrieval of the Patristic theological models of unity in diversity

---

11. To be precise the expression *extra ecclesiam nulla salus* (outside the church, no salvation), attributed to Saint Cyprian seems to have played a crucial theological role. See Theisen, *The Ultimate Church and the Promise of Salvation*; D'Costa, "Extra Ecclesiam Nulla Salus Revisited." Every era appears to have uncritically adopted the aphorism without engaging the time and context of its emergence. Unfortunately, this understanding has undergirded the relationship between the church and cultures until contemporary times. The church, while holding in abeyance other non-Christian cultures, did not pay attention to the fact the "Christian" culture emerged from the appropriation of local cultures, reinterpreting the same in the light of the Gospel.

12. "Colonial difference" as used in this context indicates the meeting point of local history and global design, which ordinarily should give birth to a new culture, where global designs have to be adapted, reintegrated. In a sense, a dialogue between the cultures, between the missionary drive and indigenous wisdom, was not to be in West African evangelization. See Mignolo, *Local Histories*, ix.

13. Buhlmann, *The Coming of the Third Church*; Allen, *The Future Church*.

demonstrates this *ressourcement and aggiornamento* and openness to different cultures beyond the one culture that has been associated with Christianity. The council recognized differences in cultures,[14] and this new development portends an acceptance of "cultural pluralism by the Catholic Church; the universality of the Church was no longer considered in terms of monocultural uniformity, but of cultural diversity in a bond of communion."[15] No doubt these shifts significantly affect Catholic theology generally and give rise to the formal recognition of contextual theology.

A clear impact of Vatican II on African Catholic theology is the emphasis on inculturation as a major theological trend. In fact, *Ecclesia in Africa*, John Paul II's exhortation on the *Church in Africa*, considers inculturation to be "one of the greatest challenges facing the church on the Continent on the eve of the Third Millennium."[16] Inculturation becomes a necessary evangelization strategy to give a Christian response to contemporary African issues, and, importantly, to rewrite the perceived missionary negligence. Expressing the sentiments of most African theologians, Laurenti Magesa, a Kenyan theologian, unequivocally states, "Contact between Christianity and African religion has historically been predominantly a monologue, bedeviled by assumptions prejudicial to the latter, with Christianity culturally more vocal and ideologically more aggressive."[17] One must not, however, deprecate the pre-Vatican II theological orientation outside of its historical context. The emphasis is really on the shifts we have been discussing. Nevertheless, it is important to listen to the past theological and missional paradigms as a guide for the future. It may be important to state,

> In the colonial era Africans were made to feel ashamed of their culture. They were made to accept alien values and alien ways. They were completely passive. Their very being was conferred on them from outside. Today, there must be a complete break with the mentality of the past, with the inferiority complex of Africans in the colonial period. A deep decolonization must take place at the level of culture.[18]

African theologians have been motivated by the conciliar openness to and appreciation of cultures and non-Christian religions to investigate

14. AG 6.
15. Olikenyi, *African Hospitality*, 21.
16. John Paul II, *Ecclesia in Africa*, 3.
17. Magesa, *African Religion*, 5.
18. Shorter, *African Christian Spirituality*, 21.

ways of giving Christianity an African face and coloration by incorporating into their theological reflections and research the beauty and insights of African traditions and cultures. This is an important aspect of decolonization. According to Paulinus Odozor, "Perhaps the greatest achievement of African theology in this regard since Vatican II has been to remind the church of a somewhat forgotten truth, namely that all theologies are contextual and the product of the circumstances within which they arise."[19] Nevertheless, contextual understanding and access to the divine revelation do not negate the unity in God's self-revealing love and the dialogue that should exist among different cultural theologies.

Particularly, this work engages the theology of Uzukwu. I have chosen to focus on Uzukwu for two basic reasons. First, his interest in the intersection between Christianity and indigenous cultures remains profound, if not unparalleled, from an African sacramental theological perspective. His theological trajectory can be framed in the following question: how can Christianity become more relevant and truly a way of life through symbols that are familiar to contexts? This is a delicate and important aspect of theology since theology from the beginning has reinterpreted borrowed categories from cultures in the light of the Christian faith. To retrieve this primordial theological undertone that was suppressed, or not fully implemented, during the evangelization of much of Africa, Uzukwu's theology engages Christianity as received through the Jewish-Western cultural elements in conversation with the African cultural context.

Uzukwu takes popes Paul VI and John Paul II seriously in their calls for inculturation[20] by creating liturgical and sacramental rites that acknowledge African proclivities. Hence, the first part of his theological endeavor is precisely on the development of rites that reflect an African sensibility, especially in worship. His doctoral dissertation, on "Blessing and Thanksgiving among the Igbo," and his work on liturgy proper, *Liturgy: Truly Christian, Truly African,* emphasize the indigenization of liturgy and

19. Odozor, *Morality*, 37.

20. In 1967, Pope Paul VI made the call for inculturation, stating that Africa has something to contribute to the Catholic Church, especially the African perception of the universe. See Paul VI, "Africae Terrarum"; John Paul II made a similar statement in 1980, when he expressed admiration for the African ancestral heritage, "Africa constitutes a real treasure-house of so many authentic human values. It is called upon to share these values with peoples and nations, and so to enrich the whole human family and all other cultures." Continuing further on the value of African tradition, he asserts that the Church is a body at home in all cultures, without identifying itself with any given culture. See John Paul II, "Address to the Bishops of Kenya," 5.

sacramental theology. He argues that various liturgical families always leave imprints of their sensibilities and the spirit of their provenances, which make their liturgy responsive and relevant to their times and places. This is precisely what he intends to achieve for the contemporary church in Africa. He undertakes a deep study of the history or genesis of liturgical rites and underscores the coexistence of multiple rites, each regarded as valid, during the early times of the church. The suppression of rites during the Middle Ages remains in contrast to the attitude of the pristine ecclesiology, for example, and respect for rites was restored by the Second Vatican Council. With its general attitude of openness to non-Western cultures, the council restored respect for indigenous voices (rites) and made room for plurality in recognition of the beauty of difference.

Tracing the origin of the Roman liturgy, Uzukwu underlines the gradual progress from improvised written texts to the compilation of texts of successive popes into the modern-day sacramentaries.[21] These rites, to a large extent, reflect the cultural differences of their provenance. Consequently, having a liturgical expression that is properly African, Uzukwu argues, not only will be contributing to the beauty of the universal church, but will also make the Roman Catholic liturgy more relevant to the African spirit.[22] This approach, according to Uzukwu, would be a return to the patristic position on the multiplicity of rites, insofar as true doctrine and central Christian faith are preserved.

Recalling the positions of the Second Vatican Council, popes Paul VI and John Paul II, Uzukwu underscores the attitude of deep respect for traditions that are not opposed to Christian practice. According to the council, "In the liturgy, the Church has no wish to impose a rigid uniformity in matters which do not involve the faith or the good of the whole community. Rather, she respects and fosters the spiritual adornments and gifts of various races."[23]

Unlike previous councils, Vatican II's position, which appears revolutionary, has given a new lease on life for liturgy that is relevant and more meaningful; however, according to Uzukwu, the caveat on maintaining the substantial unity of the Roman rite while encouraging racial and regional inculturation appears to weaken the earlier expressed position of the council in favor of the recognition of the beauty and adornment of various

21. Uzukwu, *Liturgy*, 17.
22. Uzukwu, *Liturgy*, 3.
23. SC 37.

rites.[24] More precisely, Uzukwu, relying on the openness of the council and the openness of popes Paul VI and John Paul II, argues against mere adaptation in favor of a "new Christian African culture," which liturgically he calls "African rites."[25] To this extent, inculturation of the rituals becomes a delicate but essential aspect of contemporary theology.

Inculturation as a term, though a neologism, characterizes the story of Christianity. On this account, James Hitchcock avers, "the entire history of the Church is really the history of inculturation, which occurs continuously, whether or not consciously. This must occur to make the Gospel meaningful, even though it carries the risk of betraying the Gospel."[26] To Uzukwu's mind, the incarnation in a particular cultural location, which has been deeply appropriated by Greek thinking and the Christian West, should speak adequately and in proper terms to the peoples of Africa. In his seminal work, his doctoral thesis, he studied the development of the eucharistic prayer with African contexts in mind. His subsequent works have concentrated on the emergence of a Christianity that can respond more adequately to African issues and concerns.

The independence of most African nations in the twentieth century and the Vatican II event have had wide implications for Christian theology in sub-Saharan Africa, especially the emergence of a recognizable systematic theological reflection in the region. Consequently, African theology is making a significant contribution to theological method by its dialogical relationship with indigenous religions and "distant" theologies. However, in the opinion of Kwame Bediako, a Ghanaian theologian, "African theology may have been charting a new course in theological method. It is not that this discourse has no parallel in the totality of Christian scholarship. . . . Rather, this new theological approach has no counterpart in the more recent Western theological thought forged within the context of Christendom."[27]

---

24. SC 38.

25. Uzukwu, *Liturgy*, 22.

26. Hitchcock, *History of the Catholic Church*, 15. He notes that inculturation has always been part and parcel of the Church, with its adoption of elements, cultures and practices that were once termed pagan.

27. Bediako, *Jesus and the Gospel in Africa*, 53.

Conclusion

This chapter demonstrates the inevitable anthropological foundation of sacraments—symbols and gestural behaviors, which has ethnic basis. it examined how gestural behaviors interact with the divine to reenact foundational events and stories of a community. Further, it presents the performative dimension of language beyond its instrumental perspective. Ritual language, therefore, realize what it celebrates. While the Christian faith cannot be reduced to its anthropological and phenomenological expressions, they remain important in realizing a relevant and realistic community.

Chapter 2

History and Theology of Christian Sacraments

Introduction

To SITUATE OUR ENGAGEMENT with sacramental theology, this chapter presents a brief history and theology of the Christian sacraments from a Roman Catholic perspective. The historical development of the sacraments reveals not only the Christological dimension that has been dominant in Roman Catholic sacramentology, but also anthropological and sociological perspectives. Indeed, the phenomenology of the Christian sacraments has enriched the meaning and relevance of the sacraments to practical Christian living. It has overcome mere ritualism, which is often disconnected from indigenous cultural frameworks. Consequently, the current disposition of the church,[1] in post-Vatican II sacramentology, makes it possible to reimagine the sacraments from various anthropological loci. It is from this perspective that our exploration of Uzukwu's contribution becomes a project consistent with the current theological orientation of the church, which recognizes the diversity and cultural plurality that characterize all humankind.

---

1. The Second Vatican Council (1962–65) recognized the need to express the faith in varied cultural patterns and affirmed the possibility of rethinking the sacraments. It asserted, "The Church has existed through the centuries in varying circumstances and has utilized the resources of different cultures in its preaching to explain the message of Christ, to examine and understand it more deeply, and to express it more perfectly in the liturgy and in various aspects of the life of the faithful." See GS 58 in Flannery, *Vatican Council II*.

Methodologically, this chapter demonstrates the incorporation of the concept of Christian sacraments from the Jewish religious and cultural worldview as a necessary starting point of the budding of Christian identity. It further presents the rethinking of the sacraments from the Jewish to the Greco-Roman conceptual framework, as Christianity moved from Jerusalem to the Hellenistic world. This procedure presents eloquent instances of the possibility and malleability of the divine self-unfolding through various human cultural frameworks. Hence, the mediation of the divine is not limited or tied to any particular thought system or cultural paradigm.

The chapter, therefore, lays the foundation for exploring Uzukwu's efforts in reimagining the sacraments, and concludes by introducing postmodern sacramental theology, which critiques the traditional understanding of the sacraments and illustrates the relative inadequacy of any particular philosophical or theological system in mediating the divine (which cannot be circumscribed or constrained to a formula), and the danger of a monolithic theological approach. The critique of the traditional sacramental thinking and the express openness of the Second Vatican Council to non-Western cultures are positive motifs that underscore the significance of this project.

A Brief History of the Concept of Sacrament

The emergence of the Christian concept of sacrament is an instance of the appropriation of an existing (Jewish) narrative and conventional religious practice of the infant church. To think of the possibility of human relationship with God involves some level of mediation, since the mode of divine existence is radically different from that of humans. Theologically, revelation then involves the free self-disclosure of God to humans according to human (finite) capacity. The incarnation of Jesus in a particular human culture illustrates this point clearly. By adopting cultures akin to human society, the "totally other" acquiesces with the sociological and anthropological make-up of a particular people. Herbert Vorgrimler expresses this idea well in asserting, "Sacramental structures and events characterize the history of God with human beings from the beginning, i.e., as long as humans have existed, and therefore they are formative for all areas of theology, since theology is constructed in the form of salvation history."[2] In this way, God's transcendence is nuanced and mediated by his sacramental presence. Yet

2. Vorgrimler, *Sacramental Theology*, 3.

the sacraments do not exhaust God's self, since they communicate God's love and graciousness to humankind in limited cultural terms. Thus the idea of the sacred that sacraments convey inevitably uses cultural (and secular) categories in realizing the presence of the divine; however, we must posit faith as an essential precondition for assent to divine mediation (revelation), the foundation of sacramental possibility.[3]

In further examination of sacramental mediation of the divine, Joseph Martos argues that every religion makes use of sacraments, although with different names for the reality of sacraments, since no other religion has borrowed its theological words from classical and medieval Latin as has the Catholic Church.[4] Before its adoption by the early church to describe the mystery of the revelation of Christ, the term *sacramentum* served to describe a pledge (of money or property) deposited in the temple by parties in a lawsuit. Consequently, the pledge was forfeited by the party that lost the lawsuit.[5] *Sacramentum* also described an oath of allegiance made by soldiers to their commander and the gods of Rome. From these, we see that *sacramentum* obviously had a religious undertone.[6]

The Christian writers of the second century used the term *sacramentum* to describe the initiation of neophytes into the Christian religion, by which they pledged allegiance to Christ and life of service to God.[7] More precisely, Tertullian (160–220), is credited with being the first Christian writer in the second century to use the Latin *sacramentum* to translate the Greek *musterion*,[8] (μυστήριον), which connotes the idea of a hidden reality, or secret doctrine.[9] In this sense, we can appreciate the Pauline use of *mystery* to describe God's revelation in Christ,[10] for there was no way to gain coherent access to God and his Christ without God's self-revelation, which depended absolutely on God's gratuitousness; indeed, a privilege. However, in contrast to *sacramentum*, the Latin *mysterium* had a much broader

---

3. Vorgrimler, *Sacramental Theology*, 3.
4. Martos, *Doors to the Sacred*, 3.
5. Martos, *Doors to the Sacred*, 3.
6. Martos, *Doors to the Sacred*, 3.
7. Martos, *Doors to the Sacred*, 4.
8. See Martos, *Doors to the Sacred*, 29. See also Osborne, *A General Introduction*, 21–22.
9. See "Mustérion."
10. For the Pauline use of the term mystery see 1 Cor 2:7.8; Rom 16:25; Col 4:3; Eph 3:3, 4; 5:32.

spectrum: it translated the mystery of things beyond human comprehension that were made available to the human mind by the light of faith, and not any specific Christian acts or rituals. Put differently, *mysterium* expresses the mysteries of the Christian faith generally.[11] *Sacramentum*, in contrast, expresses the specific Christian rituals, the seven sacraments, as conclusively defined in the Middle Ages.[12]

In all of this, we can easily see the influence of Greek thought-forms and cultural worldviews in expressing the reality of the Christian sacraments. In fact, in the fifth century, Saint Augustine of Hippo (354–430) gave a seminal definition of *sacramentum* that has been consistent in the history of the Latin sacramental tradition as a sign (*signum*) of sacred reality (*res*).[13] The sign was the appearance, while the reality was hidden and not visible or perceptible to the senses. John Chrysostom corroborates this idea by insisting that "a mystery is present when we realize that something exists beyond the things that we are looking at."[14] Arguably, appearance and reality of the Platonic and Neo-Platonic philosophical tradition had supplied the conceptual framework for the description of the Christian sacrament. The metaphysics of *Being* as *One and transcendent* makes the presence of *Being* available only through signs,[15] which again, engages the visible matter. By the twelfth century, the usage of the term *sacramentum* was restricted to seven church rituals, and later by Protestant reformers of the sixteenth century to two or three. The Council of Trent (1545–60), however, reaffirmed the church's definition of the sacraments and the fixed number of ritual acts that are aptly called the sacraments as seven.

Other uses of the term within human sciences and religion convey the idea of a reality hidden, beyond symbolization. To this extent, "Any ritual or object, person or place, can be considered sacramental if it is taken to be a symbol of something that is sacred or mysterious."[16] This broad understanding has the advantage of safeguarding the precise ritual acts through which the divine is experienced, without limiting the possibility of manifold other encounters with God. It may be important to add that

---

11. Vorgrimler, *Sacramental Theology*, 44.

12. Vorgrimler, *Sacramental Theology*, 52–53.

13. St. Augustine, *Letter 138*, 1, cited in Martos, *Doors to the Sacred*, 43.

14. John Chrysostom, *Commentary on I Corinthians 1*, 7, cited in Martos, *Doors to the Sacred*, 29.

15. Bisong, "The Eucharistic Mystery," 137–54.

16. Martos, *Doors to the Sacred*, 4.

sacramentality affirms the mysteriousness of God, who eludes the full grasp or comprehension of the human mind.

Traditionally, sacraments have been defined in a static way, in a descriptive and logical manner, which seems to follow a particular formula. This tradition has been informed by the ontotheological tradition emanating from the Greek philosophical system. This tradition describes precise words and moments in the sacramental process. This orientation reached its climax in the Scholastic movement of the Middle Ages:

> Scholastic theology had indeed defined the sacrament in terms of its ritual action, its immediate and remote matter, and its form that resided in specific words. But this reduced the essence of sacraments to certain actions and words of the minister, isolated from the rest of the celebration for the sake of defining essence.[17]

The basic challenge of this theology is its minimalism and confinement of the sacramental ritual to the minister's words and actions. Such a theology excluded the laity and their participation at sacramental celebrations. It exalted the clergy to the extent that it became synonymous with the Church, with sacraments conceived as quantifiable objects. To say the least, sacraments became understood as remedies. Consequently, sacramental understanding was truncated, and its practical relevance to Christian living marginalized.

Historical Development of the Christian Sacraments

The history of the Christian sacraments begins in the Jewish narrative that was helpful to the first Christians in imagining the divine reality of Jesus the Christ, and it continues through the patristic period, the Middle Ages, the Renaissance (especially in the climax of the Council of Trent), and in modern times as seen particularly in the Second Vatican Council, which inspired postmodern contemporary sacramental theology.

The Jewish Roots of Christian Sacraments

The Jewish cultural and theological worldview prepared the way for the emergence of Christianity and provides the key to understanding

17. Martos, *Doors to the Sacred*, 37–38.

the earliest distinctive Christian practices.[18] As established by Daniel Boyarin, Christian sacramental thinking was heavily indebted to Jewish cultural and religious phenomena. Boyarin demonstrates that the distinctive Christian doctrines of Incarnation and the Trinity are not foreign to Judaism: he argues that Judaism had these ideas in its religious and cultural experience. Hence, Christian creativity "is not a scandalous departure from the hermeneutical method and spirit of ancient Judaism."[19] The story of Jesus in all its nuances is biblically based, and the differences therein are exegetically obtained through a concordance of scriptural passages. Hence, for Boyarin, Christianity simply fitted the Jesus story within an existing Jewish narrative.[20] In this way, he seeks to establish the Jewish roots of the Christian identity.

Boyarin finds an important connection in the fact that the early church attributed to Jesus the title of Son of God. This phrase and Lord are prominent designations of Jesus, especially in Pauline Christology and soteriology, where they characterize Jesus's identity and mission. The Pauline understanding of the title *Son of God* is the foundation of Christology, since by adoption we are elevated as coheirs, as sons of God.[21] This brings to light the soteriological and mediatory role of Jesus as the Son of God. The salvific dimension is premised on the ontological unity of the Son and the Father. Nonetheless, while both terms (*kyrios* and Son of God) existed side by side as designation for Christ, "*Kyrios* became the current title in worship and in the individual life of the believer, while the form 'Son of God', with its more complicated language, was kept for exceptional use, at the climax of certain theological statements."[22] Martin Hengel, a biblical theologian, identifies the provenance of these terms in religious expressions that

---

18. Some authors agree on the indebtedness of the Christian sacramental tradition to the Jewish religious and cultural system. For instance, the eucharistic vocabulary, including oblation, sacrifice, to offer, banquet of God, and the like, are overwhelmingly Semitic. See Rordorf et al., *The Eucharist of the Early Church*, 133. Tertullian especially engages these Semitic terms in expressing the eucharist. The engagement of the Semitic worldview makes it possible to think of the anthropological and sociological dimensions of the sacraments and to explore Uzukwu's contribution to the imagination of the sacraments. For authors who subscribe to this view, see Gavin, *The Jewish Antecedents of the Christian Sacraments*; Monika, "Christian Eucharist in Relation to Jewish Worship," 322–28; John, "The Sacred Meal," 52–69.

19. Boyarin, *The Jewish Gospels*, 134.
20. Boyarin, *The Jewish Gospels*, 134.
21. Boyarin, *The Jewish Gospels*, 8.
22. Boyarin, *The Jewish Gospels*, 14.

ante-date Christianity. He locates divine sonship in somewhat archaic form in Hebrew Scriptures: angels and Davidic kings are called sons of God, and Israel is called a people of God.[23] In addition, ancient Judaism recognized specially gifted people as sons of God; the Enochic-Metatron is one such figures in Jewish history.[24] Yet these do not parallel Jesus because of the latter's ontological unity with the father, pre-existence, and mediation, which are solely his.[25] Nevertheless, one can see an existing nomenclature into which the identity of Jesus was placed.

The presence of Hellenistic mystery cults about gods and divinities also ante-date Christianity and its Christological formulation. Although the Greek mystic religions contain elements of miraculous births and incarnation (in the sense of descent from gods), they are devoid of the idea of pre-existence of the Son.[26] The idea of *sending* by a god in ancient Greek religion is present in the sense of pre-existing souls which differs from what Hengel calls *hidden epiphany*.[27] In contrast to the Christian understanding of Jesus, none of the accounts has an instance, where a Greek god takes the human condition—suffering and death—upon himself: the Greek gods that do take on human life are distinguished from human beings because they do not die.[28] These illustrations point to the radical difference between Jesus the Christ and the narratives of ancient religions, which may otherwise parallel the Christ event. However, we must recognize the existence of these narratives and their religious significance, which were helpful in the Christian understanding and articulation of the identity of Jesus.

The Jewish idea and religious experience of Yahweh continued to resonate in the early Christian description of Jesus and the messianic hope. Explaining this fact, Larry Hurtardo holds that the first Christians were Jewish, and entertained the cardinal Jewish belief and hope of a messiah who would be sent by God to redeem Israel and usher in a new age.[29] The exis-

23. Hengel, *The Son of God*, 22.

24. Following Gen 5:24, where Enoch was caught in the heavens, Enoch enjoys a special privilege in Jewish mysticism and is often designated as Metatron: "As 'Metatron' he is set on a throne alongside God, appointed above all angels and powers, to function as God's vizir and plenipotentiary. He is possibly given the title 'prince of the world', indeed he is even called the little Yahweh." See Hengel, *The Son of God*, 46.

25. Hengel, *The Son of God*, 45.

26. Hengel, *The Son of God*, 32.

27. Hengel, *The Son of God*, 39.

28. Hengel, *The Son of God*, 40.

29. Jacob, *A Jewish Theology*, 292.

tence of this narrative, in a sense, predisposed the first Christians to the new reality—the dawn of the messianic age in Jesus the Christ. Hence, in the first century Christians recognized Jesus as Lord (messiah) and accorded him the corresponding honor, worship and devotion.[30] He is the exalted messiah, perfectly fitting the idea of the messiah expected in the Jewish religious narrative. This argument becomes more plausible precisely because the first Christians were Jewish and shared the messianic hope.[31]

The recognition of Jesus as Lord had far-reaching implications in later Christological controversies:

> The binitarian devotional pattern began so early that no trace is left of any stages of development; it is also taken for granted as uncontroversial among Christian circles in the Pauline letters, which, again, are our earliest extant Christian writings. In all of Paul's letters cultic devotion to Christ is presupposed as already characteristic of Pauline congregations.... Indeed, important data such as the *marana tha* formula . . . and the lack of indication that the devotional life of Pauline churches constitutes any major innovation in previous Christian practice, combine to make it necessary to attribute the origins of the cultic reverence of Christ to Aramaic-speaking and Greek-speaking circles, and to the first years of the Christian movement (the 30s).[32]

Larry Hurtado thus identifies the time and locates the early beginning of the devotion to Christ and the binitarianism associated with it, with the first Christians. The Christological consequences of such binitarianism are posterior to worship and praxis. Subsequent Christological controversies that led to the definition of the ontological and functional status of Jesus as consubstantial and equal in majesty with the Father helped express Christianity's seeming duality within a monotheistic tradition.

The strict monotheism of the Jewish faith, which acknowledged a transcendent God, is mitigated and mediated only through sporadic epiphanic visitations and theophanies. These visitations, frequently found in the Old Testament,[33] say something of the nature of God. Thus, the Hebraic

---

30. Hurtado, *Lord Jesus Christ*, 135.

31. Jacob, *A Jewish Theology*, 292.

32. Hurtado, *Lord Jesus Christ*, 136.

33. By epiphanic visitations and theophanies, I mean unique divine manifestations—for instance, the call of Abraham (Gen 12), the strangers by the Oak of Mamre (Gen 18), Jacob's fight at Jabbok (Gen 32), the revelation of God to Moses (Exod 3), to mention but a few. James White further elucidates this point by insisting, "The Jews held in

theology of presence alludes to two facts: the transcendence of God and God's mediated presence through concrete elements and events in history. Samuel Terrien captures this sentiment:

> Alone in their cultural milieu, the Hebrews developed a unique theology of presence. They worshipped a God whose disclosure or proximity always had a certain quality of elusiveness. Indeed, for most generations of the biblical age, Israel prayed to a *Deus Absconditus*.[34]

Seen in this light, Israel's festive celebrations become commemorations with the potency of reliving the initial divine encounter of the God who is by nature elusive. It is in this sense that the sacred meals and, indeed, the Passover attain a new meaning and theological relevance. Hence as Terrien remarks, "Standing ceremonially between sacred protology and sacred eschatology, she [Israel] summed the beginning and the end of time into a liturgical present, but she could remember only a handful of ancestors, prophets, and poets who had actually perceived the immediacy of God."[35] An acknowledgement of the hiddenness and manifestation of God, with a balanced idea of the same, is the theological challenge that should become an integral part of the consideration of our theological language.

We can draw an inference from the absence-presence of the Judaic theological tradition to establish the mediated presence or sacramental presence of God. In this way, we can clearly see the elements of continuity and discontinuity between the Hebraic theology of presence and the sacramental presence. In this light, for the first Christians, divinity was no longer mediated only through the temple cult and liturgical celebrations, but through Jesus the Christ, risen from the dead, proclaimed as Lord. Clearly, these Christians sought to explain the new cultic reality within the conceptual framework of Judaism.

---

tension the transcendence of God with God's concrete involvement in the actual events of human history. God was made known through events and objects that disclosed the divine will but were never confused with the Deity." See White, *Introduction to Christian Worship*, 177. Nevertheless, the Hebrew understanding of divine manifestation was not to be localized to specific places and times, even if theophanies and certain revelations happened at specific places like a huge tree or a mysterious stone. All we can safely say is the existence of two typologies: *numen personale* (personal God) and *numen locale* (local god), in accounting for the divine. See Ratzinger, *Introduction to Christianity*, 122–23.

34. Terrien, *The Elusive Presence*, 1.
35. Terrien, *The Elusive Presence*, 1–2.

From the viewpoint of the Christian sacramental communion, many authors point to the relevance of Jewish meals as foreshadowing such a sacramental relationship. To the Jews, meals are sacred and important opportunities of encounter with the other, and ultimately communion with God. The place of meals within ancient Israel and Jewish culture is attested by the numerous regulatory prescriptions that undergird it:

> From Judaism also comes a profound understanding of each meal as a sacred event. This most common of human social activities became, for Judaism, an opportunity for praising and thanking God as well as for forming a bond of unity between partakers. Far from being simply [a] physical necessity, the meal became a means of encountering God as provider, host, and companion.[36]

The concepts of *praising* (blessing) and *thanksgiving* are indispensable in thinking about the Jewish meal. From its etymological derivative, the Greek verb *eulogesas* (he blessed) or its *infinitive* form *eulogein* (to bless), expresses the Hebrew *berakah* (blessing). *Berakah* presents the idea of praising, extolling, and speaking well of.[37] The Christian Eucharist is therefore a celebration of praising and thanksgiving to God. From this perspective, the human person is in debt of thanksgiving to God, which is done in ways and manners that are in sync with the proclivities and sensibilities of various anthropological groups. For instance, the Marcan narrative of the institution of the Eucharist highlights these verbs. Mark 14:22 says: "and while they were eating, he took bread, he *blessed*, he broke, and he gave to them" and Mark 14:23 similarly states: "and when he took the cup, he gave *thanks*, he gave to them." The striking point here is the fact of *giving thanks* and *blessing*, which are synonymous with the Jewish meal practice, fussing the cultic and social dimensions of meal. Joachim Jeremias identifies the existence of such motifs in the various meals of ancient Israel.[38] In addition, he underscores similarities between the Jewish meal rituals, especially Passover, and the last supper celebration of Jesus and his disciples.[39] For our

---

36. White, *Introduction to Christian Worship*, 178.

37. See Arndt and Gingrich, *A Greek-English Lexicon of the Old Testament*, 322.

38. The *kiddus* meal, *Haburah* meal, and *Essene* meal, which could be described as regular meal of social dimension contained moments of blessing. A good understanding of the last supper would necessarily take the Jewish concept of meal into consideration; however, the striking contrast between these meals is that the last supper was a nocturnal celebration. This points to the theological importance of meals in rethinking the Christian sacraments. See Jeremias, *The Eucharistic Words of Jesus*, 26–36.

39. Such gestures as reclining at table with his disciples and the pre-meal washings

purposes here, we agree with Jeremias that "the ritual interpretation of the special elements of the Passover meal was the occasion for the interpretation which Jesus gave to the bread and the wine at the last supper. That means, structurally, Jesus modelled his sayings upon the ritual of interpreting the Passover."[40] From this cultic perspective, then, meals—ordinary and profane reality—serve to ratify pacts between humans and between humans and the deity.[41] Ernest Lussier correctly observes,

> The sacrificial meal symbolized the harmonious relationship existing between the offerers and God. God does not appear as previously with terror—inspiring accompaniments of thunder, lightning, and smoke . . . but in grace and mercy. Far from being consumed, they feast in God's presence in the glory of unsurpassing beauty.[42]

The highest expression of cultic and secular meals coalesces for the Hebrew people in the Passover meal, which, though signifying liberation from Egypt, is re-enacted every year; for it is the story of freedom and liberation continued. Hence, we can safely assert that, "It is in the liturgical assembly of the children of Israel that, to look from a Christian theological point of view, we find the Old Testament sacraments."[43]

The rituals of the Old Testament, then, are helpful in delving into the Christian sacramental mysteries. The highlights of this (Old Testament) celebration present some convergence and strong overlap with the Christian eucharist, which is central to Roman Catholic tradition. Joseph Ratzinger traces the prefiguring of the eucharistic meal through the Pentateuch and the prophets, integrating the high moments of Israel's covenantal celebrations—the Passover and the Sinaiatic covenant—as attaining their climax only in the new covenant (eucharist): "The association of this primordial cultic basis, upon which Israel was founded and by which it lived,

---

(cleaning), according to Jeremias, reflect the regular Jewish practice. See Jeremias, *The Eucharistic Words of Jesus*, 48–49. Also, Joseph Ratzinger argues that Jesus transformed the Jewish Passover to an entirely new worship and in the process inaugurated a new covenant by abrogating the old. This would reflect the time of the new covenant foretold by prophet Jeremiah. See Ratzinger, *Called to Communion*, 26.

40. Jeremias, *The Eucharistic Words of Jesus*, 60–61.

41. Examples of this idea can be found in the pacts between Jacob and Laban (Gen 31:54), and among Jethro, Aaron, and the elders of Israel (Exod 18:12), and in the covenant of Sinai, which constituted Israel as a nation under God (Exod 24:10–11).

42. Lussier, *The Eucharist*, 33.

43. Vorgrimler, *Sacramental Theology*, 29.

with the core words of the prophetic tradition fuses past, present and future in the perspective of a new covenant."⁴⁴ In the same way, the sacramental expression fuses the past with the present celebration, as it anticipates the eschatological banquet of eternal life. Hellwig Monika agrees that "the basic themes of our Christian sacramental celebrations and the very sense of sacrament and of sacramental celebration is [sic] a precious heritage that we Christians have from Judaism."⁴⁵ Against this backdrop, James White asserts, "Without this Jewish mentality and these practices, the sacramental life of Christianity would never have been born."⁴⁶

Sacraments in the Early Church and Patristics

The sacramental practice of the early church, much like other liturgical expressions, developed gradually from Jewish social and cultic life. The new group of believers assembled by the proclamation of Jesus gradually understood itself to be part of the people of God. This understanding, however, does not obliterate the identity of the Jewish people as the original people of God. Hence, we can speak of a continuation with the faith of Israel and a transformation of the same faith based on certain unparalleled events within the Christian faith. An element of the continuity with the Hebraic faith is underlined in Joseph Ratzinger's assertion:

> Yahweh, thy God, is an only God. . . . This fundamental profession, which forms the background of our (Christian) Creed, making it possible, is in its original sense a renunciation of the surrounding gods. It is a profession in the fullest sense of this word, that is, it is not the registration of one view alongside others but an existential decision.⁴⁷

44. Ratzinger, *Called to Communion*, 27.
45. Monika, "Christian Eucharist in Relation to Jewish Worship," 324.
46. White, *Introduction to Christian Worship*, 178.
47. Ratzinger, *Introduction to Christianity*, 111. In the same way, we can appreciate the identification and revelation of the name of the biblical God as "I AM WHO I AM," in the dialogue with Moses (Exod 3:13–15). Ratzinger establishes a theological connection between Yahweh, as the name of the founding God of the Hebrew nation and its (Yahweh) root in the Hebrew *hayah*, ("to be"). Theologically, then, Yahweh is another way of saying "being." The emergence of the understanding of God as being inevitably beckoned to other philosophical categories to illuminate this God and his relationship with the world. In the development of the doctrine of God, which employed Greek philosophy, the attributes of being from a Greek perspective became a ready tool to demonstrate the faith. Such attributes of immutability, impassivity, uncaused cause—attributes

The environment of the early church was suffused with a plurality of gods. The choice of the Hebrew theological narrative, which early Christians redefined, introduced the naming of God through the Greek concept of being. Ratzinger notes the challenges occasioned by the translation of the Hebrew faith to Greek cultural space, and the subsequent translation of the Hebrew "I AM WHO I AM" (Exod 3:14) to the Greek "I AM HE THAT IS." The biblical name for God inevitably, under this translation, became identified with the concept of the Greek deity.[48] With this bent, the Christian God became molded to the Hellenic concept of God, and, perhaps unfortunately, acquired the static orientation that triumphed over the dynamic Hebraic understanding.

The early church, and indeed the whole patristic era,[49] had the unique privilege and burden of giving a foundational definition to the Christ event and the nascent faith. The Christological controversies of the early times and the various councils can be understood as efforts to grapple with the unprecedented instance of God-as-man (Jesus the Christ). As has been described in the previous section, the initial reaction and conceptual framework for the expression of the new religious experience was provided by the Jewish religious and cultural worldview; however, as the infant church quickly found itself outside Jewish territory,[50] it needed to reimagine the faith within another conceptual and philosophical framework, the Greco-Roman.[51]

---

synonymous with the Greek concept of being, have served to describe the Christian God without due recognition and deference to his apophatic and apocalyptic nature. With the philosophical approach to God as being, it becomes difficult to highlight the nature of God's hiddenness and the revelatory character of human knowledge of him. In this instance, the logical formula of causality keeps God at the mercy and utter liberty of the human mind. Thus, we see elements of Greek philosophy that overarch Catholic theology. It is from this perspective that our human language of and naming of God remains in need of renewal.

48. Ratzinger, *Introduction to Christianity*, 119.

49. We understand the Patristic era to represent the formative stage of Christianity when seminal understandings were forged. Arguably, Ignatius of Antioch and Irenaeus of Lyons were among the first to receive the title that designated their entire era. See Hitchcock, *History of the Catholic Church*, 78.

50. The persecution of the Christians in Jerusalem and the prevalence of Diaspora Jews to some extent, account for the fast expansion of Christianity to the Greco-Roman world. Hitchcock, *History of the Catholic Church*, 19–36. See Gonzalez, *The Story of Christianity*, 13–19.

51. The emergence of the trilingual approach to God, condemned as a heresy by the Church in the ninth century, emanated from the overwhelming dominance of Hebrew,

Christianity at first did not have its own formal philosophy, and the heavily charged philosophical atmosphere of the empire demanded a philosophical demonstration of any knowledge worth attention from the populace. One of the first Christian apologists, Justin Martyr, in his *Dialogue with Trypho,* argues, "Philosophy is indeed one's greatest possession, and is most precious in the sight of God, to whom it alone leads us and to whom it unites us, and in truth they who have applied themselves to philosophy are holy men."[52] In fact, later in the work, Justin Martyr, establishes the unity of the Hebraic prophetic tradition and the philosophers, who also lead to the knowledge of the one and the true God.[53] Probably, in modern parlance, we would rightly describe this relationship as the unity of faith and reason. Conversely, the *Apostolic Preaching* of Irenaeus engages the philosophical categories in demonstrating the eternal existence of Jesus Christ, and indeed, as the fulfilment of the prophetic preaching.[54] We thus see the beginning of the Hellenistic influence, which has remained within the Church and its theology into contemporary times. It can be discerned through the Roman destruction of the temple of Jerusalem and the city in a bid to destroy or mitigate Hebraic influence and any symbol of Jewish unity.[55] The inevitable consequence of the diminished Hebrew presence was the overwhelming Greek outlook in Christianity, with occasional references to its Hebraic origin. In addition, the expansion of Christianity in the Hellenistic world and the diminished number of Jewish Christians further reduced the Jewish presence. Nonetheless, liturgically, the early church remained close to its Jewish roots.

The early Christians continued to celebrate those unique moments and events in the life of Christ. They continued to celebrate the rituals of the Jewish faith, but now with the intention of reliving the presence of Christ,

---

Greek, and Latin as the only acceptable liturgical languages. See Benedict XVI, *Holiness is Always in Season,* 52–54. Benedict XVI discusses this heresy in the context of his allocution on the feast of Saints Cyril and Methodius, champions of the use of the vernacular in liturgy. He praises their heroic work of translating the liturgy into the Slavonic language. This idea was condemned in the ninth century as heretical, but the Second Vatican Council (1962–65) recognized and allowed the use of the vernacular in the liturgy.

52. Justin Martyr, *Dialogue with Trypho,* 2.1.

53. Justin Martyr, *Dialogue with Trypho,* 8.1–3.

54. Irenaeus of Lyons, *On the Apostolic Preaching,* 2.43–47. The Son of God is identified as the one foreseen by Abraham, Jacob and speaking with Moses. In this way, Irenaeus demonstrates the pre-existence and activity of the pre-incarnate Jesus.

55. Martos, *Doors to the Sacred,* 22.

though not all sacramental practices had yet been dogmatically defined. The fathers were not homogeneous in their understanding of the sacramental practices, yet a certain commonality can be established in their opinions, particularly, in the implication of the sacraments in the daily life of Christians. The importance of the sacramental celebrations, to the fathers, would appear to be rooted in the practical life of the Christians. Irenaeus of Lyons acknowledges this idea clearly, "Our manner of thinking is conformed to the eucharist, and the eucharist confirms our manner of thinking."[56] The eucharist thus engenders solidarity or communion with Christ and communion with fellow participants at the eucharistic table. Furthermore, from the fathers of the church, especially Ignatius of Antioch, we glean two important sacramental motifs as ecclesial action and action of the Spirit. As concerns the former, in his letter to Smyrna, Ignatius writes:

> Let no one do anything relating to the Church, except in dependence on the bishop. Let only that eucharist be regarded as legitimate that is celebrated under the presidency of the bishop or someone the bishop appoints. Wherever the bishop is, there let the community be, just as wherever Christ Jesus is, there is the Catholic Church. Only in dependence on the bishop is it permitted for anyone to baptize or celebrate the agape; whatever he appoints is also pleasing to God.[57]

This shows the ecclesiological and sacramental thinking of the early church: the sacraments are celebrated and give life to the participants. Even up to the early Middle Ages, sacraments, especially the eucharist, were understood as ecclesial actions, and the priest acted as representative of a church.[58]

Though a few fathers of the church gave practical teachings on the reality of the sacraments, it was, perhaps, Saint Augustine more than any other, who has had, arguably, the strongest impact by defining the sacrament as signs that contain what they signify. The visible form he named *sacramentum,* and the power of the sacrament, *res.* In the same way, he named the source of the sacrament as divine agency, not within the domain of the human.

---

56. Irenaeus of Lyons, *Adversus Haeresus*, IV.18.5, cited in Rordorf et al., *The Eucharist of the Early Church*, 95.

57. Ignatius of Antioch, *Letter to the Smyrnaeans*, 8.1-2, cited in Rordorf et al., *The Eucharist of the Early Church*, 59. The same ecclesiological dimension of the eucharist is found in the letter of Ignatius of Antioch to the Ephesians.

58. Kilmartin, *The Eucharist in the West*, 134-38.

The seeds of the development of Catholic sacramental theology were sown at this time in Augustine's work in response to the Donatist heresy. Augustine held that the effect of the sacrament of baptism remained, irrespective, of the minister's moral state, and the seal of the sacrament remained, even in the baptized sinner. Hence, the sanctifying grace of baptism could be lost through sin, but never the baptismal seal.[59] Future Catholic theology would identify three sacraments endowed with an indelible character: baptism, confirmation, and holy orders. In Augustine, we find the enduring definition of sacrament as, "a sacred sign."[60] From this, we see an underlying metaphysical and objective dimension of the Christian sacrament: a correct celebration of the ritual and its wording necessarily produced the sacramental effect, the endowment of grace. Postmodern sacramental thinking introduced below, would challenge this mechanistic scheme of grace; however, the sacramental reasoning of the Middle Ages continued the trajectory of the patristic tradition. One clear fact is that the fathers of the church explained the sacraments according to the cultural framework and sensibility of their environment. Indeed, "They thought about their sacraments using the concepts of their culture, and they wrote about them using the words at their disposal. They were putting into words the sacred meanings of the rituals and symbols that they lived with, and they were verbalizing the nonverbal experiences of the sacred meaning that their sacraments opened up to them."[61]

The fathers, especially Platonists and subsequently Neo-Platonists, used available tools in reflecting on the sacraments. It would therefore not be surprising to see the prevalence of duality in theological thinking of that period—a concept that survives even today. Enlightenment following the Modernity was engrossed in a totalizing approach, which excludes and divides, in a bid to unify. Consequently, it saw the climaxing of Greek dualisms. To redirect the modern totalizing tendency, contemporary theology has retrieved the pre-Augustinian theological axioms,

---

59. The North African Church of Augustine's time was torn apart by a group who insisted on re-baptism of lapsed Christians: the Donatists held the view that "sacraments as channels of grace, depend for their efficacy upon the dispositions of their ministers," consequently an unworthy minister could not confer efficacious sacrament. And second, those who had renounced the faith in the face of persecution must be subjected to re-baptism. These constitute the historical emergence of Augustine's seminal teaching on the sacrament. See Jurgens, *Faith of the Early Fathers*, 3:63.

60. Augustine, *Letter 138*, 1, cited in Martos, *Doors to the Sacred*, 43.

61. Martos, *Doors to the Sacred*, 44.

apophatic and apocalyptic, which seem to have been forgotten or rejected in modern theological reasoning. These axioms serve as an antidote to the Enlightenment and the modern totalitarian theological approach. The apophatic inclination resonates with the hiddenness of God, which delimits and challenges any absolute Christian claim on the nature and revelation of God. According to Thomas Guarino, "Both [apophatic and apocalyptic] forms are important because both are profoundly resistant to systems of totality and closure, thereby challenging Enlightenment and even earlier classical forms of thought."[62]

Sacraments in the Middle Ages

From a sacramental theological perspective, the Middle Ages had strong continuity with the earlier era. An overriding concern of the Middle Ages was the determination of proper rites, or proper conditions that make the divine present in sacramental celebration, and the number of rites that would be described as sacraments. To this extent, great emphasis was placed on the proper words (acting as form) of the sacrament. From a purely Aristotelian metaphysical perspective, it is the form that gives the determination of the matter. Thus, the definition prevailing in the Middle Ages centered on the causal principles and functionality of the sacraments; however, the erosion of collegiality and theological unanimity between the Western and Eastern blocs of the ancient Roman Empire led to the emergence of different sacramental practices and multiple rites in them. Hence, we can easily identify the cultural leanings of the various Christian blocs, even with an appeal to a common patristic ancestry.

The development in the Western tradition reached its apogee in the thirteenth century, with the emergence of Thomas Aquinas and his retrieval of Aristotelianism as a philosophical tool for Christian theology and its sacramental practices. From a sacramental perspective, the philosophy of act and potency, matter and form, substance, and accident, offered sacramentality a solid grounding. Aquinas, it may be useful to point out here, is overwhelmingly indebted to Aristotle, whose theory of hylomorphism[63] established the relationship between matter and form as the relationship

62. Guarino, *Foundations of Systematic Theology*, 256.

63. Hylomorphism is a doctrine that holds that substances are made of matter and form: the form inheres in matter. We posit that matter in Aristotle is different from matter in physics: the later holds that matter is in motion, but for the former, every object is made of matter.

between *act* and *potency*. Hence the idea that form is the determinative element of matter. This implies that although something exists in actuality, it may undergo further changes from one state of being to another. So, matter and form are the constituents of every physical substance, *form* being that which makes the substance what it is, and matter being the substratum underlying the form. Because of that, we cannot think of a being in a way that is devoid of matter and form. Matter is defined by Aristotle as "that which in itself is not a this," form, as "that which is precisely in virtue of which a thing is called a this."[64] Insofar as the form makes the object what it is, it is equated with actuality, while matter is equated with potentiality. Although the form and matter exist simultaneously in a particular substance, the form is the active principle of change. Philosopher Pierre Conway supports this idea when he states, "the principle which is called active potency is the principle of change in another, as it is the other; since even though it may happen that the active principle is in the same subject as that which undergoes, nevertheless, it is not there accordingly as it is the same, but as it is other."[65] Similarly, passive potency requires an external principle to be moved, even if the capacity of undergoing a change is already there. One can then say that every actuality was at some time in potency. Thus, we can assert that sacramental matters, though in active potency, are actuated by the form, the words of the minister in the sacramental celebration.

Under the proper recitation of the form, the matter—water, oil, bread, wine—acquires a potency (in the sense of *potentiae*); made capable of conveying grace. This model signals the beginning of an understanding of grace that gained full maturation in Scholasticism. This period similarly grappled with the determination of the proper minister of the sacraments and the qualification that would lead to the presence of Christ in the sacraments or the sacramental grace. In a word, it was, following the Greek philosophical system, overly concerned with *causality*.[66] To this extent, a legalistic, juridical, and ritualistic approach became the hallmark of the sacramental thinking of the Middle Ages.[67]

---

64. See Aristotle, *De Anima* 2:1, in Mckeon, *Introduction to Aristotle*.

65. Conway, *Metaphysics of Aquinas*, 211.

66. The adumbration of God from the perspective of causality, following the Aristotelian understanding of God in Aquinas's *Quinque Viae*, lays emphasis on the necessity of causality, even of the sacraments.

67. Vorgrimler, *Sacramental Theology*, 51.

To establish the indispensability of the divine in the sacramental process, the expression *opus operatum*, ('work already done'), emerged. It indicates that, the grace of the sacraments flows from the merits of the redemptive work of Christ, and does not depend on the holiness of the minister or even of the recipient.[68] Karl Rahner elucidates the meaning of *opus operatum* as "the grace conferred on the recipient through the positing of the sacramental sign itself, and neither the merit (holiness) of the minister nor that of the recipient is usually involved."[69] The grace of the sacrament is inextricably tied to the accomplished work of Christ.

From the foregoing, it is obvious that Aristotelian philosophy was invoked to demonstrate the causality of the sacraments. To this extent, sacramentality was conceived in a minimalistic sense and the precise definition of conditions under which divine grace is made available. In the definition of the sacraments, an effort was made to demonstrate the Christological foundation and absolute condition of the sacraments. To this extent, the union of the minister of the sacrament with Christ was the only condition necessary for sacramental efficacy.[70] Such a collapsing of identities, even momentarily, had far-reaching consequences in sacramental thinking. Its basic consequence is the emergence of an overarching clerical ecclesiology.

The influence of Peter Lombard in setting the number of sacraments as seven was characteristic of this period. Earlier, the specific number of sacraments had been a matter of serious disputation. The Second Council of Lyons (1274) determined the sacred rituals that reflect Christ's proper

---

68. The corollary expression *opus operatis* would imply the merits of the human agent in the sacramental process, to the point of attracting God's favors. This would subject sacramental grace to human efforts: however, the right disposition of the individual is necessary in making of the grace present. Vorgrimler elucidates this point by arguing, "In order to guarantee the effectiveness of the sacraments, in addition to the teaching about *opus operatum*, further minimal conditions were discussed: the minister's possession of power, and the existence of an intention to do what, in this particular sacrament he does" (Vorgrimler, *Sacramental Theology*, 52). The consequences of these include the overwhelming emphasis of the power and role of the clergy in the church (clericalism), to the exclusion of the laity. Vatican II's emphasis on the role of the laity and the addition of the word *capitis* to the Tridentine *in persona Christi capitis*, can be appreciated only as a review of this earlier teaching on sacraments. Sacraments then must have an active matter actuated through the form—the minister's words that gives determination to the ordinary matter. Under proper conditions, then, grace can be produced.

69. Rahner, *Inquiries*, 207.

70. For example, in the celebration of the sacrament of the eucharist, only the words of institution (and the consecration) were emphasized.

actions, attitudes, and abiding presence, and seven of them became known as sacraments, while other actions became known as sacramentals.

One must not gloss over the academic atmosphere of the era—basically an aftermath of the Enlightenment, and the enormous impact it had on Catholic theology. The Enlightenment beckoned to theology to revalidate its claims rationally. Thus, the cult of reason became inaugurated by the objective, universal and perpetual claims to reality. This claim further became reinforced by a metaphysical realism and correspondence theory of truth.[71] Language in this context became a reflection and expression of reality as it is, or more precisely put, the world became mediated by language. For Guarino,

> In the enlightenment quest to uncover the essential structures of human life, thought, and discourse, modernity leveled and homogenized the irreducible multiformity and polysemy of life itself. Further, the Enlightenment concern with methodology as the path to truth caused it to veil the encompassing nature of historicity and, by necessity, to ignore the nuances, complexities, and ambiguities of being and knowing.[72]

This overarching logic of modernity reduced the uniqueness of particular narratives and universalized a particular narrative as the norm and absolute, yet the logic of life itself is naturally pluriform and diversity is the Trinitarian mode of existence, and indeed in the whole of nature, points to the contrary. The imposition of unmitigated uniformity and suppression of diversity can be identified with the Scholastic theology. Consequently, the Aristotelian-Thomistic synthesis has remained dominant in the Western sacramental tradition.

Sacrament in the Era of Reformation and Counter Reformation: The Council of Trent

From a purely sacramental perspective, we can view the reformers' objection as a consequence of the notion *opus operantis*—which implies that sacraments effect what they signify when the human agent does not place obstacles. Put differently, the obtaining of sacramental grace is measured

---

71. We shall explore this idea further in this book. The correspondence theory of truth and metaphysical understanding of language as an instrument that reflects the external world, like a picture, has been challenged by contemporary theology.

72. Guarino, *Foundations of Systematic Theology*, 6.

depending on the subjective merit, and not where God acts according to his own generosity and good pleasure.[73] This would require the contribution of the human agent to the sacramental process. In a sense, "If the person is a believer, that is, if she or he accepts the word of Christ as foundation and fastness and gives him—or herself freely without trusting in human works, the faith proclaimed in the sacrament effects salvation."[74] The *Decree* of the Council of Trent, defined the precise functionality of the sacraments in a way that reaffirmed the teaching of the church without further explicating the theology undergirding its theological assumptions. For instance, in Canon VI, the Council stated, "If any one saith, that the sacraments of the New Law do not contain the grace which they signify; or, that they do not confer that grace on those who do not place an obstacle thereunto; as though they were merely outward signs of grace or justice received through faith, and certain marks of the Christian profession, whereby believers are distinguished amongst men from unbelievers; let him be anathema."[75] And in Canon VII, "If any one saith, that grace, as far as God's part is concerned, is not given through the said sacraments, always, and to all men, even though they receive them rightly, but (only) sometimes, and to some persons; let him be anathema."[76] And Canon VII, "If any one saith, that by the said sacraments of the New Law grace is not conferred through the act performed, but that faith alone in the divine promise suffices for the obtaining of grace; let him be anathema."[77] These stipulations simply reiterate the teaching of *ex opera operato*, as against the reformation insistence on the faith as the primordial condition for salvation.

The Reformation mainly acknowledged two sacraments, baptism and the eucharist, as explicitly instituted by Jesus. The exponents of the reformation held on to the objective value of the sacraments to confer grace based upon the recipient's faith. In response, the Council of Trent (1545–63), dogmatically reaffirmed the direct institution of the seven sacraments, and indeed, defined sacraments as outward signs instituted by Christ to give grace. The theology of sacraments as channels or instruments for reception of grace remained standard Roman Catholic thinking until the Second Vatican Council.

73. Rahner, *Inquiries*, 208.
74. Vorgrimler, *Sacramental Theology*, 55.
75. *Dogmatic Canons and Decrees*, 60.
76. *Dogmatic Canons and Decrees*, 61.
77. *Dogmatic Canons and Decrees*, 61.

The sacramental theology developed by the Council of Trent was largely, an affirmation of existing theology and the silencing of contrary views. For instance, the theory of transubstantiation, which the council appropriated to explain the real presence of Christ in the eucharistic species, leaves the question of the existence of substance, which accidents must inhere unanswered. Put differently, if substances are converted and not accidents after the consecration, there would be no more substances for the accidents to inhere, since the sign must be different from the reality—*res et sacramentum* must be different from the sign (*signum*), using Aristotle's logic. This situation bequeathed a static sacramental tradition and did not enhance a relational dynamic possibility of the sacraments. Edward Kilmartin, a renowned sacramental theologian, identifies some of the challenges of the Tridentine and post-Tridentine sacramental tradition as overlooking the ecclesiological and eschatological aspect of the eucharist—which a relational understanding would have evinced.[78]

In retrospect, although the Fourth Lateran Council (1215) derived the eucharistic presence from the theory of transubstantiation, the question of the real presence continued to be an issue for the reformers. In addition, the Reformation begun by Martin Luther queried three basic aspects of the traditional Catholic sacramental practice: the justification of reception of the communion under one species, a preference for the theory of transubstantiation, and identification of the Mass as a true sacrifice.[79]

The Reformation and Counter-Reformation can be said to have emphasized uniformity and suppressed diversity. Thus, the Council of Trent's declarations were definitional and exclusionary, even as they revived the duality of the ancient Greco-Roman world. Post-Tridentine theology continues to bear the burden of unity as uniformity, challenging emergent local voices and context-based theological methodology. The Enlightenment and the rationalism that ensued emphasized reason as the guarantor of authenticity and reality. Without due reference to contexts and concrete issues, such a methodology would simply continue to maintain the gap between theology and life.

---

78. Kilmartin, *The Eucharist in the West*, 150.
79. Kilmartin, *The Eucharist in the West*, 156.

HISTORY AND THEOLOGY OF CHRISTIAN SACRAMENTS

Vatican II's Understanding of Sacraments: Christological, Pneumatological and Ecclesiological

The most distinctive feature of the Second Vatican Council's sacramental thinking emphasizes the ecclesiological and pneumatological dimensions of sacraments. The council sought to strike a balance between an overly Christological reading of the sacraments and Tridentine theology.[80] Sacraments,

---

80. The Second Vatican Council's redefinition of the role of the priest from acting *in persona Christi* to *in persona Christi capitis* (in the person of Christ the head) justifies this claim. The Council of Trent, appropriating the Aristotelian-Thomistic term transubstantiation, defined the Eucharistic presence from a Christological perspective. The expression, *in persona Christi*, points to the Christological perspective of the sacraments, whereas *in persona Christi capitis* accentuates the role of the priest as head of the assembly, and hence, sacraments as the work of God (Spirit) through the assembly. The dominant theology of the Eucharist, especially in the Western tradition understands *in persona Christi* from the affiliation of the priest to Christ in celebrating the Eucharist. Thus, after the recitation of the words of consecration, Christ is truly present under the Eucharistic species. The Decree for the Armenians of the Council of Florence speaks of "the words of the Savior, by which this sacrament is confected, since the priest confects the sacrament speaking in the person of Christ. For by the power of the words themselves are converted the substance of the bread into the body of Christ, and the substance of the wine into the blood: in such a way, however, that the whole Christ is contained under the species of bread and the whole (Christ) under the species of wine. Also, the separation having been made, the whole Christ is under the consecrated host and consecrated wine." (*Decretum pro Armenis*, AD 1439 [DS 1321] cited in Kilmartin, *The Eucharist in the West*, 129). This would imply a collapsing of two identities—the identity of the priest and that of Christ, at least at the moment of the eucharistic consecration (see John Paul II, *Coena Domine*). In this, we see an understanding of *presence* from a purely onto-theological perspective, an over emphasis on the philosophy of causality: the causal principle of the eucharist is the recitation of the institution narrative. Hence, the Christological dimension of the sacraments does not properly accentuate the ecclesial and pneumatological dimensions of the sacraments, and the understanding of sacramental reality as gift and presence. Consequently, the *in persona Christi capitis* formula allowed the Council to accentuate the priest's representative role, the epiclesis, and sacraments as ecclesial action. This formula relates the priest in a closer union with the community since Christ is the head of the community. Again, the ministerial priest is subordinated to Christ and anchored on the general priesthood of believers. At the sacramental celebration, the ministerial priest, first and foremost a participant in the common priesthood, concomitantly acts *in persona Christi capitis*. Precisely because the ministerial priest is subordinate to Christ, he is other than Christ, and we must maintain the distance and difference. To think of the ministerial priest otherwise would be drifting toward the borders of idolatry, which must be avoided. Hence, the expression *in persona Christi capitis* echoes the recovery of the *communio* and the communal nature of the Church as a people of God. This is another instance that mitigates the clericalism of pre-Vatican II ecclesiology and sacramentology. See LG 10, 28; PO 2; for the view of sacraments as ecclesial actions see Schillebeeckx, *Christ the Sacrament*, 54–89. Directly flowing from the preceding, we can conceive of the

then, are to be understood as Trinitarian action in and through the church. This understanding of the sacraments further helps the appreciation of the church as a sacrament itself. In this way, the council retrieves the patristic sacramental thinking. In brief, the phenomenological aspect of sacraments seeks to make the recipient an active participant in the sacramental process. The whole idea of the renewal of the liturgy at the Second Vatican Council captures this new thinking: "The patristic renewal had advocated a return to the great tradition of the Church fathers (Greek and Latin), a tradition that was more theological and less juridical, and was prior to European Christendom and the myth of an exclusively European Catholicism, especially from a cultural point of view."[81] The reform agenda and new methodological approach that the council represents are visible in its first document, *Sacrosanctum Concilium*, approved November 1963. *Sacrosanctum Concilium* and *Lumen Gentium* underscore the participatory aspect of the liturgy. The basic approach emphasizes the church as a communion. The African synod's understanding of the church as a family further illustrates the reality of the new image of the post-Vatican II church.

Coming to a similar conclusion, the council recognized the need for plurality, especially in liturgical matters and the gamut of the life and practice of the church. For the church in Africa, with a deep historical and cultural hegemony, the council's openness serves as a new beginning, indeed a new Pentecost. Thus, inculturation has taken a prominent stage in the theological reflection of many African theologians. Inculturation goes beyond liturgical matters to reach the entire life of the church in a way that renews Christianity in Africa in a profound way. The vitality of the church and the whole Christian experience represents a refreshing experience for communities and even for non-Christians. Hence, the thesis of this book

---

sacraments as both Christological actions and ecclesial actions. Dennis Ferrara argues for an understanding of the eucharist as *in persona Christi* and *in persona ecclesiae*. By appealing to Thomas Aquinas, he argues that the axiom *in persona Christi* is properly ministerial or instrumental and not an efficient cause, which imposes the challenge of holding the Christological and ecclesiological dimensions of the sacrament in equilibrium. See Ferrara, "Representation or Self-Effacement?," 195–224. Further on the eucharist as ecclesial action performed *in persona Christi*, see Ferrara, "In Persona Christi," 65–88. In the same vein, Avery Dulles gives more prominence to the general priesthood of believers since its sphere is ubiquitous, while the ministerial priest has a representative function only in the assembly. While not denigrating the ontological configuration of the ministerial priest to Christ, Dulles emphasizes its functionality which is more restricted than the common priesthood. See Dulles, *The Priestly Office*, 10–15.

81. Faggioli, *Vatican II*, 4.

argues that inculturation of sacramental theology from an African perspective is a practical approach to the mission of the church in the contemporary Africa. Elochukwu Uzukwu is one of the authors who have done the most research in this aspect of African theology. This work will therefore be engaging his contribution to African sacramental theology.

In many ways, the council attempted to return the church to its roots—by retrieving patristic practice that had been silenced or suppressed by modernity. A precise way of doing this was the novel understanding of Christ as the primordial sacrament of God and the church as a sacrament.[82] Indeed, these two expressions theologically reinforce and shed light on each other, for it is Christ in his concrete humanity that is the sacrament of God. The humanity of Christ and his ministry reflects the divinity that is hidden. Similarly, it is in the ordinariness of the elements of nature that God through the instrumentality of the Spirit makes himself present. The emphasis on the mediation of divine presence deserves due recognition.

Because of the development and understanding of the church as a sacrament, contemporary sacramental theology owes much to the theological reflection of Otto Semmelroth, a Jesuit, who in 1953 published *kirche als Ursakrament* (The Church as Original Sacrament).[83] This thought was developed by Karl Rahner, who in 1961, published *Kirche und Sacrament,* and Edward Schillebeeckx, who in 1960 published *Christ the Sacrament of Encounter with God.*[84] No doubt, these works, read before Vatican II, enhanced the reflection of the council fathers on the church. When the church is considered as a sacrament of salvation, it becomes truer to its nature as a sign of salvation and the herald of the same salvation and not the kingdom of God.

From the sacramental theological perspective, the Second Vatican Council, unlike any other, signifies cultural, anthropological, and sociological shifts from the assumptions of previous councils, and encourages profound adaptation of the sacraments and liturgy in non-Western

---

82. At several instances in the council's documents, we find this novelty in the understanding of the church. For example, "By her relationship with Christ, the church is a kind of sacrament or sign of intimate union with God and of the unity of all mankind. She is also an instrument for the achieving of such union and unity" (LG 1); "Rising from the dead (Rom 6:9), he sent his life—giving Spirit upon his disciples and through this Spirit has established his body, the Church, as the universal sacrament of salvation" (LG 48). Other references to this description of the church are LG 9; GS 45; SC 2, 5, 26; AG 5.

83. See Osborne, *50 Years after Vatican II,* 4–5.

84. Osborne, *50 Years after Vatican II,* 2–3.

cultures.[85] It is precisely in this context that we can safely situate and locate the foundational assumptions of this book.

Jesus as the Primordial Sacrament

Edward Schillebeeckx articulates the idea of Christ as the primordial or fundamental sacrament by arguing from his status as God/man. In Jesus the Christ we find the highest revelation of God. The recurring idea of sacrament underscores a combination of the divinity and humanity, a nexus between the ordinary and the extra-ordinary. The Council of Chalcedon (AD 451) defined Christ as having two natures and one person. By this definition, Christ became consubstantial with humanity. According to Schillebeeckx, "The dogmatic definition of Chalcedon, according to which Christ is one person in two natures, implies that one and the same person, the Son of God, also took on a visible human form. Even in his humanity Christ is the Son of God. The second person of the most holy Trinity is personally man; and this man is personally God."[86] So Jesus, in his concrete humanity is the sacrament, the primordial sacrament, as he realizes the redemption of humanity.[87] In his humanness, he is the eschatological sacrament of the mercy of God for the world; he is the revealed-revealer, *sacramentum et res sacramenti*—sign and reality.

Hence in ordinary human events Jesus the divine is made manifest. According to Schillebeeckx,

> Because the saving acts of the man Jesus are performed by a divine person, they have a divine power to save, but because this divine power to save appears to us in visible form, the saving activity of Jesus is sacramental. For a sacrament is a divine bestowal of salvation in an outwardly perceptible form which makes the bestowal manifest; a bestowal of salvation in historical visibility.[88]

From this perspective, we can understand the Incarnation as the convergence of divinity and humanity: the divine breaks into the human world as a strong vehicle of revealing God-self, for Jesus is the only mediator between God and men (1 Tim 2:5). Revelation is totally God's free act,

---

85. The Second Vatican Council expressly endorsed profound adaptation in the whole sphere of Christian life. See SC 36, 39–42; LG 13, 17; AG 9, 22.

86. Schillebeeckx, *Christ the Sacrament*, 13–14.

87. Schillebeeckx, *Christ the Sacrament*, 13–14.

88. Schillebeeckx, *Christ the Sacrament*, 15.

a self-revelation to humanity, yet "this manifestation is always filtered, by necessity, through human concepts, symbols, linguistic conventions, and historically and culturally conditioned perspectives."[89]

The greatest revelation of divinity is in Christ Jesus.[90] Thus, we can affirm that "The man Jesus, as the personal visible realization of the divine grace of redemption, is *the* sacrament, the primordial sacrament, because this man, the Son of God himself, is intended by the Father to be in his humanity the only way to the actuality of redemption."[91] Jesus becomes the sacramental mediation of the godhead, the revealed reveler, the God-with-us, and his human acts of redemption become the source of grace and salvation. The effects of the obedience of Christ to the Father extends and pervades humanity, such that the acts of Christ, in an elaborate sense, can be seen as the acts of humankind.

Directly flowing from Jesus as the primordial sacrament is the contemporary understanding of the church as the basic sacrament. The Second Vatican Council clearly declares, "The Church, in Christ, is a sacrament—a sign and instrument—of communion with God and of the unity of the human race."[92] The fundamental question Kenan Osborne raises about the principle of sacramentality *of* what and *for* whom is the sacrament?[93] finds a fitting response in the consideration of Jesus as the primordial sacrament of God and the church as the sacrament of Jesus. Thus, a sacrament must be sign of a higher reality, pointing to something or someone other than itself, and for a people. Just as Jesus in his humanity is the sacrament of God, his salvation for humanity, the church is the sign of his mission and salvation for humanity. The church receives its life and ministry from Christ and diffuses the grace of Christ through her ministry and vocation ministry. So, we must posit and acknowledge the sacramental priority of Christ and the church as the basis for the sacramental rites of the church. The seven sacramental rites, therefore, have an indispensable Christological and

---

89. Guarino, *Foundations of Systematic Theology*, 1.

90. The name Jesus Christ, at the same time, expresses the humanity and divinity of his identity. Jesus the man, while Christ refers to the anointed. Hence, Jesus Christ is truly man and truly God. The understanding of this unparalleled and irreplaceable event has often been the cause of great controversies. The Christological debates and controversies of the early times of the Church highlight the challenge of the man Jesus.

91. Schillebeeckx, *Christ the Sacrament*, 15.

92. LG 1.

93. See Osborne, *A General Introduction*, 78; Osborne, *50 Years after Vatican II*, 2–4; Osborne, "Methodology and the Christian Sacraments," 43.

ecclesiological dimension.[94] We deepen this thinking by turning our attention to the church as sacrament of Christ.

The Church as Sacrament

Much has been written about the Second Vatican Council, with increasing emphasis on its proper hermeneutics. Some authors tend to give a restrictive reading of it, but others engage in a hermeneutic that may be more consistent with its spirit, which is a hermeneutic of continuity as pope Benedict XVI categorically declares. In any case, the approach of the council fathers from the perspective of ecclesiology retrieves the ecclesiological tapestry and theological motifs of the patristics. Such a model introduces concepts and imageries that modernity had forgotten, not fully utilized, or overtly rejected.[95]

The council provided an opportunity for a thorough-going reflection on the nature of the church, which was no longer to be understood from purely a juridical society, but as a people of God. The *qahal* Yahweh expresses the belongingness to God that is made more theologically appropriate by the incarnation and redemptive cross of Christ for humanity, for Christ belongs to the whole human race by the will of the father: "Since Christ is man, a human nature is divinized, thanks to the hypostatic union, through the sanctifying grace that necessarily ensues from the union, and shares in the immediate presence of God by direct vision and love."[96] The contemporary understanding of the church, the body of Christ, while a supernatural sign of salvation, is preceded by the consecration of the human race already begun by the incarnation and culminate at the cross. Hence, in a sense, Christ is the real presence of God, an unsurmountable manifestation of God in the world. On this account, Karl Rahner articulates:

> There [in Christ] the grace of God appears in our world of space and time. There is the spatio-temporal sign that effects what it points to. Christ in his historical existence is both reality and sign,

---

94. Osborne, *A General Introduction*, 36.

95. We can say that prior to the Second Vatican Council, the church's understanding of itself and mission was very *ecclesio-centric*, *soteriological*, *euro-centric*, and *parochial*. After Vatican II, the church made a great shift in its self-understanding and mission in the world. This is clearly expressed in some of its major documents, like *Lumen Gentium*, *Gaudium et spes*, *Ad Gentes Divinitus*, and post-conciliar documents on mission, like *Evangelii Nuntiandi* and *Redemptoris Missio*.

96. Rahner, *The Church and the Sacraments*, 12.

sacramentum and *res sacramenti*, of the redemptive grace of God, which through him no longer as it did before his coming, rules high over the world as the as yet hidden will of the remote transcendent God, but in him is given and established in the world, and manifest there.[97]

The documents that guide our understanding of the council in this work are basically *Sacrosanctum Concilium* and *Lumen Gentium*. An important image used for the church is the sacrament of Christ. The church is therefore in the service of Christ and indeed a sign to the world. In the opening paragraph of *Lumen Gentium*, the document describes the church as "the sacrament of salvation for the world." Commenting on the designation of the church as sacrament during the council and its future consideration, Karl Rahner asserts that future students of the council will be amazed that the new understanding of the church was presented quietly and spontaneously and without opposition.[98] This was in sharp contrast to the ecclesiology of earlier years, which considered the church "the plank of salvation in the shipwreck of the world, the small barque on which alone men are saved, the small band of those who are saved by the miracle of grace from the *massa damnata*, and the extra *ecclesiam nulla salus* was understood in a very exclusive and pessimistic sense."[99] The church is not insulated from the troubles and pains of the world but it remains the sign of salvation, a sign of grace, especially through its sacramental practices and life of active witnessing.

Sacraments are not extrinsic to the church: they constitute its heart. Indeed, as Richard McBrien succinctly states, "They are expressions of the nature and mission of the Church. The sacraments are not simply actions which the Church performs or means by which the Church makes grace available. They are moments when the Church becomes Church, manifesting itself as Church to itself and to others."[100] Recipients of the sacraments are united to Christ through the church, the sign of universal salvation. In this, we see that sacraments have a clearly ecclesiological dimension, since the sacraments are entrusted to the church as their custodians. It is in this

---

97. Rahner, *The Church and the Sacraments*, 15-16. On the nature of the church as sacrament, Karl Rahner adds, "It is Christ who is encountered in the sacraments, and it is Christ who acts in the sacraments. It is Christ's worship of the Father that is carried forward in the sacraments." See Rahner and Dych, *Foundations of Christian Faith*, 733.

98. Rahner, *The Christian of the Future*, 82.

99. Rahner, *The Christian of the Future*, 82.

100. McBrien, *Catholicism*, 733. Sacramental celebration is then the celebration of the intrinsic nature and missionary thrust of the Church.

sense that we appreciate the seven sacraments as rooted in the understanding of the church as the basic sacrament. This reinforces the theological hermeneutics and liturgical confinement or celebration of the sacraments in the church—as sacraments of the church. Osborne remarks,

> The Church is a sacrament of the Christ event; it is sacrament of a sacrament; it is the basic sacrament of an original sacrament. This maintains the primacy of Christ and the auxiliary position of the Church. The Church is the basic, historical and abiding sacrament of the original, revelatory and one salvific self-communication of a God who so loved the world that he gave it his only Son.[101]

The renewal of Vatican II therefore has a strong impart on sacramental theology. Ecclesiological renewal of the council finds a clear expression in sacramental renewal; a renewal of the church implied a renewal of the identity and characteristic feature of the people of God—worship—through liturgy. It is unsurprising that *Sacrosantum Concilium* is the first document of the council to be promulgated. Thus, the renewal involved the development of new rites and new ways of celebrating the rituals of the faith. Since the council recognized and endorsed various cultural expressions of the faith; cultural expressions that are not opposed to the fundamentals of the Christian faith help to make sacraments more relevant and realistic. So, Aristotelianism currently is not the exclusive or privileged philosophical system through which the divine can be imagined and accessed. The council spoke about the relationship of the sacrament to Christian life:

> The purpose of the sacraments is to sanctify people, to build up the body of Christ, and finally, to worship God. Because they are signs they also belong in the realm of instruction. They not only presuppose faith, but by words and objects they also nourish, strengthen, and express it. That is why they are called sacraments of faith. They do, indeed, confer grace, but, in addition, the very act of celebrating them is most effective in making people ready to receive this grace to their profit, to worship God duly, and to practice charity. It is, therefore, of the greatest importance that the faithful should easily understand the symbolism of the sacraments and eagerly frequent those sacraments which were instituted to nourish Christian life.[102]

---

101. Osborne, "Methodology and the Christian Sacraments," 45.
102. SC 59.

Sacrament and Grace

The Christian tradition makes enormous reference to grace,[103] and various Christian traditions proffer different understandings of grace. The overriding meaning lies in the graciousness of the triune God in bringing humans into the communion of the Trinity. Our interest here lies in the dominant understanding and appreciation of grace. The Greek *charis* and Latin *gratia* have been designated and described so variously that the term no longer enjoys homogeneous usage. Nonetheless, it designates a participation in the life of God—a communion, an unmerited favor. Yet, over the centuries understanding of it was linked dangerously to the sacraments as mediators and dispensers of grace. Grace therefore became the end point of the sacramental life.[104] The Catholic tradition has always associated sacraments with grace.

The grace of the sacraments flows from Christ, the expression of grace *par excellence*, for Christ is the visible manifestation of the Father's love. He is the only mediator between God and humankind.[105] Central to the understanding of sacrament is the grace aspect of it: the participation of the individual in the divine life is central to the meaning of the sacraments. Hence, we can say that, "Grace is an active love of God for an individual in the wholeness of his or her personhood. At the same time, this active love is expressed in the *koinonia*, Church fellowship. Individual participation in divine life and ecclesial fellowship are two inseparable aspects of the one reality of grace, especially in the context of sacraments."[106] This presents the ecclesial dimension of grace not in the sense of the celebrating the ritual acts alone, but in the sense of being the visible sign of the kingdom and leading all men and women to the realization of the kingdom of God. In this way, we see the intimate connection between the Christological and ecclesiological and eschatological

---

103. The concept of God's grace refers to God's graciousness, benevolence, and goodness toward humankind. Varying traditions attribute grace to either human fallenness (due to sin) or human finitude; attitudes subscribed to by the Protestant and Catholic traditions, respectively. One thing we can safely say about grace is that it is all about God's relational character, his relationship with humans. See Worgul, *From Magic to Metaphor*, 153.

104. Worgul, *From Magic to Metaphor*, 154.

105. One can then argue that visible grace is mediated grace. The sacramental rituals of the church in this sense mediate grace; they dispose the individual recipient to a life of communion with the Trinitarian God.

106. Worgul, *From Magic to Metaphor*, 157.

dimensions of the sacraments and grace. The parting words of Christ[107] further demonstrates the historical presence of Christ in every space and time. However, the church is not Christ, and not the kingdom of Christ, but the indispensable reminder or visible manifestation of the hidden reality of Christ and his continuing ministry in the world.

From the fathers of the church, we have received the idea that sacraments always convey what they signify, a convergence of sign and reality. The Second Vatican Council highlighted Christ as the primordial sacrament or ground of grace. We therefore keep in mind the relational attribute of grace, stemming from the indwelling of the Trinity in the community and the individual; however, from the fifth century, the relationship of the sacraments and grace has been integral to the Catholic understanding of sacraments. Grace and sacraments have been explained from the point of view of causality—cause and effect. On its face, such a philosophy would be seen as presumptuous of divine grace, and restrictive of divine liberty to bestow grace or not to. On a deeper level, the relationship of sacrament and grace refers to the infallible promise of God for salvation of humankind due to the vicarious death of Christ, the source of sacraments. Thus, the grace of the sacraments is the grace of Christ. Thomas Aquinas explains the sacraments as a prolongation of Christology,[108] in which the merits of Christ overflow to the recipients of the sacraments. Consequently, such terms as *opus operatum* and *opus operati* signify that the grace of the sacraments is not dependent on the holiness of the minister or of the recipient, but on God's infallible promise due to the merits of Christ.

Postmodern Sacramental Imagination

Although the postmodern sacramental project is not the focus of this book, we consider it important to introduce the concept here as a development in the history of sacramental thinking. This development attests to the inadequacy of any philosophical system in demonstrating the interaction of the divine and human in the sacramental process. We must

---

107. Such words as "he who sees you, hears you, hears me, I will be with you until the end of time," and the like, acquire new meaning and force under this consideration. Again, the communion imposed by how everyone will know his disciples through the communion (love) they share is an imperative. And the relationship of the early Christians, for better or worse was a compelling factor to the unbelieving world (see Acts 2).

108. Thomas Aquinas, *Summa Theologiae*, III.60.3.

acknowledge that the word *postmodern*,[109] does not have a universally agreed denotation. Scholars, nonetheless, seem to have an appreciation of it as a reaction to modernity and its undergirding principles. A commonly running idea would be a unanimous reaction against the metaphysical and foundationalism that is synonymous with modernity, and its disdain for duality or binaries: "Broadly speaking the term postmodern implies the rejection of certain central features of the modern project, such as the quest for certain, objective, and universal knowledge, along with its dualism and its assumption of the inherent goodness of knowledge."[110] With the emergence of various cultural shifts, and the emergence of new epistemologies and theologies, it becomes imperative to reimagine our basic epistemological and theological claims. And from a Christian theological perspective, the shifts in demographics of the centers of gravity of Christianity in contemporary times imposes a new reconsideration of an overtly homogenized understanding of Christianity. Postmodernity embraces the narratives of particular peoples, and their histories and symbol systems, without forcing a grand scheme.[111] The recognition of local cultures and the retrieval of the local church which the Second Vatican Council clearly endorsed give way to a new theological formulation, with emphasis on local epistemologies and phenomenologies. To think of theology otherwise in contemporary times would be stifling the emergence of authentic local theologies and by extension local churches. Generally, the works of Ludwig Wittgenstein and Martin Heidegger are referenced as the starting point of postmodern thinking.

Philosopher Wittgenstein's seminal project, especially his *Philosophical Investigations*, draws attention to the contexts and particularities of cultures, and in the process repudiates the metaphysical universalist outlook of the picture theory of language, propounded in his earlier work, the *Tractatus*. The new awareness makes it imperative to reimagine and recast some of our philosophical claims and theological structure built on that assumption. *Tractatus* conceived language as a mirror of reality. Thus, just like Immanuel Kant with his categories of human knowing, Wittgenstein devised symbols (conditions) that make human language

---

109. Stanley Grenz identifies two aspects of the postmodern project that concern theological enquiry as, its fundamental critique and rejection of modernity and its disregard for epistemological foundationalism. See Grenz and Franke, *Beyond Foundationalism*, 19.

110. Grenz and Franke, *Beyond Foundationalism*, 21–22.

111. Grenz and Franke, *Beyond Foundationalism*, 23.

possible, that is, conformity of words to things beyond experience. If the mind pictures reality, the external world, as it is, independent of the mind, then one can safely make several claims that border on humanity, and universal epistemology. In other words, if there were uniformity in every conceivable human experience, a universal claim would become plausible; otherwise, universal claims become a universalizing of a particular history, a particular narrative.

Nevertheless, in his later work, *Philosophical Investigations*, Wittgenstein significantly revised his earlier position on language as a mirror of reality. Indeed, he repudiated his earlier position, the so-called picture theory of reality. He categorically states at the beginning of his book, "I had occasion to reread my first book and to explain its ideas to someone. It suddenly seemed to me that I should publish those old thoughts and the new ones together: that the later could be seen in the right light only by contrast with and against the background of my old way of thinking."[112] The shift was occasioned by the realization that a proposition can have different meanings depending on its use at various times and circumstances. The meaning of propositions, then, does not necessarily consist in truth conditions (conditions that make a proposition true or false), but in the setting, or contexts, where the proposition occurs: "For a large class of cases—though not for all—in which we employ the word *meaning* it can be defined thus: the meaning of a word is its use in the language. And the meaning of a name is sometimes explained by pointing to its bearer."[113] Thus, there was a radical shift from truth conditions (*Tractatus*) to justification conditions (*Philosophical Investigations*). A justification condition implies that the use and meaning of words depend on circumstances and occasions: it takes serious consideration of the contexts, and from a theological perspective, it would imply the recognition of difference and diversity of contexts.

From a purely sacramental theological perspective, postmodern thinkers appeal to phenomenology and an understanding of sacraments as *gift* and *presence*. In contrast to the traditional understanding of God, from the Greek philosophical category of *being* and *causality*, postmodern theological thinking emphasizes the starting point of theological investigation of God from the point of view of charity. There is then, a reversion to the naming of the Christian God, from its self-revelation other than an appeal to the traditional Greco-Roman philosophical understanding of God as being.

---

112. Wittgenstein, *Philosophical Investigations*, x.
113. Wittgenstein, *Philosophical Investigations*, 43.

The naming of God is an important issue of theological concern. The classical definition and understanding of God from Aristotelian (Greek) thought, as used by Thomas Aquinas, has remained dominant in the Christian imagination of God. Not a few scholars would disagree that in as much as the Scholastic explication of the doctrine of God and sacramental principles helped the cause of Christianity, it has left contemporary theologians with the task of reimagining its assumptions and categories to keep these in sync with the level of awareness occasioned by the human and positive sciences. High Scholasticism, responding to the challenges of its time, gave precise definition of sacramental presence with exactitude of moments as in the words of institution. In this way, it sought to determine and define the utter liberty and freedom of God through a philosophical formula of cause and effect. From the eucharistic sacramental perspective, the understanding of Christ's presence metamorphosed into somatic eucharistic presence in the twelfth century,[114] unlike the sacramental presence of the fathers. Edward Kilmartin, argues that, "the identification of the exact moment of consecration of the Eucharistic elements, the essential form of the Eucharistic liturgy, and the attribution of the consecration of the elements exclusively to the presiding priest, are the three elements which constitute the kernel of the later scholastic orientation in Eucharistic theology."[115] On the contrary, the orientation of earlier ages had concentrated on various aspects of the eucharistic mystery, in response to the sensibilities and pastoral concerns of its time.

Martin Heidegger's critique of metaphysics arguably marks the starting point of postmodern sacramental imagination. The critique of traditional Western metaphysics challenges all theologies and epistemologies constructed with the aid of such metaphysical paradigm. These, therefore, stand in need of confronting the problematics offered by nascent sacramental thinking. From a theological perspective, future sacramental thinking would battle with a new mode of presence that revalidates *causality* and *being*. The whole of postmodern sacramental thinking could be described as responding to this theological impasse.

Historically, postmodernity attempts to let *Dasein* speak for itself—a resurrection from a dominating and universalistic epistemology. Modernity considered truth as timeless, static, while the human mind was set on discovering it without its contribution. The major shift from the pre-Socratic

---

114. See Kilmartin, *The Eucharist in the West*, 127.
115. Kilmartin, *The Eucharist in the West*, 128.

understanding of *being* was the conception of the being of God from the ontotheological perspective. Ontotheology, therefore, emphasizes the metaphysics of presence and ignores the interplay of *absence* and *presence*. By shifting attention to the suppressed reality of absences, historicity and facticity, Heidegger laid the foundations for postmodern thinking. From this perspective, he veered from the Husserlian understanding of phenomenology and the *transcendental ego*. The later does not offer sufficient opportunity for manifestation of truth and reality from concealment.

Conclusion

This chapter is concerned with delineating the general historical development of the Christian sacraments. Arguably, such a task would require volumes, if justice were to be done to the topic, yet a presentation of that kind would not be necessary since our topic is not limited to the history of sacraments. What is presented here necessarily involves some broad strokes. Nevertheless, we believe it conveys important general characteristics sufficient to help us situate our dialogue with Elochukwu Uzukwu in articulating the interplay of faith and culture from the African theological space.

The chapter underscores Christian sacramental thinking originated in Jewish religious and cultural worldviews and was shaped by the Hellenistic influence that has become preponderant in contemporary sacramentology. In the same way, it acknowledges the anthropological dimension that is inevitable in a human community and the possibility of divine acquiescence to human societal necessities. Similarly, it highlights the current position of the church, beginning at the Second Vatican Council, in recognizing diversity and plurality inspired by the consideration of Jesus as the primordial sacrament and the church as sacrament of Christ, and in giving express permission for profound adaptation in every aspect of the life of the church. These developments, we must say, have given rise to the recognition of contextual (African) theology, and constitute the template upon which we shall explore our topic in subsequent chapters.

Chapter 3

Anthropology and Sociology of Sacraments

Introduction

THE PREVIOUS CHAPTER INDICATED the development of a phenomenological dimension of the Christian sacraments and noted the express desire of the Second Vatican Council for a profound adaptation of the Christian faith, especially in non-Western cultures. The chapter underscored how the Hebraic and Greco-Roman worldview were instrumental in the development and recognition of certain rites as sacred. This chapter focuses on the anthropological and sociological undertones undergirding sacraments.

Sacramental Rituals

Sacramental rituals engage gestures and symbols—anthropological elements (with ethnic origin)—which highlight the possibility of adaptation/appropriation of the sacraments. Sacramental Christian gestures commemorate, reenact, and immerse participants in the original Christic events, so while the gestures serve the purpose of communication in the human sphere, they simultaneously establish connection with the divine. However, we must recognize the varied understandings of human bodies and gestural behaviors, which have occasioned a mitigated or robust engagement of the body in liturgical celebrations. As Uzukwu demonstrates, African celebrations make elaborate use of the body because of the African understanding of the body as revelatory of the person in totality, and not in compartments.

Ritual behaviors follow a particular anthropological and sociological awareness. The arrangement of rites that follows the "general" human anthropological set-up reflects social order. Thus, many cultures have rites that mark the coming to life, adolescence, maturity, marriage, assumption of office, and death or departure. Such rites make it easier to handle human experiences like pain, tension, conflicts, and joy,[1] which are associated with the various changes in life. It is in this perspective that Gérard Fourez states, "Rites always relate to tensions of existence: What is solely factual is not the object of a rite. An existential tension, however, whether it is lived or is being resolved, cannot be conveyed by a language that is rational or factual; it demands a ritual."[2] From this perspective, while rituals communicate, they speak more than can be expressed in words.

In the same way, sacraments help people bear with the transitions, tensions, and conflicts in life. This could be described as the central thesis of Gérard Fourez, for whom well-celebrated rites must emphasize this aspect of anthropological and societal need, not just the theological aspects, which however he does not downgrade. In fact, without referring to the tensions and conflicts in describing the sacraments, he argues, they become pointless: "Celebrations which do not evoke and symbolize the conflicts and tensions of existence are quickly swallowed up in the banal and the insipid; they often become static and boring."[3] Sacraments, indeed, celebrate human reality and experience. Their communal and personal benefits emphasize the two aspects that Fourez highlights. While they relate the foundational story of the group, rituals help individuals grapple with the changes of life and so are open to the transcendental dimension of human reality. In the Christian sacraments, we come face to face with the divine. Thus, rites place the individual and the community in the mainstream of the ultimate view of life—a combination of humanity and divinity. They are a place of encounter with God.

Rituals and Communal Memory

Social groups, by their very existence, need rituals that embody collective meaning, memory, and identity. Rituals ensure the survival of any group of people by perpetuating values and traits that are central to the group.

---

1. Crichton, "The Sacraments and Human Life," 15.
2. Fourez, *Sacraments and Passages*, 14.
3. Fourez, *Sacraments and Passages*, 23.

Therefore, rituals enact and re-enact communal memory.[4] They involve bodily expressions, and such expressions help identify members of a group. Sacramental expressions also involve bodily expressions, in the manner of celebrating, giving, and receiving the sacraments.[5]

Expressing the faith inevitably involves the use of certain corporeal gestures. For instance, initiation rites serve the purpose of socializing neophytes, and passing on the tradition from one generation to another.[6] In most cultures, the task of initiation is considered important, and as a result is executed with utmost care. The rites that ensure a smooth passage from childhood to adulthood, and the various moments of life, are well guarded with rituals and rules.

The sacramental structure of the church follows this organic anthropological and sociological need. Of great importance, therefore, is the study of traditional initiation (rituals) processes that leave most indigenous peoples inextricably bound to their native cultures. Again, we must make reference to rites of passage as a classical way of handing on tradition. *Rites of passage* is a technical term for various initiation rites: it can be used interchangeably with rites of initiation. The word *initiation*, from the Latin *initium*, calls to mind the idea of a new beginning, an introduction.[7] Rites of passage, then, would imply a growth, dynamism, or progress. Initiation into a group implies commitment and self-involvement as a member of the group. Initiation implies a binding that recreates the narrative of the community. Initiation rites have collective and communal appeal because they embody a people's myths and can serve as a root metaphor for the study of any sociological group. Victor Turner, in his study of the Ndembu people of central Africa, began with the study of rituals. According to him, rituals relate a people's culture.[8] Therefore, the study of rituals is a good starting point for the study of a group of people. The study of the Christian sacramental rituals, similarly, establishes the inevitable anthropological aspect of the sacraments. This is a necessary consideration for an anthropological rethinking of the sacraments.

---

4. Worgul, *From Magic to Metaphor*, 82.

5. Thomas Aquinas believed that human access to the life of the spirit is through bodily action: alternatively, he alluded to the correspondence between natural symbols and spiritual reality. See Aquinas, *Summa Theologiae*, III.61.1.

6. Rasing, "Passing on the Rites of Passage," 97.

7. Paterson and MacNaughton, *The Approach to Latin*, 279.

8. Turner, *The Ritual Process*, 5–7.

Arnold van Gennep, credited with the sacramental interpretation of rites of passage,[9] early in the twentieth century, acknowledged the role of rituals in enacting change in social status through cultural initiation. For him, these rites fall into two major categories: one personal, the other chronological.[10] Personal rites are concerned with the passage of an individual from one social status to another in the course of life, while chronological rites determine recognized moments in the passage of time like the new moon, the New Year, the change of seasons.[11] According to van Gennep, "whenever there are fine distinctions among age or occupational groups, progression from one group to the next is accompanied by special acts, like those which make up apprenticeship in our trades."[12] Thus, there are "ceremonies of birth, childhood, social puberty, betrothal, marriage, pregnancy, fatherhood, initiation into religious societies, and funerals. In this respect, a man's life resembles nature, from which neither the individual nor the society stands independent."[13] A basic underlying assumption in discussing rites is therefore the inevitable reference it makes to the individual and communal life. Indeed, we can conceive of the seven sacraments in a similar way:

> Each of the seven sacraments responds to a deep personal need we have of God's redemptive presence at the critical moments in our individual histories. In the sacraments, God works to place our major life-decisions in a meaningful context of graced service of him and of others. God recalls us from rootless wandering and the morass of isolated choices in the face of life's central problems. We need not seek in darkness for the meaning of life, growth, guilt, illness, sex, vocation, death, and relating to other people.[14]

We can thus see that the sacraments appeal to the anthropological constitution of the human person. Through the sacraments, God reaches into the deepest parts of what it means to be human. In a sense, then, we can

---

9. Barnard et al., *Encyclopaedia of Social and Cultural Anthropology*, 489. Arnold Van Gennep is accredited with the use of the expression, rites of passage in 1903. See also Barfield, *The Dictionary of Anthropology*, 409; Crim, *Abingdon Dictionary of Living Religions*, 426.
10. Gennep, *The Rites of Passage*, 3.
11. Gennep, *The Rites of Passage*, 3.
12. Gennep, *The Rites of Passage*, 3.
13. Gennep, *The Rites of Passage*, 3–4.
14. Wicks, "Sacraments," 24.

say that "the sacramental organism is an adapted organism,"[15] a point of union between the human and divine, a point of intersection between anthropology and theology. This intersection remains a necessary condition in the understanding of sacraments.

Sacraments: Rituals and Symbols

Rituals and symbols serve as dominant concepts in worship and Christian sacramental practices, and they are native to sociocultural groups as they seek to understand the universe and the world around them. One of the bedrocks of Uzukwu's argument is that ancient Greco-Roman culture has influenced Christianity in various ways. He states, "The Greco-Roman gestures deriving from a particular worldview influenced Christian practice—liturgy, ethics, preaching and spirituality."[16] However, Christianity is not irredeemably chained to these gestures as the only way of mediating the divine. Hence, Uzukwu's theological efforts and our topic of reimagining the Christian sacraments in West African contexts seek to highlight and incorporate difference and relevance of indigenous gestural practices to global Christianity.

The idea of sacraments as rituals of the church dominates Uzukwu's reflection on the sacraments and liturgical celebration. Gestures and words express rituals that are owned by the community. He speaks of Judeo-Christian rituals as constituting the "livewire" of the community. He traces this understanding of gestural practices to the prominence of the Judeo-Christian exodus and cross/resurrection events in the ritual celebrations of Judaism and Christianity, respectively. These rituals commemorate events endowed with renewed potency when reenacted, which under the appropriate environment, bring forth a renewed presence of that which is being celebrated. The environments set apart for ritual celebrations can be described as sacred spaces, which not only become unique, but also become laden with the divine and the mysterious. Thus, these spaces become the locus where the timeless interrupts time and the divine interrupts the ordinary. Sacred space, according to Mircea Eliade, "Implies a hierophany, an irruption of the sacred that results in detaching a territory from the surrounding milieu and making it qualitatively different."[17] The significance

---

15. Crichton, "The Sacraments and Human Life," 32.
16. Uzukwu, *Worship as Body Language*, 6.
17. Eliade, *The Sacred and the Profane*, 26.

of the space lies especially in the event it commemorates, an occurrence beyond daily human oddities. In language and significance, rituals bespeak divinity. Roger Grainger puts it clearly:

> The language of religious ritual is the code of human actions of reaching out towards God because it speaks of an ontological rupture in the fabric of human reality, giving rise to a chasm between created and Creator which calls out to be crossed—a wound which, if it is not to prove fatal, must somehow be healed.[18]

Rituals mitigate this distance as they acknowledge the inward spiritual pull of the human soul. A basic assumption in discussing sacraments is the indispensability of rituals and symbols. Sacraments are expressed in words and rites that involve the use of language, both verbal and gestural.[19] The centrality of language in human symbols and communication informs the study of language. Indeed language, or the ability to communicate, is native to humankind. Aristotle gave a definition of man as the living being who has language.[20] The Greek philosophical tradition developed the correlation between thinking and language in its conception of language. Plato argued, "the soul when thinking appears to me to be just talking."[21] He similarly added, "Are not thought and speech the same with the exception that what is called thought is the unuttered conversation of the soul with herself."[22] From the above, we clearly see the merger of thought and language as inseparable parts of the same reality. This idea runs through much of classical philosophy and continues in the modern period. In his earlier work, Ludwig Wittgenstein categorically stated, "Thinking is a kind of language. For a thought too is, of course, a logical picture of a sentence and therefore it just is a kind of sentence."[23] This picture theory is a philosophy that assumes the existence of reality outside the mind in which language perfectly describes and communicates.[24]

---

18. Grainger, *Bridging the Gap*, 27.
19. Chauvet, *The Sacraments*, 1.
20. See Heidegger, *On the Way to Language*.
21. Plato, *Theaetetus*, 190, cited in Edwards, *Encyclopedia of Philosophy*, 5:458.
22. Plato, *Sophist*, 263, cited in Edwards, *Encyclopedia of Philosophy*, 5:458.
23. Wittgenstein, *Tractatus Logico-Philosophicus*, 201.
24. See Hector, *Theology without Metaphysics*, 20–24. The logical consequence of this approach was that in the long philosophical tradition, truth and reality have been conceived as outside the mind, which language aptly mediates. The contrary position would be to think of these are discoverable in the events and contexts of their location.

The above instances demonstrate the origin of the instrumental concept of language from the Greek philosophical tradition. Language is no more or less than its metaphysical dimension. The instrumentalist view of language takes the existence of a concrete external world expressed by language for granted. It is often controlled by the desire to grasp reality immediately, with logical certitude and permanence over transient.[25] This theory of language finds expression in Augustine's allocution,[26] where language serves as an instrument in gaining access to objective reality, and there was so much hope in the ability of language to express external reality. This traditional understanding of language has experienced a profound revision in contemporary times. Louis-Marie Chauvet articulates the challenges of the instrumentalist scheme thus: "What unconsciously dominates the conception of language as instrument is the presupposition that sensible mediations are obstacles to truth. It is this very supposition that has been questioned through the epistemological revolution led by contemporary sciences and philosophy of language."[27] For language to be conceived as instrument, it would have to preexist the speaker. Language is unlike other instruments that humans created to serve some purpose; to stretch to the extreme, it is creative. Chauvet adds, "To be able to 'invent' language, one must think of it; but in order to think of it, one must already be in language. It is therefore true that "language teaches us the very definition of human being."[28]

Martin Heidegger contributed importantly to the revision of the idea of language, a movement from the instrumental classical scheme to the mediatory role of language. To debunk the argument of the instrumental view of language, he argued that language preexists human beings and cannot be manufactured like every other instrument. In fact, humans discover themselves inevitably embedded in language. He pointed out:

> According to an ancient understanding, we ourselves are, after all, those beings who have ability to speak and therefore already possess language. Nor is the ability to speak just one among man's many talents, of the same order as the others. The ability to speak

---

25. Chauvet, *The Sacraments*, 6.
26. Sluga et al., *The Cambridge Companion to Wittgenstein*, 264.
27. Chauvet, *The Sacraments*, 6.
28. Chauvet, *The Sacraments*, 7. Chauvet asserts that from the time of gestation, the fetus is already introduced to human culture. In a sense, inculturation begins then in the womb. This reality points to the situatedness of the human person and further attests to the fact of absence or suppositionless (abstract) conditions.

is what marks man as man. This mark contains the design of his being. Man would not be man if it were denied him to speak unceasingly, from everywhere and every which way, in many variations, and to speak in terms of "it is" that often remains unspoken. Language, in granting all this to man, is the foundation of the human being.[29]

In this consideration, language brings forth reality from its hiddenness; language mediates reality. For Heidegger, the original Greek *logos* (commonly translated as "discourse" or "word") does not mean speech or discourse, nor does *legein* mean "to speak." He adds that *lego* with its infinitive *legein* signify "to gather," "to collect." This is the sense in which Aristotle, according to Heidegger, used the term in his *Physics*, to express a 'gathering'.

Since we may logically surmise that the essence of the gathering is for disclosure, *legein* shoulders the meaning of disclosure. So, language, in this Heideggerian sense, is a creative gathering, which reveals a new reality, giving import and credence to sacramental language. Thus, language ceases to be just an instrument that mediates, but one that also constructs reality, as seen in liturgical language. As performative language, liturgy brings to reality that which it commemorates.

Contemporary studies indicate that reality is culturally mediated according to various linguistic communities. In a sense, just as language belongs to the community, so is its translation of reality a communal possession. Through the language and symbols of the community, a unique meaning is attached to reality and the events of human life. Such an interpretation of reality gives rise to particular behaviors and gestures. Chauvet uses the expression "symbolic order" to describe the united witness and the reinforcing nature of various aspects of the communal life into a coherent meaning: "To speak of 'symbolic order' is precisely to indicate that all the elements of the cultural puzzle are joined to one another and that each element acquires its significance only by being put back into this conventional ensemble as diversified as human societies are."[30] Symbols acquire their meaning by bearing a unified witness to specific meanings. And just as the human community cannot do without different modes of symbolization, human social and cultural groups have devised symbols to serve this purpose. Symbols then can be specific to cultures and societies if the words, gestures, and actions evoke a particular value within specific

---

29. Heidegger, *On the Way to Language*, 111–12.
30. Chauvet, *The Sacraments*, 15.

groups.[31] Since symbols reveal more than ideas, we can say that "symbols are a means to convey not only an idea but the value of the idea, they are 'charged,' like a battery ready to deliver power when it is grounded in a ready receiver. A symbol is a channel which somehow 'connects' the viewer with the power of the value."[32]

Symbols mitigate or bridge the difference between two unlike realities, like human reality and the mystery of the divine. They are always minute in their representation of the real, making that which is invisible concrete.[33] Further, they are communal and social in character, introducing the individual into the community. This is evident in the Christian sacraments, which embody the various aspects of the life of the community, such as sacraments of initiation, reintegration after misdeeds, leadership, and intimate relationships (for the continuation of the human community). Thus, reinventing the Christian sacraments takes the symbolic order of the group into consideration, as well as the rituals that constitute a communal memory.

Consequently, rituals have been classified as secular and sacred. While both evoke objects of profound meaning, in most cases the past memories of the group, the object of sacred rituals, is as O'Malley says, a *Mysterium Tremendum*.[34] The sacraments, major rituals of the church, celebrate and reenact an event in history, the foundation or root metaphor of the community. It is presumed that ordinarily they do not produce belief, since they open the mind to the divine. To this extent, "ritual is effective only if there is that 'connection'—not with the words—but with the transcendent God present in immanent reality. Reality means connection."[35] Thus in the sacramental celebration, the reality of the human and the divine are realized. Put differently, the rite or ritual that reenacts or recreates historical events brings the celebrating community into

---

31. O'Malley, *Sacraments*, 98. Importantly, most scholars differentiate natural from culturally conditioned symbols. Natural symbols like smoke are differentiated from culturally conditioned symbols, which have meaning only for those within a particular cultural tradition.

32. O'Malley, *Sacraments*, 97.

33. In fact, Chauvet identifies sparseness as one of the qualities of symbols, for instance, water representing baptism into the death of Christ, and bread and wine representing creation and the work of human hands, which becomes the Eucharist. See Chauvet, *The Sacraments*, 101.

34. O'Malley, *Sacraments*, 104.

35. O'Malley, *Sacraments*, 105.

communion with divine persons, since the divine in the commemorated event entered the human world through human cultural activity (food, drink, limitations). These human elements assume a higher level through the mystery they commemorate. This aspect reveals the theandric nature of sacraments as human and divine realities.

Sacramental mediation is the condition for access to the divine. In *God without Being*, Jean-Luc Marion makes subtle distinctions between idols and icons, based on the phenomenon or significance of the gaze. While the idol seizes and is characterized by the gaze,[36] the icon surpasses the gaze into infinity and never seizes the visible.[37] Sacramental mediation serves the iconic purpose of making the divinely invisible visible; it is the only way of reaching the divine, whose mode of existence is radically different from that of humans. To this extent, belief in direct access to the divine becomes idolatrous, reflecting the human imagination about the divine. In contrast, sacramental mediation is predicated on the iconicity of the sacraments, simultaneously concealing, and disclosing divinity. Hence, only by acknowledging God's otherness and absence, or the distance and separation between two dissimilar realities (God and human beings) is God truly mediated and encountered. The acknowledgment of God's absence is the condition for mediated presence. Chauvet authenticates this position by pointing out the episodes of the two disciples on the way to Emmaus, the conversion of Saul, and the Ethiopian Eunuch as examples of an encounter—a presence—that is fostered by absence.[38]

Uzukwu's sacramental reinterpretation involves the rigorous evolution of ritual studies with the endorsement of the current theological position of the church. He understands rituals from their anthropological foundation in the nature of the human body. He has argued, "Human consciousness makes human gestural activity a design and not a simple instinctual response to external or internal stimuli. There is a style or strategy in the rhythm of human body movement. This measured motion is intimately connected with speech (verbal or gesture)."[39] Precisely from this perspective, he identifies the ethnic basis of various gestural behaviors—religious and profane. Thus, he identifies rituals as a community celebration that eschews the individualism and isolationism of the modern

---

36. Marion, *God without Being*, 11.
37. Marion, *God without Being*, 18.
38. Chauvet, *The Sacraments*, 20–28.
39. Uzukwu, *Worship as Body Language*, 3.

era, for liturgical and sacramental celebration are corporate acts of the church. Individualism challenges the idea and essence of the communal celebration. From this perspective, one understands Uzukwu's insistence on inculturation of sacramental celebration through indigenous gestures as a response to gestures and languages that resonate with the meaning system of each anthropological group.

Conclusion

This chapter demonstrates the inevitable anthropological foundation of sacraments—symbols and gestural behaviors which have ethnic basis. It examined how gestural behaviors interact with the divine to reenact foundational events and stories of a community. Further, it presents the performative dimension of language beyond its instrumental perspective. Ritual language, therefore, realizes what it celebrates. While the Christian faith cannot be reduced to its anthropological and phenomenological expressions, they remain important in realizing a relevant and realistic community.

Chapter 4

Encountering Uzukwu and His Theology

Introduction

THIS CHAPTER ATTEMPTS TO identify both the worldview and the theological and cultural background of Uzukwu's theology, and how he engages these resources in responding to the need of the church in Africa. This background constitutes the basic world-sense from which Uzukwu crafts his theology. This chapter presents his theological methodology, which will help us to articulate his contribution to an African sacramental reinterpretation.

A Brief Biographical Sketch of Elochukwu Uzukwu

Uzukwu's biography reveals a personality that has a strong foundation in both the indigenous traditional community and the church of Vatican II. His upbringing and closeness to the village traditional setting serve as an ally to his theological thrust. Born August 18, 1945, during the colonial era, in the village of Nnewi in south eastern Nigeria, a cultural region of Igboland, he first experienced Christianity at the hands of missionaries. In an interview about what influenced his theological thinking, he remembers his early childhood years in the village, a communitarian setting: "What has influenced me is the village, right from my childhood, up to this point I'm talking to you, it is the village."[1] He adds, "You will not understand it when I say the village,

---

1. Oral interview with Elochukwu Uzukwu on, January 16, 2015.

because many young people today do not know the village. So, the village, its indigenous rituals, my village rituals, and when I talk about rituals, I mean the traditional rituals."[2] The village, had its own calendar, which portioned off the week in a four-day cycle, variously named in such a way that work was not to be done on certain days. The New Year was a big celebration involving traditional rituals for consecrating the year and its activities: "You clean out everything and then the heads of household who are still not Christian . . . put [coconuts] at the crossroads, and the children run out of school and rush at the coconut[s] and eat the coconut[s] and we are the children of the year. The year itself was considered a deity."[3]

The indigenous rituals and practices clearly left a deep impression on the young Uzukwu, revealing the emergence of his theology from these practices and indigenous worldview. He grounds his theological orientation in the village: "I opt for a theology that arises from the resources of the living community,"[4] which he sees as the embodiment of religion and culture. Consequently, one sees the impact of the local community as it matures and manifests in Uzukwu's idea of the local church.

From the local community and its practices, a mustard seed of the importance and significance of the local church was planted, which would blossom as Uzukwu's theological journey developed. He recounts how his grandfather, and some elders of the church would debate with the local catechist on the true meaning of church, and where it existed. He recalls how his grandfather in 1914 had opted for a church in their village, instead of having the whole community travel several miles to the parish center; this move was aimed at bringing the church closer to the people: "My grandfather, it was said, established the church, moved the church from another king's compound, you know, to the place that was called "evil forest." They cleared ground there, and started gathering from 1914."[5] Therefore, he says, "My ecclesiology is radically rooted in my grandfather's ecclesiology. He was right in his understanding of the local church."[6] In addition to village rituals and practices, Uzukwu loved to watch the elders debate the faith with the local catechists who conducted

2. Interview with Uzukwu in appendix.
3. Interview with Uzukwu in appendix.
4. Uzukwu, *A Listening Church*, 9.
5. For an oral interview with Professor Elochukwu Uzukwu, held January 16, 2015, see the appendix.
6. Interview with Uzukwu in appendix.

church services and shared the Gospel with the natives on Sundays in the absence of limited priests. These were the catechetical influences on the young Uzukwu during his primary school days.

In successive years, Uzukwu enlisted in seminary formation, from a minor seminary to the major seminary (Bigard Memorial Seminary, Enugu, Nigeria), during the 1966 Nigerian civil war. His critical mindset and thought patterns were developed during these years, including his curiosity about the phenomenon of oracles, particularly a talking bird that he investigated in 1969. He recalls his fascination at the interpretation given by native experts who understood and interpreted the bird's utterances.

After his priestly ordination, on September 15, 1972, Uzukwu was deployed to serve as bursar and assistant novice master in the Novitiate of the Holy Ghost Fathers and Brothers Congregation. The following year, he was reassigned as rector of a minor seminary in *Umu owa*,[7] and placed in charge of a parish in the locality. He recalls his encounter with pastoral problems of sickness and the experience of unwed couples cohabiting in the area. Consequently, he undertook to investigate the cultural practice of various marriage rituals, from betrothal to the final marriage rite. This study, according to him, revealed some inconsistency in the official Roman Catholic marriage teaching, which disregarded the richness and meaningful symbolism of the traditional marriage rituals. Again, he saw no difference in the essential structures and significance of both traditional and Catholic wedding ritual expressions, attributing his refusal to specialize in moral theology to this theological impasse in his understanding of the sacrament of marriage.

In contrast, the dynamism of the youths in the parish where he was serving as a priest bolstered his interest in liturgy, prompting him to delve deeper into liturgical studies. This impetus for liturgical and eucharistic studies started in the seminary through the lectures of Reverend Father Ifeanyi Anozie, who associated the Eucharist with the Jewish ritual meal, as recounted in *The Shape of The Liturgy*, a book by Dom Gregory Dix, published in 1945. According to Uzukwu, transubstantiation and similar ideas seemed too magical to him, so locating the Eucharist within the normal Jewish meal setting, gives a new meaning to the sacrament.

In his graduate studies, Uzukwu concentrated on historical theology, and since the clearest way of grasping Christian tradition was through its liturgy, he decided to focus on liturgical theology, in particular, on

---

7. *Umuowa* is the name of a community in South Eastern Nigeria.

memory and tradition, beginning from the Jewish perspective. His doctoral dissertation, "Blessing and Thanksgiving among the Igbo: Towards Eucharistia Africana," applies this approach in reimagining the Eucharist from the indigenous Igbo Prayer of Thanksgiving and Blessing.[8] Upon the successful completion of his doctorate in St. Michael's College, University of Toronto, Uzukwu was deployed to teach theology and sundry courses in the Congo Brazzaville. He recalls the challenge of having to relearn his theology to acquiesce to the French theological and academic climate operative in Congo, in addition to learning the French language itself. Consequently, he undertook this task. From the Congo, he returned to his alma mater (Bigard Memorial Seminary, Enugu, Nigeria), in 1982. He recalls the rigidity of the seminary climate and the unwillingness to reduce the Roman control of the curriculum, which inspired him to champion the establishment of the Spiritan International School of Theology in Nigeria. As the pioneer rector of this institution, he courageously applied his academic resources for the emergence of a true local church.

Uzukwu's theology is informed by and distilled through the post-Vatican II church. He anchors his distinctive contributions to the subject in a church that is open to dialogue and development. He makes a unique contribution to global Christianity through West African epistemological and transcendental realities, focusing on the understanding of God within this context. He is arguably the first West African author to delineate a distinctive theological methodology that departs radically from the dominant Western paradigm yet remains consistent with contemporary Catholic theology. In his theology, we find a novelty that does not overstretch the Vatican II teaching, yet serves the purpose of giving voice to West African Christian proclivities.

Brief Sketch of the West African Worldview: Epistemology and Cosmology

A detailed presentation of the West African worldview is beyond the scope of this work. We will therefore focus on its epistemology and cosmology since they greatly assist in understanding the undergirding assumptions in Uzukwu's works. Therefore, this section attempts to respond to a way of comprehending reality that is discernible from the West African perspective. This section further helps us situate and deepen Uzukwu's methodology,

---

8. A detailed analysis of this dissertation will be presented in the following chapter.

FAITH AND CULTURE

which has been largely drawn from traditional African wisdom. There is thus a correlation between West African epistemology and cosmology, and his theological reflections emerging from that geolocation.

A fact that a casual reader quickly notices about the African worldview is the overwhelming cultural influence of a set of beliefs and practices that can conveniently be called African Traditional Religion. A study of either religion or culture is inevitably a study of the other. The main emphasis of Uzukwu's religious thought is human-oriented, focusing more on human flourishing than on otherworldly. Uzukwu argues that religion is perhaps the most sensitive aspect of the culture and reveals the fundamental structures of any society. An important study of African theology cannot do without African religion.[9]

Uzukwu argues that religion serves the basic purpose of human flourishing in Africa. In this regard, the transcendent God breaks into human space and makes his authority felt,[10] ennobling human dignity and restoring human wholeness. African Traditional Religion constitutes the basic root metaphor for understanding the African culture and worldview. In this context, religion and culture reinforce each other. For Uzukwu, the prevalence of the spirit and recognition of diversity is analogous to Semitic experiences: "Just as there are allies and enemies of life in African Traditional Religion, Hebraic experience, drawing from a primitive Semitic pool, has a clear place for divine council, and there are allies as well as opponents of Yahweh."[11]

Epistemologically, we can identify some distinctive features of a generalized African way of knowing. The locution and modes of symbolization jointly describe an African way of knowing and expression. Robin Horton clarifies this supposition:

> The symbolist approach divides human thought and discourse into two great categories: the expressive, which involves the production of symbolic imagery as an end in itself; and the instrumental, which involves the use of literal, discursive thought and language to achieve the ulterior end of practical control of the world. In the first category fall art, magic and religion; whilst into the second fall common sense, technological and scientific thinking. Although both expressive and instrumental categories

---

9. Uzukwu, "Inculturation," 6.
10. Uzukwu, "Re-Evaluating God-Talk from an African Perspective," 55–71.
11. Uzukwu, "Liturgy, Culture and the Postmodern World," 174–75.

are within the compass of all human minds and are to be found in all cultures, the expressive is said to predominate over the instrumental in Africa and non-Western cultures, and the instrumental to predominate over the expressive in the modern West.[12]

The expressivity of African symbolism is an area dear to Uzukwu as he envisions a liturgy and sacramental practices that take African sensibilities seriously. This expressive liturgy makes ample use of gestures consistent with African mindset and will be further examined in the next chapter.

Another characteristic feature of African worldview is a strong sense of community,[13] or, broadly speaking, relationship. Uzukwu captures this tendency in his methodology, which can be summarized simply as: "nothing stands alone." The community is the rallying point and meaning-making process for knowing. Indeed, "Among the numerous cultural values and the heritage of Africa one stands out that is the ability of African traditional society to social cohesion on the basis of community life understood as common brotherhood."[14] However, the communitarian orientation does not mitigate, but celebrates individual liberty and personal traits. This approach supplies an alternative to the understanding of the individual as "a rational substance of individual nature."[15] Therefore, the African view of the individual ("I am because we are") is in direct contrast to the Cartesian "I think therefore I am."[16] This emphasizes the indispensable value of the community and interpersonal connections for the authentic human actualization in the presence of the other.

From this perspective, Uzukwu critiques and relativizes the negative view of the body. He traces this from the ancient writings of Plotinus that greatly influenced Saint Augustine and later Western thinking on the body. Nonetheless, Uzukwu has been quick to add that, "this Western viewpoint, based on a set of experiences and philosophical assumptions, is legitimate and has created the Western human type. But it must be stressed that it is one cultural attitude among many others."[17] The African view of the

---

12. Horton, *Patterns of Thought in Africa*, 6.

13. Essentials of African traditional thinking includes the community, the spiritual/religious universe and African concept of time. See Chike, "Proudly African, Proudly Christian."

14. Asouzu, "The Heuristic Principle of African Ethics," 102.

15. Aquinas, *Summa Theologiae*, I.29.1.

16. Mbiti, *African Philosophy and Religions*, 106.

17. Uzukwu, *Worship as Body Language*, 7.

person, in contrast, encompasses relationships and plurality as the ground of being.[18] This contrasts sharply with the dominant understanding and preoccupation with being as one. An epistemological orientation of this nature, traceable to Greek philosophy, lays claim to totality or monism as universality. Suffice it to say that this monism excludes, oppresses, and annihilates. According to Catherine Keller,

> Ontology emanates from Greek metaphysics. But it was absorbed by Christianity; indeed, it became the foundation for Christian theology. It conceives being as changeless self-identity over and against change and difference.... Once Christianity converted the Roman Empire, this logic of sameness over difference stimulated a Christian allergy to difference.[19]

On the contrary, in West Africa, as Uzukwu articulates, ambivalence, collaboration, and the hermeneutic of suspicion, especially the suspicion of absolutes, are the rule for accessing reality, and the ground of being. This orientation facilitates the search for a "second point of view," or what he describes as "looking at everything twice." What is not relational would be a degeneration and would not constitute an object of knowledge. Consequently, this relationality and diversity serve as a direct antithesis to absolutism and monism.[20]

The Idea of the Local Church

Uzukwu's theology revolves around the idea of the local church. The idea of the local church involves the dynamics of the relationship between the universal and the particular. It is basically a recognition of the theological validity and necessity of the local church that would give rise to the emergence of difference in liturgy and sacramental expression. Recognition of this possibility is a basic assumption of this book. Uzukwu understands the church as being fundamentally local, and the universal church as a communion of local churches.

---

18. Uzukwu, *God, Spirit, and Human Wholeness*, 11.
19. Keller, et al., *Postcolonial Theologies*, 10.
20. Uzukwu, *God, Spirit, and Human Wholeness*, 60.

Biblical and Patristic Understanding of the Church

Yves Congar traces the notion of the church to ancient Israel. The encounter between God and Abraham (Gen 12) culminated in the alliance with Israel through Moses in the Sinaitic covenant (Exod 19-20). The inheritance God promised them at this time was material and earthly, just as the relationship was based on race or on carnal affiliation. This imperfect union became broadened, especially during the exile, with the promise of becoming more spiritualized, as revealed by the prophets. Jesus, at the beginning of his ministry, inaugurated the messianic age promised by these prophets. Thus, the eschatological age began with the ministry of Jesus is the beginning of the constitution of the church. According to Congar,

> In this new order, the inheritance promised to Abraham and called "the land" is radically transformed. It is still an inheritance received from God; but what we are called to, the goods of which the people of the new alliance are to enter into possession, is no other than the patrimony of God himself. What the alliance, the Blood of the New Testament, opens out to us is access to the heavenly inheritance (Hebrews 9:15; Colossians 3:24).[21]

In the new dispensation, Christ becomes the source of inheritance for Christians, who are now co-heirs with Christ. However, in the New Testament, the Church is presented as a kingdom, a community, a city, even the body of Christ, with visible characteristics that tell of invisible realities. The condition for the new alliance is realized by sacramental symbols, no longer carnal generation, and the sacraments form the members of this alliance into a people. Congar identifies the three-fold character of the sacraments as commemorating the past in the passion of Christ (the source of reconciliation of the whole world), the present in the reality of grace and the future as consummation in glory.[22] So the church emerges directly from the life and ministry of Jesus, above all, the passion and resurrection of Christ.

The church of the New Testament was one of unity in diversity: Jewish-Christian, Hellenistic, Pauline, and Johannine communities.[23] One quickly

---

21. Congar, *The Mystery of the Church*, 61.

22. Congar, *The Mystery of the Church*, 63-64.

23. Rausch, *Towards a Truly Catholic Church*, 2. Perhaps, the Vatican II description of the church as a mystery best fits the nature of the church. Scholars identify different dimensions of the church as Christological, pneumatological, historical, and eschatological. While some ecclesial bodies try to emphasize these aspects, to some extent one aspect is inevitably dominant. Whereas the Roman Catholic relies more on Christological

observes that a legitimate diversity was prevalent in this early ecclesiology. Nonetheless, the pluralism of the early church did not undermine its essential unity. We may describe this early experience of the church as one of unity in diversity. Roger Haight notes this important characteristic of the early church: "While the pluralism is obvious, the value of unity suffused the community wherever it existed and according to all of its historical witnesses. The metaphors for the unity of the Church abound."[24] The unity and diversity of the church is expressed with the analogy of the body of Christ, where Christ is the head of the church (Col 1:18; Eph 4:15), the church becomes a people, a people of God (1 Pet 2:10). The church is not separated from Christ: it forms a single entity, in the sense that Christ remains the head and the church is the body of Christ. In the opinion of Thomas Rausch: "Christians from different churches were able to live with considerable diversity in both theology and ecclesiology; nevertheless, they did not repudiate or reject one another. They maintained communion (Koinonia) with each other."[25] The churches established by Paul in his missionary journeys and the welcoming of the Gentiles to the faith (in the famous Council of Jerusalem, Acts 15), illustrate this dimension. The central essential, unifying element was faith in Christ Jesus, for "Faith is the ground on which we are justified, and we grow as members of Christ through acts that are animated by a living faith."[26] Sacramental and liturgical celebrations always presuppose faith as they simultaneously lead to faith.

The accounts of evangelists and writers as we have them today reflect a faith-based account of various communities in the light of the Christ event. Therefore, a search for uniformity in the inessentials in the New Testament may be a futile and unnecessary venture. The patristic church, though not having a systematic presentation of various themes, reveals that the early church had a multiplicity of expressions of the one faith, which existed side by side. To early believers, diversity was not an issue as the central beliefs remained the same.

The Pentecost experience appears to have shaped the understanding of the early church. At Pentecost, the Holy Spirit is the agent of unity;

---

foundations, the Orthodox ecclesiology relies more on pneumatological orientation with its avowed emphasis on gifts (charisms) and recognition of diversity. A healthy balance between these two dimensions is necessary to avoid the danger of relapsing into the extremes of both leanings. Rausch, *Towards a Truly Catholic Church*, 4–5.

24. Haight, *Christian Community in History*, 132–33.
25. Rausch, *Towards a Truly Catholic Church*, 4.
26. Congar, *The Mystery of the Church*, 73–74.

differences of culture and language were overcome by the miracle of Pentecost. Thus, the mandate of making disciples of all nations (Acts 1:8), can be understood as a dialogical mission, which enriched the whole by the contributions of its parts. Commenting on the implications of the Pentecost experience, Richard Gaillardetz has argued that "the Holy Spirit does not erase difference but renders difference non-divisive."[27] The miracle of Pentecost is a testimony to the inherent diversity and unity in the Trinity, which also finds expression in the economy of salvation. The same idea of difference and diversity is discernible in Saint Paul's diversity of gifts that emerge from the one Spirit (1 Cor 12).

From patristic times, one quickly notices the centrality of communion of the various churches in the bond of unity. For example, Tertullian notes the communion of churches by the profession of the same doctrine: "We are in communion with the apostolic churches because our doctrine in no way differs from theirs; this is a sign of truth."[28] In the more developed communion ecclesiology of Cyprian and Augustine, the universal church is the communion of churches, the communion of communions.[29] Communion that does not envisage uniformity becomes a basic and fundamental category of the universal church. It is expedient to point out that such communion respected the diversity that is consistent with cultural and contextual differences and delineations.

The word *catholic* can etymologically be traced to Greek: "*Katholikos* is derived from the Greek root *kat'holou*, which might be translated as "pertaining to or oriented toward the whole."[30] Richard Gaillardetz and Catherine Clifford, differentiate this meaning from the dominant understanding: "Whereas universal suggests the same everywhere, true catholicity is more about unity-difference."[31] For Ignatius (in his letter to Ephesus) and Chrysostom, the Catholic Church designated the eucharistic gathering of the assembly. If this eucharistic undertone is taken seriously, then the idea of identifying the universal church with a certain locale, namely Rome, could only be ascribed to a later historical development, which obscured the original meaning of catholicity. The term *Catholic Church* appears

---

27. Gaillardetz, *Ecclesiology for a Global Church*, 38.

28. Tertullian, *Adversus Haereses*, 21.7, cited in McDonnell and Montague, *Christian Initiation and Baptism in the Holy Spirit*, 94.

29. McDonnell and Montague, *Christian Initiation and Baptism in the Holy Spirit*, 95.

30. Gaillardetz and Clifford, *Keys to the Council*, 129.

31. Gaillardetz and Clifford, *Keys to the Council*, 129.

first, according to recorded history, in Ignatius's letter to Smyrna, where he establishes the inextricable link between the Eucharist, Jesus Christ, and the Catholic Church.[32] So the local church is the dwelling of the universal church. The whole church is found in the local church, without any ontological prioritization or considerations of historical origins. The catholicity of the church, therefore, is anchored on Christ and his ministry, which is prior to every other dimension of the church. Hence, catholicity is founded vertically on Christ and horizontally on the relationship between local churches. In this regard, Uzukwu argues about the church: "It is a local and localized community that may attract praise or blame for its role in the construction of Africa. It is a local church which is realized on many levels. But the most intensive context for the realization of the meaning of this church is the liturgical assembly in which the faithful are gathered to celebrate (especially the Eucharist)."[33]

A further buttressing of the reality and theological significance of the local church involves the early church's missionary experience, or the experience of the church during the first millennium of the Christian era. The differences and similarities in the apostolic churches of the first century and the parallel development of Western (Roman) and Eastern (Byzantine) Christianity suggest the development and tolerance of the time. The Christian expansion from its cradle in Jerusalem to Ethiopia indicates an instance of inculturation. Other early forms of Christianity in the global context include Syriac Christianity, which retained enormous Semitic character in its practices, and the Armenian church of the third century, as well as the Thomas Christians of India, who locate their origin with Thomas the Apostle in the first century. It stands to reason that these Christian centers engaged the language and, to a reasonable extent, the local culture (modes of symbolization) in expressing the Christian faith and message. Accounts of the first millennium of Christianity indicate that the Christian movement from its beginning was global in impulse, embracing a catholicity that was open to cultural differences.[34] To this effect, "By the end of the first millennium Christianity had long been transposed from its original Hebrew cultural context into a surprising diversity of cultures: Hellenist, Coptic, Armenian, Persian, Syrian, Indian, Slavic

---

32. Ignatius of Antioch, *Letter to the Smyrneans*, 8.1–2, in Rordorf et al., *The Eucharist of the Early Christians*, 59. See also Jurgens, *The Faith of the Early Fathers*, 1:25.

33. Uzukwu, *A Listening Church*, 8.

34. Gaillardetz, *Ecclesiology for the Global Church*, 42.

and even Chinese."³⁵ Subsequent development of the Christian practice of recognition of diversity and difference became hoodwinked by political and historical situations, which made the Christian movement yield more to nationalistic interest than to unity within the faith.

The Loss of the Local Church

The second millennium witnessed a paradigm shift in the understanding of the church and its unity, including a radical departure from the practices of the early church. The sense of the universal church as a communion of local churches waned, with the emergence of a pyramidal structure, consistent with the Roman socio-political system. This development had enormous consequences for the church. In particular, it suppressed the validity and legitimate differentiation that gave vent to local churches, which, in turn became understood as missions of the Roman church, an outpost of the church's administrative center, understood parochially as the universal church. This convenient administrative center, with ancestry traceable to the martyrdoms of Peter and Paul, assumed priority over all other churches. Consequently, the Roman cultural and administrative structure and style became almost indistinguishable from Christian tradition and wisdom; the civilization of Christianity, in effect, became a civilization modeled on the Roman cultural system.

Scholars ascribe a plethora of factors to this paradigm shift in ecclesiology, which we describe as theological and political. Theologically, there was the understanding of unity as uniformity, which obliterated every inkling of diversity, whereas diversity is not inimical to unity and, indeed, is its ground.³⁶ A greater unity exists in the unity of purpose than in the annihilation of God-given cultures (vehicles and carriers of the divine) in the search for uniformity in every detail of ecclesial life. Uniformity in worship and sacramental expression—products of the Tridentine era— were unknown in earlier centuries.

The centralization of the church, or the ontological priority of the Church of Rome over other churches, is a modern phenomenon, to say the least. This reality has immensely transformed the church and the papacy. Nicholas Lash has summed up the situation regarding the papacy thus:

---

35. Gaillardetz, *Ecclesiology for the Global Church*, 42.
36. See White, *Roman Catholic Worship*, 144.

> From court of last appeal to chief execution officer . . . this transformation was—from the production of the Code of Canon Law in 1917 to the system of concordats established throughout the first half of this century—deliberately planned and engineered. . . . Whatever one's assessment of the increasing power and influence over diocesan affairs of the Roman Curia and its network of nuncios, these things are recent innovations.[37]

The development of Tridentine theology sought a uniformity that eclipsed the distinctness and autonomy of the local church. Most probably, the unity understood as uniformity universalized a particular cultural and theological perspective. Hence, "Theology was culturally conditioned by the Western culture . . . [which] simply assumed that it was supernatural and universally valid. And since Western culture was implicitly regarded as Christian, it was equally self-evident that this culture had to be exported with the Christian faith."[38] This orientation finds its clearest expression in the Council of Trent, which was full of polemics. To Uzukwu, the pope's ordinary and immediate jurisdiction over the entire church often presents the papacy as the "chief executive officer" of a multinational corporation and the bishops as regional managers. This designation is consistent with the ubiquitous powers of the supreme pontiff, has now been nuanced by the decentralization of the Second Vatican Council. The renewal Vatican II set out to restore the status of local churches, with an emphasis of office in the church as service.

Vatican II and Rediscovery of the Local Church

The Second Vatican Council remains a major event of the twentieth century. Occurring at a critical moment in history (after the Second World War and with the flourishing of various rights movements, as well as the cultural/political revolution), it marks a watershed in Catholic self-identity and relationship with the world. In so many ways, it acknowledged and endorsed some of the hitherto discountenanced positions, especially its view of non-Christian religions and non-Western cultures, the nature of mission, and the attitude of the church to the world. In brief, unlike previous councils, which focused on clarifying doctrines or defining dogma, Vatican II remains unparalleled in its pastoral openness to the multiplicity of the

---

37. Cited in Gray, *Christianity*, 132.
38. Bosch, *Transforming Mission*, 448. See also Olikenyi, *African Hospitality*, 19.

world's cultures. All these influenced the recognition and restoration of the authenticity and validity of local churches.

Long before the council, the experience of the Enlightenment had drawn attention to the danger of both the naïve allegiance to authority and faith and the danger of missionary paradigm that promoted the division between Christian nations and mission lands; however, from the early twentieth century the church began to adopt a new missionary approach as exemplified in the writings of some pontiffs. For example, popes Benedict XV (1919) and Pius XI (1926) supported indigenous clergy, recognizing their indispensability in missionary work. *Princeps Pastorum*, a 1959 encyclical of Pope John XXIII, argued for the validity of human cultures, since elements of goodness are not the exclusive reserve of any human culture.[39] Again, the world wars of the twentieth century, the end of colonialism, and the abolition of slavery all prepared the stage for the Copernican turn of the Vatican II Council.[40] In the opinion of Joseph Ratzinger, theological expert to the Cardinal of Cologne during the Council, "The debate on religious liberty will in later years be considered one of the most important events of the Council already rich enough in important events. To use the catchphrase again, there was in Saint Peter's square the sense that here was the end of the Middle Ages, the end event of [the] Constantinian age."[41]

Its theology inaugurated a move to retrieve the validity and role of suppressed local churches, as an indispensable constituent of the catholicity of the church universal. This shift began in its first approved document, *Sacrosanctum Concilium*, which states,

> Even in the liturgy, the church does not wish to impose a rigid uniformity in matters which do not affect the faith or the well-being of

---

39. The pontiff stated, "Whenever authentic values of art and thought can enrich the culture of the human family, the church is ready to encourage and give her patronage to these products of the spirit. As you know, she does not identify herself with any one culture to the exclusion of the rest—not even with European and Western culture, with which her history is so intricately linked." See John XXIII, *Princeps Pastorum*, in Hickey, *Modern Missionary Documents and Africa*, 43. In other documents of the Second Vatican Council, the casual reader notes the change in tone and in emphasis. For example, in *Lumen Gentium*, the Council stated, "In virtue of this catholicity, each part contributes its own gifts to other parts and to the entire church, so that the whole and each of the parts are strengthened by the common sharing of all things and by the common effort to achieve fullness in unity" (LG 13).

40. See Bevans and Gros, *Rediscovering Vatican II*, 152–53. See also Iwuchukwu, *Media Ecology and Religious Pluralism*, 30–32.

41. Cited in Bevans and Gros, *Rediscovering Vatican II*, 51.

the entire community. Rather does it cultivate and foster the qualities and talents she respects and fosters the spiritual adornments and gifts of the various races and nations. Anything in people's way of life which is not indissolubly bound up with superstition and error the church studies with sympathy and, if possible, preserves intact. It sometimes even admits such things into the liturgy itself, provided they harmonize with its true and authentic spirit.[42]

It is obvious that such a rating of indigenous and non-Western cultures remains unprecedented. Even though the structure of the Roman liturgy remains the norm, one must appreciate the openness of the Vatican II concept, which gives rise to a renewed positive evaluation of cultures. Thus, contemporary ecclesiology is moving away from the monocultural and monolithic uniformity that excluded more than it included and, indeed, made Christianity a permanent visitor in Africa. This new understanding reverses what had been dominant in Catholic theological thinking. The council further retrieved the idea of *communio* from the patristic and biblical traditions: The church is the communion of the Trinitarian life and of the people of God. Hence it stated,

> God the Father gives life to human beings dead in sin. . . . The Spirit dwells in the Church and in the hearts of the faithful, as in a temple, prays and bears witness in them that they are his adopted children. He guides the Church in the way of all truth and, uniting it in fellowship and ministry, bestows upon it different hierarchic and charismatic gifts, and in this way directs it and adorns it with his fruits. By the power of the gospel the Spirit rejuvenates the Church, constantly by renewing it and leading it to perfect union with its spouse.[43]

In this way, the council accentuated the vertical and horizontal dimensions of the church. Uzukwu has expressed this idea in the principle of relationality that undergirds the fellowship of the churches. The council's description of the church as, "a sacrament, a sign and instrument of communion

---

42. SC 37. In fact, the Council gave an incredibly positive evaluation of cultures: "It is a feature of the human person that it can achieve true and full humanity only by means of culture, that is, through the cultivation of the goods and values of nature. Whenever, therefore, there is a question of human life, nature and culture are intimately linked together" (GS 53). In this way, the Council recognized the indispensable role of culture for human flourishing. We can thus describe the Council as a realistic one.

43. LG 4.

with God and of the unity of the entire human race,"[44] reinforced this new understanding of the church. Even as the council progressed, the Trinitarian origin and foundation of the church became a clear call to recognize diversity and plurality in the one church of Christ.[45]

One must note the terminology of *profound adaptation* as used by the council in talking about native cultures. To be precise, the council elucidated its understanding of culture thus,

> The word "culture" in its general sense indicates everything whereby man develops and perfects his many bodily and spiritual qualities; he strives by his knowledge and his labor, to bring the world itself under his control. He renders social life more human both in the family and the civic community, through improvement of customs and institutions. Throughout the course of time he expresses, communicates, and conserves in his works, great spiritual experiences, and desires that they might be of advantage to the progress of many, even of the whole human family.[46]

One sees here how the council presents a positive evaluation of many cultures, recognizing a hidden God at work in the various areas of human life. It is good, then, to agree with Clemens Sedmak in his description of this recognition, "There is an implicit theology hidden in our form of life and in our way of looking at things. Our cultures are shaped by implicit theologies, implicit beliefs about what counts in life."[47] Hence, a proper listening to cultures represents an attention to the divine reality that lies hidden within.

The council affirmed how young churches can grow by borrowing from indigenous wisdom and resources in its eloquent testimony of the goodness of cultures,

> The seed, which is the word of God, watered by divine dew, sprouts from the good ground, and draws from thence its moisture, which it transforms and assimilates into itself, and finally bears much fruit. In harmony with the economy of the Incarnation, the young churches, rooted in Christ and built up on the foundation of the Apostles, take to themselves in a wonderful exchange all the riches of the nations which were given to Christ as an inheritance (cf. Ps.

44. LG 2.

45. See AG 2. It sees the church as missionary, as the product of the *missio Dei* (the communion of the Father and the persons of the Trinity), the mission of the Father, the Son, and the Holy Spirit. So, the whole church is thus missionary.

46. GS 53.

47. Sedmak, *Doing Local Theology*, 75.

2:8). They borrow from the customs and traditions of their people, from their wisdom and their learning, from their arts and disciplines, all those things which can contribute to the glory of their Creator, or enhance the grace of their Savior, or dispose Christian life the way it should be.[48]

John Paul II, drawing inspiration from the position of the council clearly argues for dialogue of cultures and insists on the necessity of cultural dialogue rather than the displacement and replacement of one culture by another.[49] For Christians outside the dominant centers of Christian gravity, the new opening drums up a new dawn, a new beginning. Directly under this inspiration, Uzukwu has argued that, "Inculturation theology is first and foremost a reaffirmation of African culture and identity, denied by Western colonialism and Christian missionary evangelism."[50] The post-Vatican II Church initiated an attempt at reclaiming a lost history, the local church, and the goodness of human persons and cultures, which were hitherto denied of any inherent good. This was a necessary endeavor, since Christianity like every other religion, carries a culture within it. The Gospel is similarly not devoid of cultural expressions. In this light, Sedmak underscored the need to constantly renegotiate Christian beliefs; hence, "We also need dialogue between theology and culture because Christian identity is constantly negotiated within local cultures. Christians live in local cultures. They do not live within a Christian culture. There is no such thing. Nor is there any Christian religion on a culturally neutral ground. Human beings are situated beings."[51] This does not disregard the fact that some cultures have been more strongly associated with the Christian message.

Intricately linked to the understanding of the local church is the role of the local bishop in his diocese. The council speaks of the role as essential to the Eucharist and the Gospel in guiding the local church, for, "where the Gospel is proclaimed and the Eucharist celebrated under the presidency of the bishop, the body of Christ is present." *Lumen Gentium* describes the diocese or the local church along the lines of eucharistic assembly.[52] Further, on the Eucharist and the local church, the council takes note of

---

48. AG 22.
49. John Paul II, "World Day of Peace," no. 10, January 1, 2001.
50. Uzukwu, *A Listening Church*, 5.
51. Sedmak, *Doing Local Theology*, 80.
52. LG 8; SC 41.

the new People called by God, in the Holy Spirit and in much fullness. In them the faithful are gathered together by the preaching of the Gospel of Christ, and the mystery of the Lord's Supper is celebrated, that by the food and blood of the Lord's body the whole brotherhood may be joined together. In any community of the altar, under the sacred ministry of the bishop, there is exhibited a symbol of that charity and "unity of the mystical Body, without which there can be no salvation."[53]

To be precise about the theological notion and validity of local churches, the council defined a diocese as, "a portion of the people of God entrusted to a bishop to be shepherded by him with the assistance of the presbyterate, so that, loyal to their pastor and gathered by him through the Gospel and the Eucharist in the Holy Spirit, it constitutes a local church in which is truly present and active the one, holy, and apostolic Church of Christ."[54] Thus, we note the essentials of a true authentic church: the Gospel, the Eucharist, and the Holy Spirit. So, the church does not exist in isolation. This renewed position of the council reveals the recovery of the validity and identity of the local church. The council further declares, "It is only in and from these local churches that the one and single Catholic Church exists."[55] Hence the universal church is a communion of local churches.

From this perspective, all gatherings of the people of God make the church, and every gathering is a local church. We can, then, speak of the church of Jerusalem, the church of Rome, the church of Corinth, and the church of Ephesus—descriptions known in the early church. The letters of Saint Paul to various churches give credence to this understanding. The subsequent prioritization of the Church of Rome, with its attendant ontological superiority, was a later development, consistent with the mentality and uniformitarianism of the time. Hence, the church could be described as "a community of local circumscriptions."[56] A Tridentine understanding of the church, on the contrary, using juridical terms, defined the Church of Rome as the universal church and other churches as the outposts or missions of it. Vatican II was out to correct this overly juridical and legalistic view

---

53. LG 26.
54. CD 11.
55. LG 23.
56. Akpunonu, "The Universal Church and the Local Churches of Africa," 29.

of the church. *Lumen Gentium*, its dogmatic constitution on the church, avoided any definition, and described the church as a mystery.[57]

Vatican II reexamined the nature of the church and settled for a less legalistic structure, one that gives prominence to the Holy Spirit, rather than to human sociology. Brian Hearne articulates this point, "The mystical Body of Christ is found, not primarily in an organization, however majestically structured, but in the community of people who live with the faith of Christ in their hearts: a faith which needs external and structural expression, yes, but which comes before and gives meaning to all structures."[58] This presents the essentials of the church beyond the human structures. In the expression of this faith, the eucharistic sacrifice, which constitutes the community and is celebrated by the community, becomes essential.

Vatican II amply demonstrates that the Eucharist makes the church. According to the council, "the Church finds its clearest manifestation in the Eucharist celebrated by the local bishop surrounded by his people."[59] This is the reality of the particular church, and it similarly states that, "This Church of Christ is truly present in all legitimate local congregations of the faithful, which, united with their pastors, are themselves called 'churches' in the New Testament. For in their own locality, these are the new people called by God in the Holy Spirit and with much fullness."[60]

A recognition of the identity of the church as present in all local congregations is a recognition of legitimate diversity and difference in the local churches. Consequently, this gives rise to the acceptance of differences in worship, differences in the manner of addressing local problems, and differences in a variety of Christian patterns of life. Different situations and different communities require different approaches and solutions. Uniformity is no longer a mark of Catholic unity—a decisive moment in the history of Catholicism and the entire ecumenical movement. The council points out:

> The Christian life will be adapted to the mentality and character of each culture, and local traditions, together with the special qualities of each national family, illumined by the light of the gospel, will be taken up into a Catholic Unity. So new particular churches,

---

57. This reversion is further attested by the definition of ministry as service. The Constitution on the Church more emphatically places the laity and general priesthood before ecclesiastical offices. See LG 3.

58. Hearne, "Conciliar Fellowship and the Local Church," 130.

59. SC 41.

60. LG 23, 26.

each with its own traditions, have their place in the community of the Church, the primacy of Peter which presides over this universal assembly of charity, all the while remaining intact.[61]

One of the council's greatest insights concerning the church is its identification of the true church of Christ wherever the community gathers around its bishop to celebrate the Eucharist. This point is crucial for the particular or local churches, for where you have a community of believers, there you have the Catholic Church. The supreme bond among Christians is faith in Christ who lives among them, while the church, in the last analysis, is simply the community that lives in the presence of the risen Christ. Therefore, Karl Rahner could write:

> Basic communities, in the sense of local Christian groupings built up from below as a result of free initiative and association, have just as much right as a territorial parish to be recognized as a basic element of the church. It is clear for theological reasons and in the light of the testimony of history that parishes constituted by a particular territory simply could not be the sole basic element of the church.[62]

Uzukwu's theology is solidly anchored in Vatican II's recovery of the theological validity of the local church. The local church, as rediscovered by Vatican II, is an ecclesiological paradigm that is consistent with that of first-century Christianity. Church Fathers like Cyprian knew of local churches that enjoyed some degree of autonomy while being in communion with other sister churches, like the Church of Rome. Thus, Uzukwu argues,

> The Second Vatican Council broke through this authority-conscious model of church and projected the image of the *people of God*. A basic equality exists! Each member is called to holiness, called to participate fully in the life of the church; and ministry is exercised for the good of the body of Christ. This new vision of church encouraged local churches in Africa to initiate actions responding to local needs.[63]

Local needs should provide the content of theology, which of course, the local church responds to in a manner that is consistent with her faith. In the mind of Uzukwu, over-reliance on the Church of Rome for the solution

---

61. AG 22.
62. Rahner, *The Shape of the Church to Come*, 109.
63. Uzukwu, "The Birth and Development of a Local Church," 1, 17–23.

to every problem inevitably shields the African clergy and those in formation away from the concrete realities of life on the African continent. Authentic local churches must take responsibility for numerous projects without precluding the possibility of mutual exchange of charity. To this effect, we can say that Vatican II's shift from a pyramidal pattern of ecclesiastical structure and administration makes theology more relevant to contexts and Christian life more authentic.

It is in this light that Uzukwu argues for a change in the structure of the local church in Africa. He states that a pyramidal structure with a similar authority structure is foreign to African contexts, and a new vision for the Church would encourage actions that could respond to local needs. He praises the decision of the *Association of Member Episcopal Conferences of East Africa* (AMECEA) to establish *small Christian communities* (SCC), in 1976. He recognizes the danger of the SCC, such as splinter groups, but writes, "This new style [SCC] threatens the command structure; those in power are not ready to change. AMECEA saw initiative and responsibility as fundamental to the emergence of a dynamic local church; but these must be supervised and even must originate from the clergy in order to ensure right doctrine and right practice."[64] Although it is still premature at this point, a casual reader may misconstrue Uzukwu as preferring the culture over certain essential Christian practices. Nonetheless, it would be proper to read him within the context: the desire for the emergence of a church that would bear the marks of local communities.

A necessary correlation exists between the church and her sacraments since the model of ecclesiology determines her sacramental practices. The church's understanding of herself, her nature, and her mission, determines her sacramental structure. In other words, ecclesiological structure is the major determinant of sacramental structure, as the latter anticipates and follows the former. A discussion of renewed sacramental structure is preceded only by a new way of being a church. Uzukwu's understanding and reinterpretation of sacraments follows his view of ecclesiology. His whole theological exploration can be summed up in the creation of authentic local churches. In his response to the 1994 Special Assembly of the Synod of Bishops for Africa, he articulated his vision in his *A Listening Church*. He admits that African churches are products of European missionary efforts but, argues that these churches have attained some maturity and can think for themselves:

---

64. Uzukwu, "The Birth and Development of a Local Church," 18.

The colonial and missionary ideology had as their ultimate aim the changing of the identity of the "colonized" and "evangelized." In those situations where nationalistic and evangelical interests were consciously merged, the deep-seated exploitative colonial program along with the then European prejudice against Africans failed to be lucidly examined by missionaries.[65]

One can read the concatenation of the political situation and the prevailing ecclesiological structure as intolerant to local voices in enforcing unity as uniformity, as already discussed in the first chapter. To this extent, the whole of inculturation theology from the African perspective is "First and foremost a reaffirmation of the African culture and identity, denied by Western colonialism and Christian missionary evangelism."[66] Uzukwu adds that, "This church, which sometimes speaks out and at other times appears less ready to take positions, is not a platonic institution."[67] In other words, it is not idealized, like a superstructure with outposts: "It is a local church which is realized on many levels. But the most intensive context for the realization of the meaning of this church is the liturgical assembly in which the faithful are gathered to celebrate (especially the Eucharist)."[68]

To realize a true local church in Africa, Uzukwu suggests retrieving the traditional model of African societies before the colonial era. He believes that these structures mirror the structures of the New Testament churches: "The church in Africa should allow itself to be influenced both by the traditional political systems and by the New Testament experience to assume proper patterns of ministry."[69] He gives credit for the creativity and originality of pastors in Africa who have responded to the need for a local theology, given contextual problems that are unknown to the Western world. This encompasses a retrieval of ancestral experience and profound Christian experience while bridging the alienation of the African Christian in the face of daily challenges.

The argument for retrieving indigenous organizational structure, with due modernization, could be employed for constructing authentic local churches in Africa. However, a quick reaction to this endorsement of the family model for the church in Africa is that it does not take into

---

65. Uzukwu, *A Listening Church*, 4.
66. Uzukwu, *A Listening Church*, 5.
67. Uzukwu, *A Listening Church*, 8.
68. Uzukwu, *A Listening Church*, 8–9.
69. Uzukwu, *A Listening Church*, 20.

consideration the hierarchy and often the paternalism found in the African family system. Beyond the view of family as a place for warmth, love, and concern for its members, we must attend to the patriarchy that dehumanizes and excludes females, almost to the point of denying them full humanity.[70] We may understand these as areas that require some necessary critiquing before their appropriation into Christianity.

Uzukwu's Theological Methodology

The importance of theological methods in theological discussion has gained more currency in contemporary times. This recognition is partly due to the realization of diversity and cultural plurality, which detract from a monolithic universalization. Diversity of contexts can only accommodate plurality of theological methods. The corollary is that tools for theologizing, which often determine the product of theological endeavor, must begin from contextual issues. These issues and the manner of the exercise determine the overall results. Theology to a large extent is about interpretation, for "the way one understands governs understanding itself, since understanding itself is generated by its method, [and] method reaches into the content of theology to shape the understanding of theology."[71] Understanding necessarily makes use of cultural "givens" and norms. Uzukwu engages this dynamic of faith and culture in his theological enterprise, for theology must mediate between faith and culture. From the point of view of theology, Bernard Lonergan articulates this idea, since theology, "is a product not only of the religion it investigates and expounds but also of the cultural ideals and norms that set its problems and direct its solution."[72] Uzukwu's interest in methodology therefore stems from the conviction that authentic African theology must draw its resources from the dynamic energies of the local to create alternative ways of doing theology. Such indigenous resources constitute the basic molding blocks in reinterpreting Christian life and practice.[73]

Methodologically, therefore, Uzukwu's theology invokes a different epistemological approach from dominant Western theologies. Such a

---

70. See Nyamiti, *Some Contemporary Models of African Ecclesiology*, 115.
71. Haight, *Dynamics of Theology*, 189.
72. Lonergan, "Theology in Its New Context," 58.
73. See Uzukwu and Boodoo, "Globalization, Politics and Religion in Postcolonial Africa," 83.

distancing from the European paradigm gives rise to the emergence and relevance of contextual theologies. Uzukwu realizes that a monocultural and monolithic theology will at best remain sterile outside the domains of its origins, and, at worse, become oppressive and counterproductive. The locality or contextuality of every theology, which does not preclude mutual exchange, though a novelty, calls for this break if theology is to become relevant and responsive to the multiplicity of contexts. Nevertheless, the aforementioned epistemological break does not take away from the one faith but retrieves the Patristic approach of unity in diversity. Uzukwu amply demonstrates this *ressourcement* in his theological methodology.

Hence, the question of method is fundamental to the discipline, so that, "once one grasps what a given theologian is up to methodologically, one can have a fairly accurate appreciation by anticipation of what his or her conclusions will be. For method reaches into the content of theology to shape the very understanding of the subject matter."[74] The post-Vatican II era has witnessed a plurality of theological methods, indicating a realization of a multiplicity of cultures and a diversity of existential contexts. This awareness is enhanced by the deconstruction of the classicist or parochial understanding of cultures. Consequently, it has come to involve a reinterpretation of the Christian heritage, especially in non-Western cultures. Uzukwu realized this crucial aspect of the Christian mission early in his days as a doctoral student and made a strong case for African theology from the perspective of methodology. For him, *theologia Africana* means the interpretation and explication of the Christ event in African concepts and symbols, and he sees theological methodology as an essential part of African theology. He avers, "To build a systematic theology based on African concepts and symbols, it is necessary to face the question of methodology which will help to clarify the aims and direction of such a theology."[75] To guarantee the theological status and possibility of African theology, he subscribes to the *salvation history approach*, which acknowledges the positive aspects of non-Christian religions. In this way, he avoids the radical displacement of the indigenous religions for the Christian message as espoused by some missionaries during the evangelization of Africa.

African Traditional Religion, like other major world religions, responds to the basic questions of life. The possibility of *theologia Africana* is anchored in the continuity between the Christ event and indigenous

---

74. Haight, *Dynamics of Theology*, 189.
75. Uzukwu, "Notes on Methodology," 156.

African cultures. Uzukwu states, "If there is no continuity there is no basis for a dialogue and *theologia Africana* might be mistaken for native coloring and other appendages while conceptual tools are ignored."[76] He adds, "There is yet no African theologian who . . . has considered this method as a possible tool for the formulation of a *theologia Africana*."[77] The predominant approach to evangelization, or theology in non-Western contexts has been that of radical displacement of indigenous religions and cultures. But the elements of goodness in non-Christian religions as acknowledged for the first time by the Second Vatican Council gives Uzukwu's methodology some credibility. It is only under this consideration that there can be any possibility of dialogue. The possibility of dialogue implies, at least, the presence of common elements that could serve as starting points for dialogue; however, without watering down the distinctive marks of Christianity, Uzukwu acknowledges the radical and decisive position of the revelation of God in Jesus the Christ, a position that cannot be sacrificed.[78] Furthermore, he advocates a critical dialogue between African religion and the development of the Hebrew religion that culminates in the Christ event. Besides his interest in the history of the Hebrew religion and the Christ event, he emphasizes the need for *theologia Africana* to engage in a critical examination of African worldviews to identify parallels and areas of discontinuity with the Judeo-Christian tradition.[79]

Most scholars identify five major theological methods, transcendental, correlational, existential, empirical, and socio phenomenological.[80] Correlation as a theological method aims at making the past relevant to the present using symbols that express the old in a new way.[81] As can be quickly seen, the provenance of these methods or the contexts from which they arose account to a large extent for the nature and utility of

---

76. Uzukwu, "Notes on Methodology," 158.

77. Uzukwu, "Notes on Methodology," 159.

78. Uzukwu, "Notes on Methodology," 159.

79. Uzukwu, "Notes on Methodology," 161–62.

80. See Mueller, *What Are They Saying about Theological Method?* He identifies the traditional methods of theology as Transcendental Method, represented by Rahner and Lonergan, Existential Method, associated with Macquarrie and Tillich, Empirical Method, associated with David Tracy and Meland, and Socio-Phenomenological Method, associated with Schillebeeckx and Sobrino.

81. Mueller, *What Are They Saying about Theological Method?*, 191–94. In fact, Haight sees correlation as the method of theology since it preserves the past by expressing it in present symbols. In a sense, correlation therefore preserves the tradition.

the methods. In other words, the tools of the research determine its extent. Such tools that are manufactured from or for specific contexts most probably will be deficient in responding to specific challenges of varied contexts. Jon Sobrino identifies the post-Enlightenment era as responsible for the European theological method, much unlike the method of liberation theology, which responds to the Latin American context of economic and structural injustices.[82] As classical as these methods have been, not a few African scholars have adopted these methods, especially Paul Tillich's method of correlation in articulating a theology for African contexts and issues. To the best of our knowledge, none of these writers has engaged the corpus of indigenous cultural wisdom as Uzukwu has done in his theological methodology, which is rooted firmly in an African worldview and is consistent with the Jewish religious experience.

Uzukwu's method is not simply an interpretation of the past in the light of the new realities, which would easily qualify as correlational. As early as 1978, Uzukwu began thinking about method in African theology. In his *Notes on Methodology*, he argues for the dialogical nature of African theology, taking seriously the salvation history approach. He also argues for a combination of two dominant approaches in the study of world religions, namely, salvation history and dialogue: "This combination of the Salvation-History approach with Dialogue could be the best method, presently, for building a *theologia Africana*. It is true that African religion is already disadvantaged because those involved in the dialogue have mainly passed over to Christianity, but this does not make the creation of a critical *theologia Africana* unnecessary."[83]

In brief, while not elevating the non-Christian religions to the status of de jure, he argues for the value of African indigenous religion as *praeparatio evangelica*. The task of the African theologian, therefore, becomes a critical work of delineating the parallels and differences between our indigenous religions and their Judeo-Christian counterparts. To this extent, he holds the opinion that the theology of radical displacement is inconsistent with the salvation history model, which sees the Christ event as the ultimate fulfilment of God's revelation of Godself. Furthermore, he observes that salvation history upholds the presence of divine action in African religions, which is related to the central divine intervention in human history. Drawing from the Semitic naming of God, often involved

---

82. See Sobrino, *A True Church of the Poor*.
83. Uzukwu, "Notes on Methodology," 10.

in a syncretistic appropriation of non-Jewish naming of God, he does not find it wrong to appropriate the rich tapestry of the West African non-Christian experience of God.

Uzukwu's project is well based in the vision that the West African worldview has something to contribute to the universal church. According to him,

> My basic assumption is that the West African is not utterly dissimilar from the Jewish-Christian experience of God. Because plurality of active deities that do not threaten the transcendent One God dominates the West African universe, I opt for a perception of hierarchy in divinity that is flexible and dynamic to explore aspects of the history of God in the Jewish-Christian tradition.[84]

Well informed in the West African worldview, Uzukwu engages the predominant orientation to reality: "flexibility as methodological starting point that will enable African theologians to adopt a second view-point"[85] on African and contemporary universal Christian issues. Thus, for him, a "relational tension mediates being-in-the world".[86] This approach, a constituent feature of the West African universe, argues for the need to take a second look and to be open to alternatives. "Instead of absolutizing one's conclusions, every resolution to any problem or conclusion to any discussion is left open-ended."[87] In this way, Uzukwu does not absolutize his West African influences, but makes a strong case for a healthy interface among the various theological regions. West African theologians today redefine themselves and their universe beyond the categorizations of colonial ideology: no static or essentialist model.

---

84. Uzukwu, *God, Spirit, and Human Wholeness*, 105.
85. Uzukwu, *God, Spirit, and Human Wholeness*, 6.
86. Uzukwu, *God, Spirit, and Human Wholeness*, 9.
87. Uzukwu, *God, Spirit, and Human Wholeness*, 11. Uzukwu sees this approach as a way out of the quagmire created for theology and philosophy by the enlightenment, which as a project called for a halt in traditional claims or at worst a revalidation of those claims. And to ignore the Enlightenment can lead only to more cataclysmic consequences for a people of faith: we must be able to give an account of the faith we hold (1 Pet 3:15).

Lived Experience as a Source of Theology

A major implication of the modern turn to the anthropological subject[88] is the recognition of diversity and the validity of cultural pluralism. This development has challenged some assumptions of "the universal" and "the objective" which can be apprehended without reference to contexts, in a false sense of homogeneity due to unwarranted universalism. Particular theologies dubbed universal were made to fit into every concrete situation without reference to context. This definition of a universal theology must then take local contexts into consideration. Dermot Lane rightly draws attention to the contextuality of theology, "All of theology is contextual, and one of the lessons we learned in the twentieth century was that there is no such thing as 'pure' theology. Christian theology arises out of a critical interaction between traditional faith and contemporary experience, between religion and culture, between church and society."[89] As a matter of fact, contexts and cultural differences challenge the assumption of only one, true universal theology. Stephen Bevans describes this phenomenon as a shift from the classic to the empirical understanding of culture.[90] Hence, just as we can say that there is no one ultimate culture, which every other culture should aspire toward, there is also no one ultimate theology. Instead, one must acknowledge plurality of cultures, which are legitimate in their own rights. This remarkable development has made it imperative to take seriously the epistemic location of every theology and the exigencies of that location. Contextual theology therefore engages seriously various times, cultures, and current concerns in articulating a theological response. It recognizes that every theology has developed from or within particular issues, times, and contexts, the interaction of theologies and cultures must respond to the demands of Christian life.

As already presented from the patristic and medieval times, the casual reader notes that the development of theologies often engaged prevailing thought forms (philosophical systems), to respond to the challenges of the day. While some of those challenges linger to this day, it would be naïve to

---

88. Some scholars locate modernity with the philosophy of Rene Descartes. In reaction to the challenge posed by the Enlightenment, which negated any authentic knowledge and the need for a revalidation of knowledge, Descartes came up with the formula *Cogito ergo sum*, and thus redirected the focus of philosophy (and the humanities) from the question of being to the anthropological subject. See Lane, "Theology in Transition," 4–6.

89. Lane, "Theology in Transition," 3.

90. Bevans, *Models of Contextual Theology*.

think that the whole theological work has been done and concluded by any epoch. Theology, like every other human science, responds to the mutability of human cultures. So, God's self-revelation continues to be appropriated in response to contextual and universal issues. As Bevans states, "When revelation was understood in terms of eternal truths framed in unchanging and unchangeable divinely given language, theology could only be conceived of as unchanging and having little or nothing to do with the realities of the culture and social change."[91] On the contrary, theology involves constant interaction between revelation and the changing circumstances of human existence: theology is not a finished product, and it cannot be uncritically parceled out across cultural contexts.

Theological context has revealed the multiplicity and diversity of cultures and anthropological locations. Thus, reality is not just out there, but mediated through culture and history. This implies that truth is constantly renegotiated and reconfigured according to each cultural and historical situation, reinforcing the relevance of contexts.

This recognition of context offers a renewed awareness of the importance of the interaction between the Gospel and concrete issues.[92] The context of the Gospel implies that theological reflection starts with issues of particular contexts and their experience. The fact of variations in present human experience—inescapably historically and culturally bound makes the addition of this experience necessary to traditional sources of theology.[93] Nonetheless, the relevance of such a theology is not context-bound, or specific to that context only, but has wide relevance and applicability. As theological reflection, such faith responses are open to other areas and can inspire wherever similar faith issues abound. Put in another way, contextual theology draws attention to the historical and issues of where the Gospel is preached and lived. Without this recognition, a one-world order is assumed, which does not give a good expression to the reality of the Church in its diversity. Contexts therefore become theologically important and indispensable.

Contextualization as a theological model is understood here as having the same basic meaning as inculturation, which, although theologically more accurate, involves an expression of the Christian faith in cultural models. Yet,

---

91. Bevans, *Models of Contextual Theology*, 10.

92. See Schreiter, *Constructing Local Theologies*; Bevans, *Models of Contextual Theology*.

93. Bevans, *Models of Contextual Theology*, 1.

as a theological model, inculturation is inspired by the reality of the incarnation. As an evangelization tool, inculturation should proclaim the Good News from within a culture by engaging the prevailing contextual issues. By assuming the culture, the Gospel takes root in that particular space, which concomitantly transforms and challenges the culture. Jesus often used this approach in evangelizing; his stories and parables were drawn from ordinary rural life experiences, yet he was elevating and transforming that culture as well. We can safely assert, therefore, that the mission of the church evangelizes human cultures, transforming them through the Gospel. Hence, proper inculturation engages the worldview, symbols, and anthropological and sociological givens of a particular community.

Contextualization as a model facilitates the interaction between scripture and tradition in specific situations and locations. To this extent, it is not just a culturalism or cultural theology, which would privilege or prioritize the culture over Christian tradition. Hence, "the term contextualization includes all that is implied in the older indigenization or inculturation but seeks also to include the realities of contemporary secularity, technology and the struggle for human justice."[94]

Events of modern times have made recognition of the contextuality of theology an inevitable theological model. First, a paradigm shift in the center of gravity of Christianity—the demographic shift of Christianity—makes it necessary to recognize and take seriously the location of the Christians; especially the question of inculturation as popes Paul VI and John Paul II strongly indicated. It is necessary to note an interesting study, "At the beginning of the twentieth century, eighty percent of the world's Christians were of the Caucasian origin, living mostly in the northern hemisphere. But by early in the twenty-first century, they will count for only twenty percent of world Christianity."[95] Voices from the new homeland of Christianity[96] as this book attempts to show, are an important addition to the Christian tradition. Second, the freedom and liberation of the former colonized world make it possible for the colonized to tell their own stories, presenting their unique contributions to world Christianity.

Furthermore, Pope Francis seems to have endorsed the contextual role of theology when he stated, "we see then that the task of evangelization operates within the limits of language and circumstances. It

---

94. Bevans, *Models of Contextual Theology*, 21.

95. Rausch, *Towards a Truly Catholic Church*, 11.

96. See Allen, *The Future Church*.

constantly seeks to communicate more effectively the truth of the Gospel in a specific context, without renouncing the truth, the goodness and the light which it can bring whenever perfection is not possible."[97] Theology is not an abstract reality, or a subject concerned only with the unseen and invisible but with the concrete experiences of real people. For Uzukwu, the objects of theology are the daily challenges of the Christian in living the faith in diverse cultural contexts. Experience therefore becomes an important source of theology, and theology must be concerned and inextricably intertwined with the sociology and anthropology of a people. This does not eclipse the specificity of the Christian heritage but responds to the different challenges of a different people. In this sense, the Christian faith and its God become malleable. This further makes for the imperative of Uzukwu's theological methodology, characterized by flexibility, relationality, and twinness; nothing stands alone.

Resonances of and Hebraic Foundations for African Theology

Uzukwu, to a large extent focuses on the overlap between African and Jewish cosmologies to develop a theology that is consistent with Catholic tradition. He identifies a close relationship between the West African imagination of God and the Jewish experience and reflections on God. Through this approach, he overcomes the challenges of the Greek philosophical tradition, which was quickly adopted to articulate the Christian message. It is worthy of note that Greek philosophy became a tool for expressing the faith, almost to the extent of becoming synonymous with Christian culture, while it furthers a richer appreciation of God's manifold presence.

Although unique in many ways, the Hebraic understanding of God often appropriated the expressions and symbols of Judea's polytheistic neighbors, like the Canaanites' view of God. Their numerous gods and goddesses became messengers or members of the heavenly court in Judaism. In fact, it has been argued that pre-exilian history of Israel had monotheism existing concurrently with polytheism, with monotheism emerging after the Babylonian exile.[98]

The polarity of monotheism and polytheism needs further reflection since we can have both a strict and a broad definition of monotheism. In

---

97. Francis, *The Joy of the Gospel*, No. 45.
98. Sommer, *Bodies of God and the World of Ancient Israel*, 145.

a strict sense, monotheism implies the existence of one deity, without the possibility of others.[99] While this was the professed faith of Israel as exemplified by the *shema*, the concrete experience of Israel indicates the existence of other divine beings that are variously named as angel, the heavenly court, and so on. The elusive divine manifestations to the patriarchs and the epiphanic visitations mitigate the idea of strict monotheism and attest to the plurality of divine beings. This development gives rise to the broad definition of monotheism, in which there "exists one supreme being in the universe, whose will is sovereign over all beings."[100] The emphasis in this second understanding is on the relationship between the divine beings in which only one is supreme; contrariwise, a situation where no one deity has absolute power over all aspects of the world is polytheism.[101]

In this regard, it is appropriate to underscore that "The phrase 'sons of God', which was the usual term for the gods of Canaan in Canaanite polytheism, for they were believed to be literally the children of the great gods and goddesses, was taken over in Israelite circles as a designation for God's heavenly host."[102] In such a divine assembly, from the Canaanite perspective, El was the great god, and Asherah was the mother goddess, as she was linked to fertility, through whom emerged Baal.[103] Scholars continue to debate the status of Asherah in ancient Israel, while monotheists insist that Asherah as goddess was not worshipped. However, in Israel, Yahweh took over some of the functions and identities of the Canaanite gods, as El and Baal are both used as names for Yahweh, the God of Israel. In a similar way, such natural elements and forces like storm, lightning, and thunder through which Baal had been active were now ascribed to Yahweh (Ps 18:13–14; 29; Exod 19:16–19; 1 Kgs 19:11–12). While Baal and polytheism did not make their way into the official religion of Israel, it is probable that they influenced the Jewish notion of God. In many ways, therefore, the Hebrew worldview was basically those of its Semitic neighbors.

In other ways, Israel equally repudiated some religious practices of its neighbors. It repudiated sacred prostitution (Deut 23:17–18), insisted on one God (Deut 6:4–6), who was supreme and often expressed as masculine,

---

99. Sommer, *Bodies of God and the World of Ancient Israel*, 146.
100. Sommer, *Bodies of God and the World of Ancient Israel*, 146.
101. Sommer, *Bodies of God and the World of Ancient Israel*, 147.
102. Wright, *Biblical Archaeology*, 5.
103. See 1 Kings 18–19, which records how Jezebel introduced prophets of Asherah into Israel and the subsequent battle with Elijah, the true prophet of God.

and prohibited images (Exod 20:2–4). Israelite names for God were basically drawn from human social concepts, such as king, judge, shepherd, father, and husband, unlike the Canaanite naming of God from nature. In addition, Israel disavowed goddesses since there was no word for goddess in biblical Hebrew.[104] The later history of Israel and its understanding of God became strongly defined by the Exodus experience.

Thus, to create an African theology, Uzukwu has gone beyond the Greco-Roman presentations of God to the patristic and early Jewish experiences. He states, "My basic assumption is that the West African is not utterly dissimilar from the Jewish-Christian experience of God, because the plurality of active deities that do not threaten the transcendent one God dominates the West African universe."[105] In making this claim, he draws inspiration from the Hebraic pre-exilic understanding of God, which was less opposed to other deities, although there was the prevalence of monotheism or mono-Yahwism. He contends that strict monotheism was a particular characteristic of Israel's post-Babylonian experience.[106] In other words, the absolute transcendence of the one and only Yahweh are later developments in the Deuteronomist era. In this way, Uzukwu highlights resonances between the West African dynamic and flexible understandings of God and the Semitic experiences.

Another indicator of the African experience of God is revealed in names that have been associated with West African cultures. This approach reveals that God is not just transcendent, but also near at hand. *Ere*, the name of God among the Banda people of the Central African Republic, captures both the transcendence and the nearness of God. Commenting on this naming of God, Joseph Donders states, "The Banda speak in this way of a non-personal, indefinable dimension of reality comprising everything that could be named only in a neutral way—*Ere*: thing, it."[107]

The dominant Hebraic theology of Yahweh has not been consistent from its ancestral religion. Uzukwu argues for a more tolerant and flexible Yahweh, and wider inculturation of near-Semitic religious experience into the Yahwistic experience and understanding. The emerged universal, exclusive and absolutist religious outlook of Yahweh was part of the Deuteronomistic reform of later centuries, which established monotheism and derided other

---

104. Wright, *Biblical Archaeology*, 17.
105. Uzukwu, *God, Spirit, and Human Wholeness*, 105.
106. Uzukwu, *God, Spirit, and Human Wholeness*, 105.
107. Donders, *Non-Bourgeois Theology*, 14.

gods, whereas in the ancient divine council El Elyon, Yahweh was head of the council. The metamorphosis from head of divine council to the absolute and only God is accounted for in the later history of Israel.

Retrieving the episode of Elijah and the Horeb experience that forms a major basis of Uzukwu's argument, in which, he underlines the silence, distance, and transcendence of God as factors that invite tolerance and flexibility instead of the violence and exclusivism of the Elijah circle. Indeed, Elijah's violent destruction of the priests of Baal seems to be in opposition to the subsequent revelation of God, in the still and gentle breeze. In the words of Uzukwu, "If the idea of silence, distance and transcendence succeeds in enriching theology in the cross fertilization of Hebraic and West African narratives and practice, one should not undermine or underestimate the dynamism of oneness or uniqueness of Yahweh in a theology that involves the encounter of cultures."[108]

Patristic Foundations of Theology

Uzukwu draws inspiration from the Church of Cyprian of Carthage, a third century father of the church, which was autonomous but in communion with the Church of Rome. Such autonomy would not be foreign to the church of contemporary times. To achieve this autonomy, he argues that revelation is inextricably tied to culture and can accommodate every culture. Therefore, cultural expressions of the one faith would not undermine, but rather enhance the catholicity of the church.

Uzukwu advocates for a local church that would not negate relations with the universal but would respond to its issues appropriately. He argues that the universal and centralizing tendency of the Church of Rome does not necessarily stem from the Petrine ministry, pointing out the existence of various patriarchates in the history of the church. Those patriarchates were responsive to the cultural and anthropological uniqueness of their various locations.

The desire of Uzukwu and most African champions of inculturation is probably summed up in the opinion of a committee of the Tanzanian Episcopal Conference, "The mission process . . . is not fundamentally one of 'adapting' a Christian culture to the needs and forms of expression of a non-Christian culture, a process of translation only. Rather, it is a creative process

---

108. Uzukwu, *God, Spirit, and Human Wholeness*, 125.

in which a new Christian culture comes into being."[109] Hence, Uzukwu establishes, "the fact that Christ can become incarnate, or that Christ can be recognized as already incarnate within the Igbo (African) culture."[110] Interaction of Christianity and cultures renews and transforms.

Relational Pneumatology

Jewish and Greco-Roman understandings of God embody a relational self. The Christian doctrine of the Trinity demonstrates this aspect of the Christian God. Relationality thus effectively stands against the absolute and strict monotheism. Uzukwu deepens this thought on the relational aspect of God especially in his pneumatology by drawing on the West African experience and understanding of God, spirits, and deities. Hence, the prominence of the Spirit in the theological exploration of Uzukwu cannot be overstated. The Spirit serves as the entry point into the divine in its being and operation in the human world. The Spirit guarantees God's transcendence and communion. Uzukwu has stated this idea clearly, "In the West African perception of dynamic hierarchy and flexibility in divinity, the multiplicity of spirits and the distance of God are valid ways of stressing transcendence, communion and mystery."[111]

Relationality, Uzukwu's undergirding principle of life and meaning in West Africa finds expression in the flexibility of the hierarchical understanding of native deities. This understanding includes a dynamic relationship that abhors exclusivism and absolutism. West Africans believe in the relationality of the Supreme Being, who, though top in hierarchy, is in a dynamic relationship with other deities. Those deities serve as deputies to the Supreme Being, whose supremacy does not portent aloofness or unapproachability. This is a subtle distinction, not unlike the Jewish understanding of absolute monotheism in its later religious history. Such relationality is the ground of being and mediates being in the West African world. Closely related to the divine hierarchy of beings is belief in the existence of personal guardian spirits with personal destinies and behavioral patterns assembled at the inception of a new human being. Uzukwu states, "Sacred narratives recount the pre-existence of each human in the land of the dead, the land of spirits. Each human is indeed a 'reincarnation' into

109. Cited in Uzukwu, "Blessing and Thanksgiving among the Igbo," 3.
110. Uzukwu, "Blessing and Thanksgiving among the Igbo," 3.
111. Uzukwu, *God, Spirit, and Human Wholeness*, 213.

the human world through the creative act of a guardian personal spirit that embodies individual destiny."[112] Indeed, this belief can easily be generalized about the understanding of human life and destiny in Africa.

Uzukwu and Contextualized Ecclesiology

Uzukwu refers favorably to indigenous African societal organizational structure before the advent of colonialism. He dismisses the seeming dissimilarities in the vast area of Africa by emphasizing overwhelming commonalities: "I like to consider common features which emerge from African communitarianism, such as the typical African resources to be utilized in the construction of African societies and church."[113] He has proudly asserted, "Athens may have taught the West the principles of democracy, but African communitarianism has contained these elements in African traditions as far back as memory can go."[114] He has identified two basic indigenous patterns of societal organization, "societies with dispersal authority, or with authority in the hands of many," and those with "centralized authority."[115] In the former, authority lies in many hands in the village, which comprises extended families and clans, with the eldest acting as first among equals, while the oracles served as a court of last appeal. Again, for the centralized authority model Uzukwu identifies a common element, the existence of kingship.

In either organizational structure, Uzukwu has identified a high level of consultation and deliberation before decisions are reached.[116] This is an important characteristic of local West African churches, different from the pyramidal hierarchy, under which it can be said, "Power lies in the hands of the people . . . the society or community is an active subject of right."[117] A properly inculturated ecclesial structure necessary for the local church should invoke some of the elements in the traditional organizational

---

112. Uzukwu, *God, Spirit, and Human Wholeness*, 152.
113. Uzukwu, *A Listening Church*, 14.
114. Uzukwu, *A Listening Church*, 19.
115. Uzukwu, *A Listening Church*, 14.
116. It might be necessary to relate this to the imagery of the totem of the *manja* chief in the Central African Republic, which is a large eared rabbit. These ears symbolize a great deal of listening by the chief before he takes a decision. The near-consensus decision is what Uzukwu describes as the African "palaver."
117. Uzukwu, *A Listening Church*, 18.

structure that is not inimical to Christian teaching. The church is the people of God gathered at specific places and time.

Conclusion

This chapter is concerned with articulating the background of Uzukwu's theological formation—a West African worldview in its organizational structure and systematic understanding. It has demonstrated the recovery of the theological validity of local church by Vatican II, and the express endorsement of the use of indigenous resources for the enrichment of the local church. It has elucidated how Uzukwu's theology is rooted in the Judeo-Christian tradition and yet addresses the anthropological and sociological challenges of the contemporary African Christian. In this way, Uzukwu has laid the foundations for an African sacramental theology that engages African worldviews and authentic Christian traditions. This approach is consistent with sacred tradition and responds to the dynamics of life in Africa. While faith in Jesus Christ is central to Christian theology, theology has the arduous task of responding to the deep and existential questions of people situated in every cultural context. The reinterpretation of the one faith in Jesus Christ through West African cultural context is an essential component of the African theological mission. The next chapter builds on the foundation provided in this chapter to reimagine the sacraments.

Chapter 5

Rethinking Sacraments through African Values System

Introduction

IN THE PRECEDING CHAPTER, we established the background and influences on Uzukwu as he developed his theology. We underscored his desire to highlight the theological significance of the local church as inspired by the Second Vatican Council, and the possibility of diversity in liturgical celebrations, while being consistent with the practice of the church. This orientation, rooted in Vatican II theology, recognizes cultural differences and the rich repository of anthropological and sociological goodness in non-Western cultures and religions. This understanding and revision of modern ecclesiology paves the way for this chapter.

This chapter attempts to articulate Uzukwu's reconfiguration of the sacraments through the prism of liturgy, the proper home of the sacraments. It focuses on the specific cultural anthropology and basic world view of the region under discussion for a theologically correct reinterpretation of liturgical and sacramental celebration. It begins by recounting the position of the Second Vatican Council on adaptation of the sacraments and progressively develops how Uzukwu has incorporated cultural elements into liturgical celebration. It concludes with a statement on Uzukwu's understanding of the sacraments and their relevance to daily Christian living.

Vatican II on Profound Adaptation: Reimagining Sacraments

The Second Vatican Council, correctly reading the signs of the time, called for expressing the Christian message according to various cultures.[1] This giant stride is testimony of the church's diversity of traditions and plurality of cultures; in this way, the council recognized the need for and made possible the inculturation of the Gospel. It recognized the importance of relating faith through categories that make cultural sense. This approach allows various cultures, in some sense, "possess" the Gospel and to make it more relevant. Such a rediscovery responds to the intrinsic nature of the Gospel, which addresses everyone and every culture in distinct and unique ways. Monolithic theological hermeneutics, or an extension that is merely an extrapolation, is not an adequate response to the need to evangelization. In fact, a conciliar document, the *Church in the Modern World*, holds that

> The church has been sent to all ages and nations and, therefore, is not tied exclusively and indissolubly to any race and nation, to any one particular way of life, or to any customary practices, ancient or modern. . . . It can then enter into communion with different forms of culture, thereby enriching both itself and the cultures themselves.[2]

This statement addresses the need for true incarnation of the Gospel in every culture, even as it presents mutual enrichment of cultures as the purpose of the inculturation. Documents issued after thecouncil concluded, especially *Evangelii Nuntiandi* (1975) and *Redemptoris Missio* (1990) confirm and elaborate on the church's position concerning inculturation. Although *Redemptoris Missio* uses the term insertion in talking about inculturation, it acknowledges the need to go beyond amonocultural expression of the faith. George Worgul articulates the need for inculturation from a theological perspective:

> The church, whether it admits it or not, participates in culture. It always has and it always will. At one and the same time, the ecclesial community is a product of revelation and culture, of the divine and the human. . . . Moreover "revelation" and belief system of the Christian community are expressed in and through the medium of a culture's language, patterns of behavior, and social structures.[3]

---

1. GS 44.
2. GS 58.
3. Worgul, *From Magic to Metaphor*, 9.

Putting the above statement differently would be to state that there is no theology without presuppositions, culturally and socially grounded. It is then possible, at least theoretically, to distinguish between what is cultural and what is strictly divine. Besides, what constitutes the core of the Christian faith, in some, sense remains fluid.[4] Hence, the presence of concepts and rites of passage in the culture could make the issue of inculturation easily acceptable to the culture in question. It is against this backdrop that the possibility of inculturation presents itself as an important mission of the church in contemporary times.

Rites of Christian initiation of adults, much like other practices of the church, have cultural underpinnings that must be acknowledged. If theology is to speak to men and women of every age, space, and time, then the need for serious reflection on contextualization cannot be ignored. In fact, context, as discussed in the previous chapter, is an important theological locus and a major determinant of the contemporary theological task.[5] This recognition portends a significant response to the dynamism that characterizes human experience and cultural diversity. Remarkably, the current Roman *ordo* makes inculturation of the sacrament of baptism an imperative when it declares:

> As stated in nos. 37–40 and 65 of the Constitution on the Liturgy, it is the responsibility of the Conferences of bishops in mission countries to judge whether certain initiation ceremonies in use among some people can be adapted for the rite of Christian baptism and to decide whether these rites are to be incorporated into it.[6]

This position is a direct invitation for inculturation of the rites of initiation. It is through such adaptation that universality can be attained through cultural relativity and particularities, which both recognize its immediate audience and remain open to a wider audience.

In this regard, the Catholic Bishops Conference of Nigeria, acknowledging the value of incarnating sacramental and Christian practices, issued a series of directives to effect this within indigenous cultures, having noted the yawning chasm between professed faith and its actual practice among Christians. The conference therefore issued documents targeting

---

4. I use the word *fluid* to describe the core message of Christianity because to most authors the core message appears inseparable from the Gospel message. See Orlando Espin et al., *Futuring Our Past*, 3.

5. See Tracy, *Blessed Rage for Order*, 3–34.

6. See *The Rites of the Catholic Church*, nos. 23–24.

different segments of the church in Nigeria, emphasizing the need for ongoing formation.[7] This recurring theme indicates that something more fundamental is lacking in the current manual of faith formation, revealing the need to contextualize the Rites of Christian Initiation of Adults. Whichever way one looks at it, there is a void somewhere, emphasizing the importance of *contemporizing* the manual for initiation into the faith. The bishops therefore noted: "We strongly recommend the establishment of centers for ongoing formation and renewal at diocesan and provincial levels. These will help not only priests and religious, but also every faithful follower of Christ in their spiritual and Christian life."[8] The above statement is an eloquent testimony to the need for contextualizing the faith to make it more relevant to contemporary times.

Sacraments as Rites of Passage

Having established the ethnic dimension of gestural and ritual activities and their relation to religious expression, Uzukwu further sees the various sacraments as rites of passage with the West African indigenous organization in view.

In chapter 2, we discussed the etymological and theological meaning in the historical evolution of the rites. We noted the initiatory significance of both the sacraments into the community of believers and full participation in that community, and the inevitable anthropological dimension of sacraments. In this section, we shall be discussing sacraments as rites of passage, emphasizing other aspects beyond the rite of initiation alone.

In contemporary times, rites of passage have become a crucial way of studying religion and cultures. They reveal how a group understands the universe and make sense of the world around them. They are actions and preparations that accompany transitions in life. They are not modern realities; they have been part and parcel of society from earliest times: they are, "a primary way of passing on a tradition, its ordering of the world, and its wisdom, and for initiating the young into a community. They are ways of achieving harmony with the order and rhythms of the universe and of

---

7. See the following works from the Catholic Bishops' Conference of Nigeria: *Salt of the Earth and Light of the World*, 107–18; *Ratio Fundamentalis Institutionis Sacerdotalis*, 55–59; *I Chose You*, 36–44; *Formation and Collaboration in Communion*, 30–34.

8. Catholic Bishops' Conference of Nigeria, *Called to Love*, 37.

keeping in touch with the spirits of the dead."[9] We can see them as maintaining the foundational myths of the group. Indeed, the ancients understood human society, human life, and the environment through the various creation myths involving primeval stories. In this way, the body that engages in expressing the view of the world through songs and dances so that ritual belongs to tradition, is the custodian of community memory.

Among the general claims made for rituals is that they establish a link between the profane and the sacred (foundational narrative of the group), and play a cohesive social role helping bind society together. Arnold van Gennep, who has done foundational work on rites of passage, views passage as a universal phenomenon, often ritualized through mediations in space and time that cushion the effects of changes. He has argued that "a complete scheme of rites of passage theoretically includes preliminary rites (rites of separation), liminal rites (rites of transition) and post-liminal rites (rites of incorporation)."[10] These stages are intimately connected so that one cannot be neatly separated from the other; however, the old self (before initiation) must give way for the new to emerge after initiation, which leads, in Clem Gorman's view, into newer or higher grounds.[11] Van Gennep's understanding of rites appears quite conservative. In his opinion, "The chief function of rites is to maintain and adjust social equilibrium-both for social groups and for individuals."[12] In a sense then, rites fix social limits and systematize social roles.[13]

Further information on rituals, especially on the significance of liminality, has been provided by Victor Turner,[14] an anthropologist, who highlights the contemporary nature and functionality of rituals that not only conserve, but are also creative, since society is always in the state of becoming, not a finished product. He argues:

> The social world is a world in becoming, not a world in being (except insofar as "being" is a description of the static, atemporal

9. Power, *Sacraments*, 124.
10. Gennep, *The Rites of Passage*, 11.
11. Gorman, *The Book of Ceremony*, 45.
12. See Vanderwilt, "Rites of Passage," 4.
13. Vanderwilt, "Rites of Passage," 3.
14. Earlier studies on rituals point to the fact that rituals take us backward to the foundations of the anthropological groups, or to the constants in rituals of various groups, but Turner discusses rituals from the viewpoint of ongoing process, since no culture is static, but ever growing and changing.

models men have in their heads), and for this reason studies of social structure as such are irrelevant. They are erroneous in basic premise because there is no such thing as "static action." That is why I am a little chary of the terms "community" or "society," . . . for they are often thought of as static concepts. Such a view violates the actual flux and changefulness of the human social scene.[15]

Turner then discusses the stage of transitions, or liminality, further demonstrating the changes in human society that rituals uphold and respond to. Accordingly, "Liminal entities are neither here nor there; they are betwixt and between the positions assigned and arrayed by law, custom, convention, and ceremonial."[16] Elsewhere, he likens liminality to a wilderness, a kind of eclipse, involving darkness and invisibility.[17] Through these changes and transitions, the initiate is adjusted to the environment. We may then argue that "The rites of passage have the pragmatic value of ontologically binding individuals to the ethnic group, a binding beyond what is achieved by the fact of being born into the group. The initiate deliberately takes full responsibility for his future actions, with their attendant rights and duties."[18]

Another area to which Turner devotes attention is the use of symbols, an integral part of rituals; in fact, he describes ritual as "an aggregate of symbols."[19] Such symbols carry meanings that are transcultural or crosstemporal. Together, ritual symbols offer a united witness to the meaning of what is celebrated. In this case, we may say that the whole is greater than the sum of its parts; together, they shed more light than do its individual parts. Turner puts it well, "Ritual symbols are not simply expressive, but epistemologically and sociologically constitutive units."[20] They are part and parcel of sociocultural groups and act as an individual's response to the environment.[21] Rituals then serve dual purposes: they preserve and recreate the identity of the group and renew the individuals who participate in the rituals; they perpetuate and re-envision the tradition they celebrate. "Christian ritual reproduces the shape of the Christian story. Words and actions which

15. Turner, *Dramas, Fields and Metaphors*, 24.
16. Turner, "Liminality and Communitas," 512.
17. Turner, "Liminality and Communitas," 512.
18. See Osigwe, "Ikwerre Rites of Passage and Sacraments of Initiation," 72–89.
19. Turner, *The Drums of Affliction*, 2.
20. Turner, *The Drums of Affliction*, 7.
21. The rites play the unique role of forming an individual's personal identity and relation to the group. So while the individual is the focus of the rites, the rites also function by renewing the group and its foundational story.

remember Christ's own offering of his own life on our behalf on the cross are ceremonies which celebrate a transformed awareness brought about by an infinitely closer fellowship with God than we are actually capable of imagining."[22] Just as an individual is recreated through rituals, so is a community's youthfulness renewed through ritual celebration.

Uzukwu sees rituals as carriers and revealers of religion and culture. In the traditional Igbo ritual of prayer, he identifies a spirituality that reveals something of the Igbo cosmology, divinities, and value of the human person. Such a prayer reveals the ontological hierarchy of the spiritual universe or forces. An interesting aspect of prayer rituals in the traditional Igbo setting is that they are not static; while their essence and formulary remain, they undergo subtle changes to accommodate the changes and development of modern society. Thus, the prayers are ancient, yet modern in outlook;[23] they capture the traditional ancestral beliefs while engaging social changes and contemporary events. The traditional rituals—prayers or invocations—reveal the basic assumptions of the community and their views of the universe around them. For Uzukwu, "One experiences this radical dependence on the Igbo traditional 'foundational questions' during the prayer."[24] In this sense, prayer not only reveals the indigenous spirituality, but is also an aspect of the indigenous culture.

Uzukwu's liturgical and sacramental theology draws inspiration from ritual studies that provide a window into the anthropology and sociology of human organizations. Describing sacraments as rites of passage indicates "the attainment of important stages in a person's experience as a member of the church, vital thresholds crossed in his or her progress through life."[25] In fact, sacraments are based on concrete events, not just abstract ideas. Concerning this, Grainger states,

> In sacramental ritual the tokens of our participation in God and one another, which are the symbols of our reconciliation with our own true being, are the very stuff of our common experience of

---

22. Grainger, *Bridging the Gap* 25.

23. African religions and culture are deeply connected. Discussing Igbo spirituality (prayer) rituals, Uzukwu points out how culture and religion reinforce each other. See Uzukwu, "Igbo Spirituality."

24. Uzukwu, "Igbo Spirituality," 156.

25. Grainger, "The Sacraments as Passage Rites," 215.

the world: water, fire, food, blood, flesh, secular things made holy by acting as the media for our return to God.[26]

Sacraments as rites of passage also indicate not only important milestones in the believer's Christian journey but the essential support they provide for the journey through life. As articulated by Vatican II, the sacraments acquire their efficacy through the paschal mystery (the death and resurrection of Christ), and are organized around that dominant Christian theme or narrative, technically called the "semantic core" of the Christian message.[27] Such rituals link the human and the divine. Put differently, rituals mediate divinity since no direct access to the divine is unmediated. Contemporary sacramental theologians, especially Jean-Luc Marion, have amply demonstrated this understanding.[28] The mediatory role of the elements of human culture remains inevitable after the divine template of condescending to the human level through the human mode of symbolization.

To this extent, the effect of the rites of passage on the initiates is similar to the effects of sacraments in the life of participants. Just as the participants in the ritual are renewed and recreated through the rites, so the sacraments renew and recreate participants. The change in the life of participants simultaneously renews the community and reminds it of its foundation story. Rites therefore exert positive influence on individuals and on the corporate memory of the community.

Uzukwu considers the rites of passage in describing the Christian sacraments. Just as the rites have social and religious functions, so do the sacraments. He defines rites of passage as, "rituals devised through the experience of sociocultural groups to lead 'passengers' through life cycles or crises in a universe where a happy interaction prevails between spirits and

---

26. Grainger, "The Sacraments as Passage Rites," 219.

27. The foundational stories or narratives that are reenacted through rituals are relived with their continuing effects in participants' lives. Such stories are like the Hebrew Passover and the Christian paschal mystery, especially its commemoration in the Eucharistic celebration. Immersion in the Christian foundation story (the death and resurrection of Jesus) requires a dying to self so as to live a new life. Saint Paul writes that in baptism we were buried with Christ so we can be resurrected with him (Col 3). To participate requires initiation. In the words of Mircea Eliade, "Initiation is an indispensable process in every effort to transcend man's natural condition and attain to a sanctified mode of being" (Eliade, *Rites and Symbols of Initiation*, 114). This accounts for the central position of the sacraments of initiation, especially baptism as the door to the other sacraments.

28. The human quest for unmediated immediacy has given rise to idolatry in sacramental thinking, whereas sacraments properly serve as icons.

humans."[29] This definition indicates the dual dimensions of the rites as being social and religious. Contemporary studies of rituals, especially beginning with Van Gennep, have pointed out the intricate and deep significance of rites of passage. Thus, we can safely say that rites of passage are fundamental to "being" and belongingness to a community. The experience of dying to self and gaining a new life through the sacraments can motivate rethinking the sacraments through the tripod stand of Gennep's pre-liminal, liminal, and post-liminal rites. The dominant and inevitable position of the paschal mystery to the seven sacraments endows every sacrament with the liminality that gives way to a new or renewed life. This is an area that our future theological reflection may seek to emphasize. The reality of a future eschaton, in some sense, reduces every stage of the Christian life to liminality. The Eucharist, which recalls the Christian foundation story (events of the past), simultaneously celebrates the past as it awaits the fullness of time in the eschaton. So, it is plausible to agree with Grainger that "all seven sacraments preserve the shape of the rite of passage in their individual structures, and have pre-liminal, liminal, and post-liminal phases despite the fact that their theological meaning transcends any such division."[30]

The church, like every other human institution, accords great significance and respect to her tradition and the rituals that maintain it. In fact, the church gives sacred tradition the same status as sacred scripture, since both concepts constitute a single deposit of the word of God.[31] The nexus between the two is attested by how they shed light on one another. In other words, tradition aids the interpretation and understanding of scriptures; however, the word *tradition*, in Catholic understanding is part of divine revelation. It denotes a deposit of faith like the scriptures, yet not defined as scripture. John Thiel sees tradition as "an ongoing event, a trader in which the faith is handed down from generation to generation."[32] The aspect of an ongoing event and the distinction between the *tradita* and the *traditio*,[33] provide ample room for Uzukwu's reflection on the inculturation of sacraments. For Terrence Tilley, "fidelity to a tradition may sometimes involve extensive reworking of the *tradita*. In the perspective of

---

29. Uzukwu, *Worship as Body Language*, 220.
30. Grainger, "The Sacraments as Passage Rites," 221.
31. *Dei Verbum* 10 in Flannery, *Vatican Council II*.
32. Thiel, *Senses of Tradition*, 13.
33. According to Tilley, *tradita* refers to the content of a tradition, and *traditio* is the medium or means of the transmission, often held to be part of the tradition.

communication theory, then, it may be parochial to think that *tradita* alone can carry the tradition."[34] It is precisely against the understanding that tradition can be reworked, since they are not static, that Uzukwu avers, "As African Christians, we exercise our right to live and interpret the received Christian tradition in terms of the sets of assumptions of the African practice and discourse."[35] The broader understanding in this regard is that rituals can be reworked or recreated according to socio-cultural groups, without undermining the foundational story. The argument for the possibility of change in the local practice of Christian initiation of adults is corroborated by the popular religiosity and emergence of a true local theology for a local church. On this assumption and the provision of the Church rests our effort of inculturating liturgical expressions.

Uzukwu on Sacraments of Initiation

The revisions in *Sacosanctum Concilium* and *The General Introduction* to the 1972 Rite of Christian Initiation of Adults provide conditions for inculturating the sacraments of initiation. *Sacrosanctum Concilium* clearly states, "Following the pattern of the new edition of the Roman ritual, particular rituals are to be prepared . . . adapted to the linguistic and other needs of the different regions."[36] It is in this light that Patrick Chibuko, a Nigerian liturgist, argues,

> Since Vatican II, one of the greatest challenges in reforming the liturgy is the urgent demand for furnishing the existing rites with, not just suitable alternatives, but creating entirely new ones. This is because the Roman rite is only a model intended for the entire world using it and this has to be enculturated into every local church. Besides, the Roman rite has notable deficiencies which make it impossible to satisfy every culture and people.[37]

After a careful study of the nature, structure, and theology of the Advent preface, Chibuko composed Advent prefaces along the line of the Nigerian context, while retaining the immutable parts, like the introductory dialogue. A dominant idea in his construction is the prevalence of the

---

34. Tilley, *Inventing Catholic Tradition*, 29.
35. Uzukwu, *Worship as Body Language*, 221.
36. SC 63.
37. Chibuko, "New Prefaces for the Liturgical Season of Advent," 320–33.

indigenous spirituality and modes of expressing expectations in view of the Christmas season.

Uzukwu's starting point in the sacramental theology is the living faith of the community and its rituals. For him, the celebration of the community inserts participants into the original and initial event that constitutes the community. This tradition recalls the position of the fathers of the church, for whom the sacraments were not matters of intellectual discourse, but an action, a liturgy. Sacramental worship, in Uzukwu's perspective, must be rooted within its proper liturgical domain. The people of God are constituted through liturgical celebration (prayer). The very understanding of the church, *ecclesia*, recalls this gathering, or summoning of the elect.[38] Rational and intellectual discussion of the sacraments emerging from the scholasticism of the thirteenth century, as discussed in chapter 2, continues to challenge contemporary sacramental theology. Some theologians have noted the need for a return of sacramental theology to its original domain, which Uzukwu's sacramental trajectory follows.

Uzukwu appreciates the emerging creative African liturgies that attempt to inculturate the sacraments of initiation. He sees diversity in these celebrations as consistent with the churches the apostles left behind but eclipsed in the age of unity as uniformity.[39] Thus, he approves the practice of adapted traditional initiation rites, such as the naming ceremony ritual and the Igbo rites for healing relationships called *Igba ndu*—a kind of ritual covenanting in various West African churches, notably those of the Ashanti, Yoruba, and Igbo. For him, when these cultural practices are interlaced with Christian understanding, they produce a more lasting impact and commitment in the initiates.

The Christian sacraments of initiation are baptism, confirmation, and the Eucharist, the culmination of the process of initiation. The rite of initiation as already seen in the previous sections involves a dying to self and immersion into the myth-narrative of the Christian community. These rites serve the purpose of socialization and acquisition of personal identity by the neophytes. The General Introduction to the Rite of Christian Initiation for Adults captures this transition well: "Through the sacraments of initiation men and women are freed from the power of darkness. With Christ they

---

38. Ecclesia means both the actual process of assembling and the assembled congregation itself. See Kung, *On Being a Christian*, 479.

39. Uzukwu identifies this period from the eighth and ninth centuries under the reign of Charlemagne. See Uzukwu, *Worship as Body Language*, 265.

die, are buried, and rise again. They receive the Spirit of adoption which makes them God's sons and daughters, and, with the entire people of God, they celebrate the memorial of the Lord's death and resurrection." This indicates a separation from the old and the acquisition of a new life through the mystery of Christian initiation; however, the impact of this initiation, according to Uzukwu, has remained limited due to over emphasis on cerebral knowledge, "as opposed to knowledge through action."[40] To him, the traditional initiation rituals appear more binding on the neophytes, since the culture and religion have become coterminous.

Writing on the significance of the traditional initiation ceremonies, Uzukwu discusses the myths, namely the Nri myth of origin from the Igbo of Southeastern Nigeria, the *Enuma Elish* (Babylonian myth of origin), and the Christian story of death and resurrection, as the basic metaphor of the Christian tradition. These rituals create a lasting impact on the communities that reenact them. The foundational Christian story celebrated in the Eucharist was the focus of Uzukwu's doctoral dissertation and will be analyzed later in this chapter for insights into Uzukwu's interpretation of the Babylonian and Igbo *Nri* myths.

The Babylonian creation myth, Enuma Elish, presents the domination of the forces of chaos, the war of the gods, Marduk and Tiamat, as the origin of the universe. Marduk split the body of Tiamat and formed the waters above and below, while with the blood of Tiamat's second husband, Qingu, Marduk formed human beings. Bringing order out of chaos establishes Marduk's sovereignty. Despite controversy among scholars about the dating of this epic, Marduk's ascendancy as the head of the pantheon forms an integral part of Hammurabi's code, with its wide influence over the people and its importance in their story and their ritual.

The Nri myth of origin explains the beginning of the sociopolitical system of the Igbo, the firmness of the earth, the development of the four-day week, and the provision of food. As Uzukwu recounts the myth, the founding father or civilizing hero of the Igbo nation, Eri, prayed to Chukwu (God) for food, and that was the beginning of the bestowal of yam. The essentials of the Igbo nation, its organization from chaos into an agricultural market system revolving around the four-day week are linked to the foundation story of Eri. The traditional priest-king of the Nri is the custodian and link between the past and the present; he exercises power over the people. With the conflation of the political and

---

40. Uzukwu, *Worship as Body Language*, 230.

religious life of the Igbo, his presence authenticates religious and political ceremonies. The Eze Nri is the guardian of morality and the preservation of the sacredness of the land, with no bloodshed and other taboos. In this way, the foundation ritual of the Nri is perpetuated. How this myth has influenced and continues to influence life in Igbo landforms a major part of Uzukwu's analysis of the ritual.

Other native rituals Uzukwu discusses are the ones for reintegrating estranged members of the community and those for acquiring mystical powers. In writing about the quest of the Niger Delta Youths for liberation from transnational corporations and the destruction of their ancestral lands, Uzukwu notes the significance of their initiation ritual to gain mystical empowerment and protection from Egbesu, the ancestral Ijaw war divinity.[41] The interlacing of ancestral rituals and Christian ones is perceived by Uzukwu as a "sign of the necessary impact of the local on the global."[42] We must nevertheless acknowledge that he does not give a blanket or uncritical approval of these rituals. In fact, with similar rituals all over Africa, Christians are challenged to strengthen their rituals that oppose negative forces. This leads to the prevalence of rituals for healing among religious groups that populate Africa. Rituals also exist for purification after any form of bloodshed, to safeguard humans from killing one another, and to forestall bloodshed associated with power in traditional cosmology.[43] Initiation rituals for offices limit the use and exercise of power within limits of reason. For Uzukwu, "any exercise of power or authority is preceded by initiation or passage rites that ensure that the leader, king, matriarch or chief is servant who rules under the steady gaze of God and the spirits."[44] Consequently, he proposes that liturgists create rituals of initiation that capture reality in the modern world and maintain the good use of power and authority, so that leaders would feel the shame for the naked use of power and bear the consequences for abuse of power.

Incorporating these rituals into Christian celebrations, after critical reflection on their logic and significance, would give birth to a new way of understanding and appreciating the lasting effects of Christian rituals.

---

41. Uzukwu, *God, Spirit, and Human Wholeness*, 9.
42. Uzukwu, *God, Spirit, and Human Wholeness*, 9.
43. See Uzukwu, "Liturgy, Culture and the Postmodern World," 167.
44. Uzukwu, "Liturgy, Culture and the Postmodern World," 169. While this is true of religious societies, one wonders about the applicability of this in secular post-Christian societies.

The similarity in logic of traditional and Christian rituals as commemorating real events of the past makes it possible to begin a theological exercise of this nature. The sacraments celebrate realized eschatology or events of the past as they anticipate the fullness of time. As celebrations of the community, the sacraments make the community contemporaneous with what is being celebrated. For Uzukwu, "This realized eschatology contextually promises to promote Christianity at the same time close to the African world-vision because sacraments 'epitomize the whole Gospel' and convey eschatological realities."[45] Hence, all other rituals find their culmination in the realized eschatology of the Christian vision.

Uzukwu's Understanding of Sacraments

In the previous section, we introduced the inevitable phenomenological dimension of the Christian sacraments. In this section we present witnesses who substantiate and buttress the necessity of reinterpreting the sacraments in West Africa, especially the significance of the community. Such reinterpretation is necessary for the proper incarnation of the Gospel in African culture.

Uzukwu's understanding of the Christian sacraments is deeply entrenched in his ecclesiology. For him, the sacraments belong to the church (community). Sacraments are sacraments of Christ, who is present through the gestures and symbols of the community. Uzukwu's understanding of the church is anchored on the anthropological constitution of the church as a community. The indispensability of the community in the sacramental celebration is the root and condition of the sacraments. Uzukwu criticizes an overly centralized ecclesiology of the Roman system, which obscures multiple sacramental liturgies and opts for an ecclesiological model that recognizes and encourages the local church. Hence, the local church serves as the platform for constructing his theological edifice. John Zizioulas and Richard Gailladertz share the theology of Uzukwu in this regard. Accordingly, theology must interact with other human sciences like anthropology and sociology, as was the case in the patristic era.

Uzukwu's understanding of the sacraments is firmly rooted in the community. His emphasis on sacraments as liturgical celebrations circumvents the rationalism of the scholastics, and a return to the patristic era, which understood sacraments as basically liturgical celebrations. In his

---

45. Uzukwu, "Endless Worlds, Creative Memories," 1–2.

doctoral dissertation, which focuses on Eucharist as prayer and thanksgiving, he engages a rigorous analysis of the Jewish roots of the Eucharist and delineates cultural and historical circumstances of the evolution of the Eucharistic prayers. Much like Edward Kilmartin, he is interested in the history of the Eucharistic prayers, which convinces him of the possibility that a different theology can emerge from a different context, while still communicating the mystery that is being celebrated.[46] The sacraments are not abstract or mechanical realities but acts of the community that depends on Christ. Therefore, Uzukwu makes two profound suggestions concerning the elements for the Eucharist in Africa: Africa should become an ecclesiastical region capable of developing its own liturgical rite, and liturgists should select elements of the Eucharistic memorial that compare with the original elements used by Jesus. He adds, "We have chosen millet and palm wine because they seem to respond best to African regional authenticity while at the same time possessing the capacity of comparing well with the existing Church discipline."[47]

From this perspective, Uzukwu may be seen as placing the accent on the ecclesiological dimension more than the Christological aspect in the sacramental celebration. His statement points in that direction: "In Africa the whole Christian liturgical action becomes a gestural display before God of the community confessing its reception of fullness of life in Christ, a community at peace with its ancestral heritage and environment. The African Eucharistic community expresses in a different metaphor the experience of the same unique salvation in the Christ that is the faith of the universal church."[48] Uzukwu's emphasis on the ecclesiological dimension of the sacraments may place him at odds with proponents of the Christological model. But an understanding of the ecclesiological model as anchored on the Christological overcomes this challenge. Historically from the Scholastic period, the sacrament has been understood as acts of Christ, and the presiding minister as acting *in persona Christi*. The presiding minister also acted *in persona ecclesiae*, yet the chronological prioritizing of the in *persona Christi* over the *persona ecclesiae* was inevitable. Dennis Ferrara gives an interesting interpretation when he states, "The formula in persona Christi has its true provenance in this mystery of faith and derives its whole meaning from this mystery; to see it as referring to a

---

46. See Chapp, *Encounter with the Triune God*, 59–61.
47. Uzukwu, "Food and Drink in Africa," 383.
48. Uzukwu, "Inculturation and the Liturgy," 111.

characteristic of the priest is essentially to misconstrue it."⁴⁹ The ecclesiological aspect of contemporary theology in a sense returns the sacraments to the community, reflecting "a pneumatological and charismatic understanding of the liturgy,"⁵⁰ the true home of the sacraments.

Ancient and modern theologians agree in the unity of the mystical Body of Christ as proper to the sacraments of the Eucharist. Consequently, the constitution of the mystical Body of Christ is the ground of sacramental action and causality. While the sacraments are not new acts, the novelty consists in the symbolization of the one unrepeatable event of Christ. The church does not realize something new in the sacraments, (for example, the Eucharist), but makes Christ present through the mysteries accomplished by Christ and entrusted to the Church by Christ. The sacraments therefore bring Christians in contact with Christ. The sacraments are precisely the means by which is realized the oneness, the uniqueness, of the mediation of Christ.

Revalidation of Sacraments through Indigenous Sociocultural Rituals

Right from his days as a student of theology, Uzukwu was interested in establishing the interception between the Gospel and indigenous cultures. He locates the possibility of reimagining the sacraments, rituals, and modes of symbolization in Vatican II's openness to adaptation of the Christian sacraments. This openness makes it possible to identify elements from cultural and traditional wisdom that establish, "intimate connection between the visible and the invisible, between the experienced and the mystery beyond the experience, between the verbalized and the Word beyond words."⁵¹ The current ecclesiology of the church, which allows multiple rites, is a return to the practice of early Christianity. Uzukwu argues that a rite "does not apply to a single action of, for example, sacramental administration. Rather, it touches all expressions of the faith particular to a local church."⁵² This already indicates why his theological effort resonates with diverse areas of the life of the church in West Africa. Laurenti Magesa shares his view of a proper incarnation of the Gospel. In fact, arguing from the perspective of

49. Ferrara, "Representation or Self-Effacement?," 212.
50. Kilmartin, "Sacraments as Liturgy of the Church," 530.
51. Uzukwu, "The Sacramental Imagination," 301.
52. Uzukwu. *Worship as Body Language*, 267.

incarnational theology and the culture that is integral to the Gospel, Magesa insists that the Christian mission is inevitably cultural.[53] Consequently, he argues for evangelization that profoundly accommodates African indigenous practices. He perceives this approach as the necessary route to the mature development of the African Church since evangelization and inculturation cannot be separated. In the same way, Dickson Kwesi insists on evangelization that is not mere adaptation: "The faith can only be meaningful when Christ is encountered as speaking and acting authentically, when he is heard in the African languages, when culture 'shapes the human voice that answers the voice of Christ.'"[54] He calls for decolonizing the theological and liturgical orientations that are prevalent in Africa to respond to the cultural orientation of African Christians.

Uzukwu locates the provenance of human gestural practices in the ethnic or cultural domain. The coming to being of the human person already situates him in a particular place and time, which influence each person from first consciousness. The corporeal behavioral patterns are aligned according to or rooted in an ethnic and cultural experience of the universe.[55] Even from the point of view of the sacraments, "participation in the language event of Christian sacrament is grounded in bodily ritual."[56] Verbal and nonverbal communications constitute the whole gamut of human gestural practices.

The body's actions and words are indispensable in sacramental events, for sacramental actions are developed around the body, like bread, wine, oil, water, and the laying on of hands. The body supplies the sign aspect of every sacrament and, to a large extent, the form in the minister's words. Even from ancient times, "the fabrication of tools is an extension of human gestures,"[57] which are not instinctual practices, but rationally designed and learned activities.[58] Tools can be conceived as extensions of the body, to make up for its limitations. Hence, gestures as modes of symbolization are ethnic and speak to each particular context. It is in this light that Uzukwu argues, "The Christian gesture (ritual or ethical) must be ethnic (referring to a historical human group) to be meaningful. For it will be wrong to

53. Magesa, *Anatomy of Inculturation*, 148.
54. Dickson, *Theology in Africa*, 5.
55. Uzukwu, *Worship as Body Language*, 2.
56. Power, *Sacraments*, 120.
57. Power, *Sacraments*, 120.
58. Power, *Sacraments*, 3.

think that in Jesus confessed as the Christ, a universal ritual (way of doing, body language) has been set up."[59] The Christ event is too great to be confined within a particular cultural and local expression. The cosmic nature of the event itself—with universal relevance and applicability—defies any circumscription. This warrants the appropriation of the chief ritual of the church (liturgy) according to various sociocultural groups. When this appropriation is done, "the faith becomes culture, Christ in the members of his body becomes African, an African Christianity emerges, and the liturgy becomes a sumptuous cultural experience."[60] The emergence of this particular Christianity involves the use of African instruments, hymns, drums, local liturgical art, dance and body expression, all of which indicate African celebratory proclivities. This would further involve a reinstatement of the positive African view of the body.

Historically, the body has been viewed differently, with some perspectives being more negative. Uzukwu notes the dualistic tendency toward the body that dominates Western epistemology; probably accounting for the disdain of body. Accordingly, the pessimism of the West was communicated through the great Greek and Roman classical traditions; the body movement became more suspect through the process of inculturating Christianity in the West. Africans, in contrast, see the body differently. He states,

> Because worship is concerned with body motions or gestures, African Christians see worship as a channel to display their deep experience of the mystery revealed in the Christian story. And since African sociocultural groups have successfully integrated body and spirit into interactional gestures, a healthy expression of the incarnate human in African Christian liturgy should constitute the intent of the inculturation of worship in African Christian communities. Here inculturation is understood as the experience and expression by African Christians of the mutual impact of gospel and culture in their respective sociocultural area.[61]

In contrast, some Scholastics upheld the negative view of the body and explained the sacrament as a remedial or medicinal pill for inordinate corporeal desires. We find this in Bonaventure, who followed the position of Hugo of Saint Victor. For him, the institution of the sacraments was a remedy against

---

59. Uzukwu, "African Symbols and Christian Liturgical Celebration," 100.
60. Uzukwu, *Worship as Body Language*, 270.
61. Uzukwu, *Worship as Body Language*, 15.

ignorance and a way to help humans learn the right proportion in matters of the body.[62] Aquinas was more positive in seeing the corporeal sacraments as windows to the spirit.[63] Thus the negative ranking of the body (flesh) stems from its being viewed as an instrument of sin. Augustine's development of the doctrine of original sin further deepened the distrust of the body and bodily gestures. It was more often considered the site of sin; however, it is essential to sacramental gestures and symbolization.

Referring to anthropological dimension of the sacraments, Uzukwu re-envisions the sacraments through the cultural rites of passage, such as the integration of age groups and associations like youth, Catholic Women Organization, men's groups, and traditional marriage (sacrament of matrimony). These bodies are culture specific, and they have become part and parcel of the Church structure in most West African parishes and beyond. Uzukwu views this development favorably.[64] Such structures, modeled on the indigenous age groups for propagating traditional culture, are essential for inculcating the faith in a way that is appropriate and specific to the contexts, as well as the candidates' biological and physical needs. Uzukwu suggests that inculturating the administrative structures of the local church various indigenous structures will bolster both faith and evangelization.[65] The harmonization of rites of marriage—the seclusion and training into womanhood, as well as the seclusion of the religious—could find greater expression and relevance through indigenous cultural practices. Uzukwu provides an instance of this in the approved Igbo liturgical rite of marriage, which incorporates the traditional marriage elements into the Roman liturgy, thus creating a truly Christian and truly African rite of marriage. According to Uzukwu, "Incorporating a people's organizational

---

62. Hugo of St. Victor, *De Sacramentis Fidei* II.3: PL 176: 319–22, cited in Power, *Sacraments*, 121.

63. See Aquinas, *Summa Theologiae* III.61.1.

64. These organizations follow the age groups and become viable organs for administration and ongoing formation in the Christian faith.

65. Uzukwu argues for the possibility of inculturating traditional elements of leadership, like title taking, into a recognizable structure in the church. The favorable disposition of the French missionaries toward these traditional structures is a case in point. The later demonization and disavowal of traditional elements by the Irish missionaries was consistent with the whole gamut of the colonial agenda, which was not in the interest of the Gospel. With the maturity of the Christian faith, Uzukwu is optimistic that respecting and engaging the cultural paradigms will serve a greater purpose in the evangelization and development of the Church's mission. See Uzukwu, "Traditioning and the Emerging Shape of a Local Church," 215–30.

structures into the Church administration and celebrating marriage, Christian and African in one rite, appropriates Tradition creativity. This is a witness to catholicity: a robust way of receiving, thinking through and living the faith."[66] The faith from its inception has not been devoid of cultural expression and appropriation. Indeed, a faith or Gospel without historical background would be unrealistic and abstract. To this extent, the faith remains in constant need of appropriation and contextualization according to various anthropological groups.

Analysis of *Eucharistia Africana:* Uzukwu's Doctoral Dissertation

Uzukwu's doctoral dissertation, presented at the Toronto School of Theology in 1978, can be described as a work of first impression, engaging the openness of Vatican II, which had just ended a little over a decade earlier. The basic question that runs through the dissertation concerns a Christianity that will take African cultures seriously, making them a conveyor of the good news, just as Jewish cultures in the first millennium and European cultures in the second millennium were the vehicles for the Gospel. In this exercise, indigenous African spirituality, culture, philosophy, language, and prayers are taken seriously in order to create an African Eucharistic Prayer. Uzukwu states this fact in the introduction to his dissertation: "This thesis is an attempt to put into action the fact that Christ can become incarnate, or that Christ can be recognized as already incarnate within the Igbo (African) culture. It is an attempt to provide for Igbo (African) Christians, a Christian Igbo Eucharistic Prayer."[67]

The dissertation, entitled "Blessing and Thanksgiving among the Igbo (Nigeria): Towards An African Eucharistic Prayer," focuses on the great prayer of praise and thanksgiving to God for work, which culminates in the Christ event. This prayer has variously been called the Eucharistic Prayer and the Canon of the Mass. To create a similar prayer from Igbo indigenous spirituality, Uzukwu presents a theological methodology that enables him to draw consistency between the salvation in Christianity and traditional indigenous African religions.

Salvation-history theological methodology argues for consistency in God's revelation that culminates in the Christ event. This method is

66. Uzukwu, "Traditioning and the Emerging Shape of a Local Church," 230.
67. Uzukwu, "Blessing and Thanksgiving among the Igbo," 3.

anchored in the Vatican II declaration on non-Christian religions (*Nostra Aetate*), which marks a significant shift from earlier positions of the Church. Notably, the document, in discussing non-Christian religions, avoids such terms as *pagan, idolatry* and so on. Vatican II marks an overall departure from the views of earlier councils. It has been likened to two great reforming movements in history: the Gregorian Reform of the eleventh century and the Lutheran Reformation in the sixteenth.[68] The reform of *Nostra Aetate* becomes more evident if the text is seen in light of previous derogatory, exclusivist, triumphalist postures of the Roman Church. Above all, the salvation-history model sees continuity between Jewish-Christian traditions and non-Christian religions. Uzukwu therefore capitalized on this openness and change in theological orientation.

In the dissertation, Uzukwu discusses three religious traditions: Jewish, Christian, and Igbo meal rituals. He investigates the Jewish temple, synagogue, and table liturgy in search of antecedents to the Christian liturgy, with the aim of establishing foundations for the novel Igbo Eucharistic Prayer. This involves a historical and rigorous analysis of early Jewish liturgies and their impact on the Septuagint and Christian liturgy precisely.

According to Uzukwu, the oldest Jewish prayer is that of praise and thanksgiving, especially in view of divine portents: *beraka*, in its various forms, describes simultaneously the act of praising and blessing God for his intervention in their lives and history, referring to fruitfulness or fecundity. History in this sense gives direction to Jewish spirituality, while blessing to return thanks is central to Jewish prayer. Uzukwu sees blessing (*baruk* or *beraka*) as the controlling theme of Jewish prayer, found in the creation narrative of God blessing his creatures, and subsequently in the blessing of the inferior by the superior.[69] More generally, he remarks that blessings that were originally natural became more centered on the cultic setting. Blessing consequently became the basic structure of the Jewish liturgy. Considering the blessing and synagogue *eucharistein* as having influenced Christian liturgy, he states, "The temple and the synagogue worship constitute one of the basic influences on Christian community. The prayer to accept the sacrifices and thanksgiving (which narrate in a general way God's special relation with Israel), definitely predate the Christian era."[70] While the thanksgiving motif runs through the synagogue prayer, sacrifice

68. O'Malley, *Tradition and Transition*, 17.
69. O'Malley, *Tradition and Transition*, 15–17.
70. O'Malley, *Tradition and Transition*, 56.

is associated with the temple. Christian liturgy is a combination of both motifs. Besides the synagogue and temple prayers, prayer that defined Jewish spirituality and has direct bearing on the Christian liturgy is the grace before meals, or table prayer.

The meal in its various forms like the sacrificial meal, meals of Essenes community, the meals of family events, and Sabbath and Passover meals—has influenced the Christian understanding of the Eucharist. According to Uzukwu, "What is common to all these groups is the meal; and what interests us in the meals is the blessing (and thanksgiving) for the bread and wine."[71] Blessing was said over the bread and the cup as well. Jesus's prayers at meals, it is plausibly argued, took the form of these Jewish prayers, but with a profound adaptation in the significance of the words and the interpretation of the Grace.[72] Joachim Jeremias seems to agree with Uzukwu's supposition of a combination of various meal motifs in the Eucharistic words of Jesus. He discounts the influence of a single meal motif, but argues that the Passover meal has greater influence, as seen in the eating of the Passover lamb, with unleavened bread and bitter herbs; the fact that Jesus spoke the words of interpretation over the bread in connection with the grace before the beginning of the main meal; and the last supper was totally surrounded by the atmosphere of the Passover.[73]

In subsequent sections, Uzukwu discusses the development of various aspects of the liturgical celebration, pointing out that each part has been influenced by cultural and ethnic gestural behaviors. The Christian liturgical types that emerged are the Syrian, Egyptian, and Roman types, with differing points of emphasis. He notes that although each type contained the basic elements of the Eucharistic prayers, marked cultural influences led to differences.[74]

Therefore, he logically attempts to develop Igbo Eucharistic prayers that reflect how the Igbo bless, praise, and give thanks with the use of concrete symbols, like the kola-nut. The Igbo, familiar with the existence and role of God (Chukwu), have a litany of prayers that offer blessing and thanks to God for the various roles he has played and continues to play in their history. Uzukwu identifies parallels between the Igbo and Jewish prayers with the basic motif of praise and thanksgiving. Perhaps

71. O'Malley, *Tradition and Transition*, 84.
72. O'Malley, *Tradition and Transition*, 93.
73. Jeremias, *The Eucharistic Words of Jesus*, 86–88.
74. See Uzukwu, "Blessing and Thanksgiving among the Igbo," 183–84.

the difference lies in the Igbo praise and acknowledgement of *chi*-little deitiesand not just Chukwu, the supreme God. A sample of the Igbo Eucharistic Prayer he proposes goes thus:

> "The Lord be with you.
>
> R/ And also with you
>
> Lift up your hearts
>
> R/ We lift them up to the Lord
>
> Let us give thanks to the Lord our God
>
> R/ It is right to give him thanks and praise
>
> Osebuluwa (Lord), Chukwu (God), the all-powerful,
> we praise You!
>
> Creator of the world, Chi (God), the owner of life,
> we praise You!
>
> Our Father, father of our ancestors,
>
> We gather together to praise and thank You with sacrifice.
>
> Your children stand before You, thanking, praising,
> and rejoicing in You:
>
> Because You are our life,
>
> Because You lead and protect us one by one.
>
> Because You give us life and cause us to increase in the world.
>
> Your power and glory are manifest in the heaven and the earth.
>
> The sun, the moon, and the stars, which fill the heavens proclaim
> Your glory.
>
> This goodly land in which we live, is the work of your hands.
>
> The food which gives us life, produce of the land,
> is your blessing."[75]

In this prayer, one observes a striking similarity with the Jewish-Christian tradition: God's greatness is acknowledged, and he is praised as creator of the universe, source of life and well-being, provider of food and drink, and protector. This prayer combines the ritual Morning Prayer, prayer for the

---

75. Uzukwu, "Blessing and Thanksgiving among the Igbo," 183–84.

breaking of kola-nut, and prayer for marriage. In summary, it is a prayer that covers the various daily endeavors.

By so doing, Uzukwu attempts to recapture and give relevance to Christianity through Igbo cultural practices. His work is corroborated by David Power, who sees the reality of the Spirit, Word, as not chained to a particular rite and tradition. Indeed, this makes it possible for the sacraments to have a pluriform expression. "This great sacrament of God's love is always the completeness of the divine gift, and yet always historically and culturally realized within the concreteness of the human experience."[76] The fact of being culturally realized envisages a multiplicity of expression according to different cultural matrices.

In addition, Power shows the interplay between praise and thanksgiving (doxology), which emanate from human experience and its relationship with God: "Praise is given in virtue of wonder. It allows the sheer wonder of the gift/presence of Word and Spirit to stand forth. . . . Thanksgiving comes as it were in second place, by way of acknowledging the origin of these events and their grace in God and in God's love."[77] He notes that Jesus reinterpreted the praise of God for his blessings on Israel's past activities so as to signify the fulfillment of that activity in Jesus Christ.

The question Uzukwu treated in his dissertation is the inculturation of the Eucharistic sacrifice through the African traditional prayer of blessing and thanksgiving. He responds to this challenge by adapting the Jewish prayer pattern, which formed the basis for the Christian prayer so that his dissertation begins with the pre-Christian Jewish prayer of blessing.

The Eucharistic Prayer he created resonates with indigenous cultural life and is based on the similarities between a Jewish worldview and an Igbo worldview, as seen in traditional prayers, like prayers of lamentation. In his discussion of similarities in songs he states, "what I want to emphasize is the facility with which two worlds (Jewish and Igbo) merge."[78] He appreciates the centrality of the sacrament of the Eucharist to the Christian tradition, for he understands that it celebrates the unique Christian memory and meaning system. Hence, the renewal Vatican II inaugurated in its teaching on the liturgy, clearly expressed in *Sacrosanctum Concilium*, provides a favorable condition for the proper inculturation.

---

76. Power, *Sacraments*, 86.
77. Power, *Sacraments*, 86.
78. Uzukwu, "Bible and Christian Worship in Africa," 19.

Another striking feature in Uzukwu's articulation of the *Eucharistia Africana* is the overflow of ancestral memory into the Eucharistic celebration. Thus, the explosive joy and festivity that are consistent with the African culture finds deep expression in the liturgy. Writing on this theme, Uzukwu states, "Whether one accepts the ancestor model or not, and whether or not the participants in a lively African Eucharist are able to articulate their experience verbally, we cannot fail to note the flow of ancestral memory into the Christian response."[79]

Relevance of Sacraments to Life

In the celebration of the Eucharist the Christian community gathers to commemorate the death and resurrection of Christ and to renew its commitment to God. Through the proclaimed word of God and the commemoration of the life of Christ, they glorify God for the new life acquired through baptism and initiation into the life of Christ.[80] Thus, the whole ritual shapes the fundamental attitude and the life of the believer in Christ Jesus. In a sense then, the pedagogy of the paschal mystery comes to shape in the logic of believers' daily lives. Uzukwu ruminates on this relationship of Christian commitment to the temporal world. In his recent work on eschatology, he argues for concrete human flourishing in time and relativizes the dominant view of a complete break with temporal work as often proclaimed. For him, eschatology implies a total "game over," which mitigates the aspect of human flourishing and well-being. Gaillardetz seems to corroborate this view when he argues, "As Christians, we do not live as if this world were a kind of waiting room where we simply bide our time and place all our hope in the glory of a resurrection in the afterlife.... Our resurrection is not something that we await beyond the moment of our physical death. Our new life has already begun."[81] Rather, the temporal world is a beginning of the eternal, and a life of commitment to Christ and his values is already begun at the sacrament of baptism.

---

79. Uzukwu, "Inculturation and the Liturgy," 101.

80. SC 106.

81. Gaillardetz and Clifford, *Keys to the Council*, 7. Saint Paul writing to the Romans indicates the newness of life acquired through baptism so that the old self of sin is set aside, and a new life of grace is attained through the death and resurrection of Christ. See Rom 6:3–11.

Sacraments of the church impose ethical standards upon the recipients. How Christians live and what relations they have with God find expression in their interpersonal relationships. As David Power affirms,

> A community that in worship lauds the actions of Christ in hymns, praise, and narrates them as the actions of God's Word among us, takes up the following of Christ according to the measure of this Word. At the same time, the ethical engagement itself is brought back to worship and influences the way in which worship is celebrated, in both its words and its ritual actions.[82]

He adds, "The interplay between worship and ethics is inescapable, but it is built into the character of language as such, since poetics expresses the ideal of praxis."[83] The law of celebration and belief should also be the law of life and living.

This interpretation is strongly entrenched in the West African worldview, where religion defines the manner of life: from commerce to the most profane, actions are guided by religion. Appropriating the sacraments as Uzukwu champions, from the cosmology and ontology of the people, in some sense translates into making sacraments the fulcrum of life. In this way, just as the church makes the sacraments, the sacraments in turn should renew the church in its vigor by renewing its members constantly. In a way then, "The Church in a culture is embodied on the one hand in its sacraments and in its institutions, but it's also embodied in its ethical engagement with the world that is shaped by this sacramental memorial."[84] Sacramental rituals celebrate real events in history, events that conditioned and changed lives and patterns of life, as well as a way of seeing the world and judging. Hence, commemorating such events in rituals must make similar impacts on the lives of participants in the celebration; otherwise, one becomes simply a ritualist who "performs external gestures without inner commitment to the ideas and values being expressed."[85] The essence of rituals is a transformation in participants' lives, just as the foundation events led to similar transformations. Consequently, the relationship between sacraments and ethics must remain unchanged. Uzukwu insists on this intrinsic connection in the celebrations of the church. Sacraments will be disembodied, and the community turned into ritualism without this

---

82. Power, *Sacraments*, 88.
83. Power, *Sacraments*, 88.
84. Power, *Sacraments*, 88.
85. Douglas, *Natural Symbols*, 2.

intrinsic relationship between sacraments and life, or an existential dimension to the Christian sacraments.

Christian worship, or liturgy, brings about a renewal and reenacting of the foundation stories of the Christian faith. The events they commemorate find expression in concrete life, which becomes a single expression or continuation of the liturgy. In this regard, Chauvet writes, "Consequently, it is the dailiness of life, when lived in faith and love, which through the Spirit becomes the primary place of the 'liturgy' or the 'spiritual sacrifice' to the glory of God."[86] Liturgy of daily life makes it imperative for Christians to become engaged with seeking justice in the practical social order. In this way, we become what we celebrate. Liturgy must have an indispensable and practical effect in the daily life of believers. Paul's letter captures this understanding, "I appeal to you to present your bodies as a living sacrifice, holy and acceptable to God, which is your spiritual worship" (Rom 12:1). Worship must be in harmony with heart and actions. Theology, in this sense finds a better expression in and through the anthropological. Paul underscores this idea: "You yourselves are our letter, written on our hearts, to be known and read by all; and you show that you are letter of Christ, prepared by us, written not with ink but with the Spirit of the living God, not on tablets of stone but on tablets of human hearts" (2 Cor 3:2–3). Daily lives become a better reflection and expression of the liturgy, as both reinforce each other. Chauvet has a fine expression for this: "Without liturgy, ethics can be most generous but is in danger of losing its Christian identity of response to the prior commitment to God. Without ethics, sacramental practice is bound to become ossified and to verge on magic. It is the sacrament that gives ethics the power to become a 'spiritual sacrifice'; it is ethics that gives the sacrament the means of verifying its fruitfulness."[87]

Conclusion

This chapter expressed how Uzukwu focuses on the sacraments from the viewpoint of indigenous anthropology and cosmology. We established the

---

86. Chauvet, *The Sacraments*, 63 He identifies how the Christian sanctification of the profane substitutes for the Jewish distinction between the sacred and the profane. The profane is not converted or eclipsed by the sanctified. Probably, the liturgy of daily life expresses this idea better. This idea is discernible in traditional Hebrew spirituality, where God's revelation was fundamentally via hearing (word), which demanded action by the living (Deut 6:4), Hearing elicits response, not in words, but in action.

87. Chauvet, *The Sacraments*, 65.

meeting points in these anthropologies, and the practical ethical implications of the commitment attained through sacramental initiation. We examined how gestural behaviors are particular and instrumental to the emergence of a unique and relevant Christianity. Indeed, the emergence of a relevant Christianity can be seen as the basic motif of Uzukwu's theological enterprise; this will build a truly Christian and truly African church. This concern is also the basic challenge of theologies and Christianities outside the dominant tradition. One fact that casual readers may observe is that Uzukwu appears less critical of indigenous cultures. This may give the false impression that African cultures do not stand in need of evangelization by the Gospel. However, Paul VI, in his encyclical, *Evangelii Nuntiandi,* insists on the need for cultures to be evangelized. This is an area that calls for further reflection. Indeed, the faith can and should challenge the culture to rise to what Jesus and his Gospel proclaim. In fact, the faith cannot be reduced to its anthropological and phenomenological expressions alone. In the next chapter, we shall examine the implications of Uzukwu's sacramental endeavors.

Chapter 6

Implications of Reimagining the Sacraments

Introduction

IN THE PRECEDING CHAPTER, we examined how Uzukwu envisions sacramental celebration by relying on the documents of Vatican II. We presented Uzukwu's discussion of West African anthropology and liturgical history to develop a theology for the practice of sacramental inculturation. In doing this, we underlined the consistency of this practice with the practice of early Christian times before the age of unification and uniformity. The Second Vatican Council remains pivotal in the return to the sources and to plurality in liturgical practices. In this chapter, faithful to the central thesis of this book and in response to theological necessity, we shall examine how Uzukwu's sacramental reinterpretation resonates in liturgical theology, ecclesiology, and pneumatology. These areas constitute the tripod upon which his theology stands and from which his overall theology can be assessed. Like a symphony, these aspects of his theology received ample attention and revision at the Second Vatican Council, and reinforce each other and highlight his theology. In brief, we can safely say that Vatican II inaugurated a dramatic renewal in the pneumatology of Catholic ecclesiology.

Liturgy

The most visible expression of the council's renewal is perhaps in the document on sacred liturgy,[1] the first chapter of which sets the nature of the liturgy and its significance in the life of the community: in the liturgy, "the work of our redemption takes place . . . enabling the faithful to express in their lives and portray to others the mystery of Christ and the real nature of the Church."[2] Liturgy thus serves as the fundamental point of encounter with the merits of the death and resurrection of Christ, the foundation of the Christian faith. In the liturgy, the grace flowing through the death and resurrection of Christ sanctifies the faithful.[3] It becomes easy to see why the council began its renewal with liturgical activity of the church.

The Constitution on the Sacred Liturgy, *Sacrosanctum Concilium*, was the first document to be debated and approved, on December 4, 1963,[4] setting the pace for the overall work of the council and contributing significantly to the changes taking place in the contemporary church.[5] In response to the felt need for renewal, the intention of the Constitution is boldly stated in the opening paragraph: "to adapt more closely to the needs of our age those institutions which are subject to change, as cogent reasons for undertaking the reform and promotion of the liturgy."[6] This reform and its openness have given rise to more creative liturgies. For example, instead of a single Canon of the Mass (*Te Igitur*), which prevailed over a long period of time (16th to 20th century), additional canons have emerged. These additional canons reveal and emphasize various aspects of the mystery of God. In fact, "The New Eucharistic prayers beautifully underscore the

---

1. Gaillardetz and Clifford, *Keys to the Council*, 1.

2. SC 2.

3. SC 61. The council ascribes grace of sacraments and sacramentals to the paschal mystery of Christ, the source of grace. The church has always seen sacramentals as "sacred signs authorized for use by the church that bring about some spiritual effect or occasion a personal encounter with the grace of Christ, apart from the seven liturgical signs of the church that have been designated as sacraments." See Gaillardetz and Clifford, *Keys to the Council*, 5.

4. The renewal of the document was heralded by a long process of liturgical review, dating back to early studies by the German and French bishops' conferences on the scriptures and early Christian writings. Furthermore, Pope Pius XII emphasized these studies of the early 1900s in the encyclical *Mediator Dei* (1947), suggesting a substantial reform of the liturgy.

5. See Maldonado, "Liturgy as Communal Enterprise," 309.

6. SC 1.

convergence of creational revelation and biblical revelation in the paschal mystery. They express also the unity of the salvific initiative that the Father seeks through the work of the Son and in the Holy Spirit with loving determination until the end of time."[7] These aspects complement and enrich the monistic view of the preface expressed by the *Te Igitur*. Such prefaces or Eucharistic prayers, which highlight the work of the Father in creation, the redemption of the Son and the continuing sanctification of the Holy Spirit are part of the *All-Africa Eucharistic prayers*, which Uzukwu creates. In Uzukwu's summation, the African cosmology resonates with the idea of God as Almighty Father/ Creator (*Chukwu, Orisa, Chiokike*), and this makes it possible to reinterpret the liturgy and especially the Eucharistic prayers. As we shall discuss in this chapter, the Spirit has a robust place in African cosmology. Uzukwu's Eucharistic prayers capture the African cosmology and spirituality in a unique way.

In addition, from an African liturgical perspective, the openness and latitude envisaged by the council offer a great impetus to adapt the liturgy by changing the theological and political models of the missionary age in Africa. For emphasis, Uzukwu often links the evangelization of sub-Saharan Africa to the colonial establishment. For him, the relationship between the missionaries and colonial administrators was ambivalent in most cases, except for a few instances where missionaries disagreed with other colonialists. Consequently, a movement for liturgical adaptation, or inculturation as he would prefer to call it, becomes an urgent and necessary mission of the church in contemporary Africa.

Uzukwu's theology, inspired by Vatican II, revolves around a reinterpretation of the received Roman liturgy. His familiarity with the history of the liturgy convinces him of the possibility and practice of liturgical reinterpretation. Most of his writings investigate the history of the Christian liturgy, identifying the anthropological and cultural underpinnings of various liturgies that would be sensitive to African anthropology and cultural proclivities.

Liturgy in the Life of the Church

The sacred liturgy expresses the whole activity of the Church, which is basically to worship God.[8] The Greek *leitourgia*, liturgy, properly ex-

---

7. Echema, "Liturgy," 146.
8. SC 33.

presses the role and function of liturgy as public work (worship). The fundamental task of the Church is therefore to praise and glorify God. The mystical body of Christ, the head, and its members, in varying degrees, are involved in this activity. In this consideration, the opinion of Austin Echema is quite apt, "There is nothing that the Church does in the world which has more consequence for the faith identity and agency of its people than its public work, namely, the liturgy."[9] Liturgy is an expression of faith as well as a school of learning about the ascent of faith. Just as in communal worship Israel learned about its faith (Deut 6:20–25; 26:5–9), so also the church liturgically expresses its faith.

Considering the foregoing, we delineate two components of liturgy as descending and ascending movements. The descending aspect (the *katabatic*) refers to God's sanctifying grace in the Holy Spirit; *anabatic*, on the contrary, refers to ascending movement, which describes worshiping and glorifying God.[10] These two movements in the liturgical activity of the church do not strictly represent human and divine work, as if the divine was confined to any specific *locale* or *formula*. In sum, liturgy represents these movements as the work of God and the human response.

An outstanding focus of Uzukwu's theology lies in the history of the Christian tradition, which he accesses through the prism of liturgy, identifying the cultural undertones of the major liturgical families. In fact, for him, cultural differences are partly responsible for the separation of various liturgical families. Hence diversity and difference have always characterized the liturgy.[11] The use of symbols, signs, and rituals, which often have ethnic origins, further justifies the cultural dimensions of liturgy. Although the reality of the Christ event has a universal applicability, its concrete expression adopts gestures and languages of contexts. This concrete contextual expression does not limit the veracity and authenticity of expressions outside the dominant tradition, making it possible to express the Christian story with various cultural particularities. Symbols and gestures are *not* integral to the fundamental story that the Christian liturgy celebrates.

The liturgy then inserts its participants into the Christian tradition with the wisdom of the ages and provides a moment of didactic encounter with wisdom both ancient and contemporary, and a moment for formation. The council expresses this idea when it states that, "liturgy contains

---

9. Echema, "Liturgy," 142–43.
10. Vorgrimler, *Sacramental Theology*, 22.
11. See Uzukwu, *Liturgy*.

abundant instruction for the faithful."[12] So liturgy informs as much as it transforms the participants. In other words, liturgy is anchored on faith and leads to faith. No wonder worship is the foremost activity of the church, which Vatican II theology demonstrates!

Consequently, the sacraments, which liturgy celebrates, are moments of renewal for the community as it makes the salvific work of Christ present. The council describes the work of Christ variously as, the "work of redemption," and the "work of salvation."[13] The sacramental celebration, involves the work of the Holy Spirit, the church, and faith. These variables are essential to the fruitful realization of the presence and merits of the redemptive work of Christ. Herbert Vorgrimler expresses this idea further,

> But since those works are not separable from the person of Jesus, and since faith presumes that Jesus and his saving works are living in God's presence, and that neither, through any human power, can be truly made present or brought into an existential moment of time, it is Jesus Christ himself who creates this presence in the Holy Spirit.[14]

Mediation, the central agency of Jesus in the sacramental celebration becomes the very condition for the liturgy. This sacramental reenactment of past events, precisely the paschal mystery, introduces an important theological concept of *memory* as an indispensable condition that is laden with potency.

Liturgy Constitutes and Renews the Church

Liturgy is theologically anchored on the concept of *memory*. The Hebrew verb *zakhar*,[15] (to remember), which has various nuances carries enormous importance in Jewish social and cultic life. Even as the etymological problems continue,[16] the concept, more than any other, probably explains the motif and foundation of liturgy. Louis-Marie Chauvet distinguishes two senses of the concept of memory.[17] The first sense is a simple mem-

12. SC 93.
13. SC 2, 6, 4.
14. Vorgrimler, *Sacramental Theology*, 22–23.
15. Childs, *Memory and Tradition in Israel*, 9.
16. Recent lexicographers seem to agree that the etymological problem of derivatives of the literal *zkr* will remain unsolved. See Childs, *Memory and Tradition in Israel*, 9–10.
17. Chauvet, *Symbol and Sacrament*, 233.

orization or remembrance of an act or event of the past, albeit a static one; examples of this might be found in photos, like graduation photos, swearing-in photos, or past events that have no bearing on the present and the future. The second sense of memory communicates the idea of commemoration: "It is in this act of communal memory a people or a group regenerates itself. The past of its origins is snatched out of its 'pastness' to become the living genesis of today. This today is thus received as 'present,' as a 'gift of grace.'"[18] Liturgy that celebrates this tradition and gift of love in history becomes a response in love to the initial and providential care of the divine majesty. It is precisely a gift of grace, contemporizing the past with all its significance and grace. In this act of memorial, the story of the past acquires a new and continuous life in the present. The simple Jewish profession of faith exemplifies this point:

> My father was a wondering Aramean, who took his family to Egypt to live. They were few in number when they went there, but they became a large and powerful nation. The Egyptians treated us harshly and forced us to work as slaves. Then we cried out for help to the Lord, the God of our ancestors. He heard us and saw our suffering, hardship, and misery. By his great power and strength, he rescued us from Egypt. He worked miracles and wonders and caused terrifying things to happen. He brought us here and gave us this rich and fertile land.[19]

In this way, collective Jewish history is assumed in a personal or present identity, and the promises thereof are actualized in the present.

The act of memorial also conveys the need to keep God's graciousness in mind. Past events always shed light on the future. It is in this sense that Brevard Childs considers cultic memorial as the way Israel was brought constantly to God's attention. The memorial was not simply a general human psychological act but acquired a deeply theological meaning. Consequently, "To remember was to actualize the past, to bridge the gap of time and to form a solidarity with the fathers. Israel's remembrance became a technical term to express the process by which later Israel made relevant the great redemptive acts which she recited in her tradition."[20] Childs points out the relationship between cult and memory, and how they actualize the effects of past events. This interpretation continues in the Deuteronomist

---

18. Chauvet, *Symbol and Sacrament*, 233.
19. See Deut 26:5–9.
20. Childs, *Memory and Tradition in Israel*, 74–75.

era, reinterpreting and contemporizing past events for later generations separated from the actual events in time and space. Through this approach, those who had not experienced the exodus were introduced to God's continuous redemptive acts. Subsequently, Childs identifies a second motif in Israel's memory, "Israel is commanded to be obedient to the commandments *in order to* remember the redemptive history."[21] For example, obedience to the command of the Sabbath inserts Israel into the redemption that the Sabbath commemorates. This leads to the actualization of the Sabbath promises and the blessings attuned to that end. Therefore, memory remains an important liturgical element in the above-mentioned ways.

Liturgical celebrations are then the proper context for renewing the church and handing on the faith. Pope Pius XI expresses this idea thus, "For people are instructed in the truths of faith and brought to appreciate the inner joys of religion far more effectually by the annual celebration of our sacred mysteries than by any official pronouncement, of the teaching of the Church. Such pronouncements usually reach only a few and the more learned among the faithful."[22] In other words, such pronouncements and encyclicals may speak only once, except when consulted for references, whereas liturgy speaks repeatedly. For Uzukwu, this act of repetition is fundamental to the ritual that liturgy celebrates. In fact, he sees repetition as a "fundamental property of ritual gesture," which "translates ritual behavior into an instrument of social engineering."[23] Liturgy appeals not only to the mind (intellect), but also to the heart and actions of humankind. Liturgy proper is the place of learning and teaching in worship of the mysteries of our faith.[24] In fact, in Austin Echema's understanding, the popular patristic saying *"lex orandi, lex credendi"* refers primarily to the

---

21. Childs, *Memory and Tradition in Israel*, 78.

22. Pius XI, *Quas Primas*, 21.

23. Uzukwu, *Worship as Body Language*, 41.

24. We can see this pedagogical insight in the establishment of the cult of martyrs, confessors, virgins, and devotion to Mary in the early Church, or more precisely, during persecution, as a way to inspire heroism in the face of terror, and devotion to the Blessed Virgin Mary. Liturgy is then a form of school, which inspires faith. John Paul II seems to highlight this point in his reflection on catechesis: "Catechesis is intrinsically linked with every liturgical and sacramental action, because it is in the sacraments, and especially in the Eucharist, that Christ acts in fullness for the transformation of humans." See John Paul II, *The Apostolic Exhortation*, 48.

liturgy as the normative expression of faith,[25] which leads to faith in the events liturgy celebrates.

From this perspective, Sebastian Madathumuriyil gives an iconic interpretation of the gestures in the liturgy. Each gesture signifies the activity and presence of God in the community, but above all, he suggests that the liturgy be incarnated or expressed in the lives of the participants in the liturgy.[26] He succinctly avers,

> Briefly speaking, the whole liturgical dynamics is very important in constructing the meaning of the liturgy. But the originary activity of the Spirit, which lies even at the root of gathering the assembly, is that which makes the Church's liturgy fecund so as to mediate presence and grace.[27]

Chronologically, he prioritizes God's activity in the liturgy over the human response, so liturgy does not originate from individual volition, or even the community, but is a response to divine action; it is a celebration of the excessive *givenness* of God's love.[28] Hence various liturgical gestures serve as symbols to indicate God's presence. As will be seen in a later section of this chapter, the activity and agency of the Spirit and Christ acquire profound significance in the liturgy. Liturgy emerges from the initial activity of God on the people, who gather in faith to participate in an activity that simultaneously leads to faith. Hence, we can say that participation in the mystery of Christ (liturgy) involves us in a hermeneutic circle of transformation by our incorporation, whether overtly or covertly. On the didactic nature of the liturgy, Vatican II categorically states, "Because they are signs, they also instruct. They not only presuppose faith, but by words and objects they also nourish, strengthen, and express it. That is why they are called 'sacraments of faith.'"[29] Liturgy, then, is the unquestionable for faith formation into the mystery of the Christian faith.

---

25. John Paul II, *The Apostolic Exhortation*, 143.
26. Madathummuriyil, *Sacrament as Gift*, 269–72.
27. Madathummuriyil, *Sacrament as Gift*, 272.
28. Madathummuriyil, *Sacrament as Gift*, 173.
29. SC 59.

Liturgy Expressed through African Anthropology

In 1969, while on pastoral visit to Kampala (Kenya), Pope Paul VI prophetically declared, "You may, and you must have an African Christianity."[30] An African Christianity expresses the same Christian message in an African culture and worldview. As indigenization, African Christianity is seen as a theological hermeneutic procedure in search of authentic ways to express the faith in ways that are faithful to the Gospel and to indigenous traditions.[31] The project of realizing an African Christianity begins with the most fundamental activity of the church, namely, liturgy. It involves a renegotiation of received Christianity by engaging and bringing to bear aspects of the indigenous cultures that express the Gospel and are coterminous with the current theological disposition of the church. An exercise in liturgical reinterpretation is one that responds to and furthers a realization of the plurality that characterizes the Catholic tradition.

Central to Uzukwu's liturgical reinterpretation is his articulation of a unique West African notion of the person. He identifies profound differences between the Greek (Western) and African views of the body: "The austere liturgies of the West do not project the body in the same way that liturgies in Africa have recently attempted to do."[32] This difference stems from a divergence between the African and the Greco-Roman understanding of the person, which has influenced Christian anthropology and consequently the liturgy of the Christian West. He sees the impact of the Roman juridical system and dogmatic constitution of the person as promoting individuality, instead of community and relationships. This idea shields personhood from relationships and turns the individual into itself and to God (self-transcendence). In this regard, it may be proper to indicate the subtle difference Uzukwu sees in African and Western understanding of the body and its gestures. According to Uzukwu,

> Liturgical "dances," carry a clear message about the disposition of a culture and tradition towards the "body," a message that has anthropological bearing. Africans do not share the Western suspicion of the body as "prison" for the soul or instrument of sin—a

---

30. Paul VI, "Discourse at the Closing of the First Plenary Assembly of the Symposium of the Episcopal Conferences of Africa and Madagascar (SECAM), Kampala, Uganda, July 31, 1969," cited in Healey and Sybertz, *Towards an African Narrative Theology*, 19.
31. Martey, *African Theology*, 65.
32. Martey, *African Theology*, 101.

suspicion that engulfed the West through Platonism, Neo-Platonism and the Fathers (especially Augustine of Hippo). African anthropology sees "body" as "epiphany of the person."[33]

The ensuing immobility emanating from the Greek monistic idea does not leave room for relationships and kinship. The uniformity in the Christian liturgy, following the Roman system, resulted in an immobile behavioral liturgical posture. Consequently, Uzukwu notes, "Liturgical celebration which was a community affair gradually came to project the individual over against the community under the influence of Germanic Celtic individualism and Roman law. The way the person is perceived, does influence the way worship is experienced."[34] Human gestural behavior follows a particular understanding of the person; however, John Zizioulas, in his estimation of the Roman consideration of the person, gives a slightly different interpretation. According to Zizioulas, in Roman antiquity, the view of the person was more in sync with relationships and communion. He states, "Roman thought, which is fundamentally organizational and social, concerns itself not with ontology, with the being of man, but with his relationship with others, with his ability to form associations, to enter into contracts, to set up collegia, to organize human life in state."[35] The Roman *persona* is defined from a sociological dimension, as a role one plays in moral or legal life, without reference to ontology.[36] Consequently, the enclosed individual that quickly found its way into the Christian liturgy can be explained only as a later development in the Roman anthropology. Liturgically, we can attempt to establish some convergence between Uzukwu and Zizioulas when we see the emergence of the Christian understanding of the person as dating to later Christian writings and the influence of dualistic philosophies that Platonism and Neo-Platonism typify. Uzukwu identifies the unique importance of these philosophies to the early Fathers and their definitions, as the limitations of these philosophies inevitably affect their theology. The African notion of the person is tailored toward communalism, whereas the ancient Roman notion was toward the individual and the *force* of that difference, which lies within. This current runs through the Igbo concept of reality, which is always ambivalent since

---

33. Uzukwu, "Liturgy, Culture and the Postmodern World," 162.
34. Uzukwu, "African Personality and the Christian Liturgy," 63.
35. Zizioulas, *Being as Communion*, 34.
36. Zizioulas, *Being as Communion*, 34.

everything coexists with its opposite.³⁷ For instance, body and spirit are coextensive with each other, without any strict dualism or division. Ikenga Metuh expresses this idea thus:

> The African doctrine of man does not admit the dualism which is characteristic of the Western Graeco-Roman culture. Man is not split into two conflicting principles, the body and the soul. . . . [T]here are indeed a number of principles in man, but these do not contradict his unity. They are, rather, principles which link man, 'the real person' with other beings in the ontological order.³⁸

Furthermore, the African view of the person emphasizes the plurality of the elements in the interaction of the person with his environment as essential factors. In this sense, we can state that *persona* is all about relationships. The Roman immobility of the person, handed down through the concerted efforts of colonialism and evangelization as essential to Christian comportment, remains in need of decolonization. Liturgical decolonization, which Uzukwu champions, becomes necessary for reclaiming the relational African communalism in liturgical life and for social engineering. It is precisely this aspect of African relatedness and the goodness of gestural behaviors that Uzukwu has focused on in creating a liturgy that would be sensitive to indigenous anthropology and cosmology: a community-oriented worship style. Luis Maldonado seems to suggest that the ecclesiology and liturgy envisaged by Vatican II is both communion and community oriented.³⁹

In pursuance of community-oriented celebrations, Uzukwu is interested in creative initiatory rites, those that incorporate the individual into the community. Such celebrations include changes in the biological cycle and social crises in the life of the individual and his community. Obviously, Uzukwu is unsatisfied with the practice of cerebral faith formation for sacraments, which does not properly attend to life changes and the role of the community in the life of the individual. Nonetheless, in reinterpreting the liturgical celebration of the sacraments, he cautions for attentiveness to the spirituality and prayerful context of the celebrations. By engaging various

---

37. Nwigwe and Emedolu, *Emergent and Contentious Issues in African Philosophy*, 162. It may be important to remark that "In Igbo understanding, being is seen as dual, not in the sense of sharp distinction into separate principles of mind and matter, physics and metaphysics, but in the sense of a coextensiveness of these with one another" (Nwigwe and Emedolu, *Emergent and Contentious Issues in African Philosophy*, 162).

38. Metuh, *God and Man in African Religion*, 113.

39. Maldonado, "Liturgy as Communal Enterprise," 310.

Igbo traditional rituals, he demonstrates the inculturation of the sacraments to be more pragmatic and relevant to the community.[40] To buttress his points, he does not include a systematic discussion of all the sacraments but presents insights on a few of the sacraments. The following outline attempts to capture his position on some sacraments.

Sacrament of Baptism

Uzukwu discusses the sacraments not as abstract intellectual realities, but primarily as community celebrations. As was discussed in chapter 3, regarding sacraments as rites of passage, the sacrament of baptism initiates and incorporates the individual into Christ. Consequently, the candidate is endowed with the Holy Spirit after the renunciation of evil, and a new lifestyle is thereby begun. Therefore, rites of initiation play the fundamental role of initiating the neophyte into a particular lifestyle. Uzukwu argues precisely for incorporating the prevalent rite of a *naming ceremony* in the West African baptism ritual. Accordingly,

> The naming ceremony as the major entry point of a neonate into a socio-cultural group has remarkable features in West African societies. The Igbo, Akan and Yoruba, for example, connect the child to the day of the week, to ancestral roots, and to circumstances surrounding the birth-all of which are linked to the destined course in life of the neonate.[41]

The names represent the circumstances and the family experience of the neonate so that simply hearing the name already informs one of the specifics of the person. The incorporation of this aspect of the ritual of baptism as already discussed (instructions for rite of baptism), is currently accommodated in the present disposition of the church.

Inculturating the sacraments of initiation through traditional rites was viewed with disdain before Vatican II, being considered inconsistent with the new Christian identity of baptism. Christian initiation from early times, however, accommodated and adapted ancient non-Christian practices. Uzukwu has identified the rich cultural symbolisms in the naming

---

40. Uzukwu bases this exercise on the fact that Christian rituals do not differ from anthropological characteristics. Notwithstanding, this approach does not relativize the specificity of the Christian ritual.

41. Uzukwu, "Body and Belief," 207.

ceremony as re-enacting a memorial in the sacred stories of the early beginnings, nurturing both the individual and the community.[42]

Sacrament of Eucharist

In chapter 4, we analyzed Uzukwu's doctoral dissertation, which focuses on the Eucharist. In this section, we attempt to recapture Uzukwu's model for the sacramental celebration that he situates within the Jewish meal, since its elements are typical of the Jewish family meal. Consequently, the Eucharist becomes a cultic ritual meal, through which, "the participants are related to the divinity who gives, recommends, receives or shares in such a meal. In eating and drinking, the participants commune with the divinity."[43] The Eucharist is then transposed from the ordinariness of the meal to a participation in the body and blood of the Lord (1 Cor 11). The development of the Eucharistic celebration as an adaptation by the early church recognizes the anthropological dimension of the meal, which further reinforces cultural adaptation. However, Uzukwu expresses some pain with the canonical provisions, for the elements of the Eucharist limit the extent of cultural adaptation.[44] He categorically states, "I maintain that the initiative in the choice of food items to be used in the eucharistic ritual should rest with the church in Africa as well as other native churches. . . . The functioning of a socio-cultural group or a whole geographical area in a Christian way necessarily includes gestures of eating and drinking."[45] Consequently, he argues for the use of indigenous elements for the Eucharistic celebration; however, he cautions for carefulness in selecting the elements for the Eucharist that will most authentically represent the region.

Besides the Eucharistic elements, Uzukwu sees exuberant expressive worship as necessary for the African celebration. In fact, he argues that the vitality of the assembly's worship indicates that the chosen people of God is not a frozen people.[46] One clearly sees his strong position on the

42. Uzukwu, "Body and Belief," 217–18.

43. Uzukwu, "African Symbols and Christian Liturgical Celebration," 107.

44. Canon 924 specifies the nature of the Eucharistic elements when it states: (1) the Eucharist must be celebrated in bread, and in wine to which a small quantity of water is to be added; (2) the bread must be wheaten only, and recently made, so that there is no danger of corruption; (3) the wine must be natural, made from grapes of the vine, and not corrupt. See *Code of Canon Law*, Canon 924, sections 1–3.

45. Uzukwu, "African Symbols and Christian Liturgical Celebration," 110.

46. Uzukwu, "The Sacramental Imagination," 308.

beauty of gestural behavior in the eucharistic celebration. Specific bodily gestures and prayers (presented here in chapter 4) are a right to the African church. When this is done, according to Uzukwu, "Liturgical celebration in African symbols offers the Christ to Africans in an appropriate way and offers to the universal church another unique experience and expression of the one Christ."[47]

Sacrament of Reconciliation

Uzukwu develops a ritual of reconciliation that captures and incorporates indigenous patterns of reconciliation. This approach, which has the evidence of history in its favor, responds to the challenges of the African personality.

Through the centuries, the Catholic Church has always exercised rituals for reconciliation, with alternate practice of private and communal confessions. These responded to various circumstances of the Christian faith. Hence, from the African contexts, specifically with the multiplicity of spirits that are manipulated to unleash harm and demonic possessions, reconciliation needs a model that would capture the specificities of the African personality. The reality of evil which contravenes goodness toward the individual and the community, and the very realization of individual and communal destiny, deserves no less than a communal reconciliation approach. The assertion of John Mbiti on the communality of African personality is worth recalling here: "I am because we are, and since we are, therefore, I am." The African human type is bonded to the community, as his indispensable worldview. A coherent theology of reconciliation, in this context, cannot afford to ignore this fundamental identity question.

This is precisely why Uzukwu critiques the model of the sacrament of reconciliation for being overly influenced by the Western individualistic approach. He wants to see relatedness, which undergirds the African notion of the person, expressed in this sacrament of reconciliation. Rituals of reconciliation make enormous difference and lasting impacts when rooted in the value of life and the meaning of a group. A community-oriented ritual of reconciliation, which Uzukwu discusses, like the *igba ndu* ceremony, ritualizes reconciliation and restoration of relationships. It takes into consideration an elaborate dimension of the person and the communal nature of sin/evil. Hence, he describes it as a "purification

---

47. Uzukwu, "African Symbols and Christian Liturgical Celebration," 111–12.

ritual." His basis for such inculturation is that the history of the sacrament reveals features that "characterize certain epochs and localities."[48] One instance is the change from public penance to private, which has historical reasons. Indeed, he describes the current practice of the sacrament of reconciliation as laden with the Western view of the person as individual. His proposed outline integrates the relatedness that characterizes the African view of the person so that reconciliation goes beyond the acts of the individual because the individual is a member of the community. The celebration he proposes "takes off from the truth that life has meaning for the African person when it is practiced as relationships. It accepts the traditional African perception that symbolic-ritual is effective means of resolving conflicts only when it is plunging of individuals in community into the "life-meaning" structure to recreate relationship."[49]

Joseph Martos, arguing for the reconstruction of the sacraments, agrees with Uzukwu's position. He sees the modern practice of the sacrament of reconciliation as ritualistic, magical, and separated from reconciliation with the rest of the community.[50] Individual confession as a ritual that rehabilitates the individual to the community has no impact on the one who has been sinned against. He therefore states,

> If the Catholic Church is to develop rituals of genuine reconciliation in the future, it must begin with a vision of what kind of reconciliation it wants to bring about, and it must then develop appropriate procedures to foster it. These will not be liturgical procedures, but as in the Rite of Christian Initiation of Adults, various steps or moments in the process could be celebrated ritually.[51]

This is precisely the manner of reconciliation practiced in many indigenous cultures, where reconciliation is not automatic but involves the parties in the case. Sacramental reconciliation becomes more active in a context of family, community, and individual dimensions when it engenders genuine reconciliation between people in addition to God's forgiveness.

48. Uzukwu, "African Personality and the Christian Liturgy," 71–72.
49. Uzukwu, "African Personality and the Christian Liturgy," 73.
50. Martos, *Reconstructing Sacramental Theology*, 265.
51. Martos, *Reconstructing Sacramental Theology*, 266.

Sacrament of Matrimony

The effort to express sacraments through indigenous practices is discernible in how Uzukwu discusses marriage as practiced in some dioceses in Nigeria. The traditional socio-religious rite of marriage is rich in symbolism and establishes a covenant between the bride and bridegroom's families and communities. In fact, the first National Pastoral Congress of the Catholic Church in Nigeria, held in 2002, emphasized marriage and family as major areas of inculturation according to native cultures and Christian practice.[52] In this way, the rich cultural marriage rites coalesce with the specific Christian sacramental character of Christ's presence.

The practical aspect of harmonization between the traditional and Christian rites of marriage is the indigenous practice of "fattening," a period of seclusion of the maidens for pre-marriage guidance and counseling on the secrets of a successful marriage, serving the purpose of "initiation into the 'female secrets' of married life in general and formal lessons in wifehood and motherhood."[53] Uzukwu sees the rituals within the liminality and ritual of integration as powerful ways of establishing a lasting marriage bond[54] and, therefore, he completely approves of dioceses that have undertaken this harmonization. Consequently, a joint celebration of both ceremonies, in the form of a "church wedding and a traditional one," incorporates the strengths of the indigenous marriage practices, thereby creating a truly Christian and truly African rite of marriage. Uzukwu accounts this approach as a creative appropriation of tradition.

Holy Orders

While Uzukwu does not specifically treat the priesthood in his work, one learns his view on the priesthood from his ecclesiology, the sacraments, and the liturgy. He is obviously uncomfortable with the pre-Vatican II model of the church, which was centered on the ministerial priesthood. This over clericalism is in sharp contrast with the African model of leadership, which he champions, and is contrary to the church's concept as communion, and the African synod's understanding as family. Being an ordained minister is a call to serve and to promote charity among the people of God, who are

---

52. See Catholic Bishops' Conference of Nigeria, *The Church in Nigeria*, 2.
53. Uzukwu, "Traditioning and the Emerging Shape of a Local Church," 228.
54. Uzukwu, "The Sacramental Imagination," 312.

equally gifted with the charism that flows from the Holy Spirit. Initiations into leadership elevate the leaders and keep them under the watchful gaze of the community's ancestors. Similarly, leaders in the church are under an obligation to lead but not dominate the flock.

Sacrament of Healing

African traditional religion is centered on human flourishing. A multiplicity of deities and spirits function for the good of humankind. Hence, healing is an important aspect of West African cosmology. In fact, Uzukwu describes African religion as, "a therapeutic religion in contradistinction to religious experiences elsewhere in the world."[55] The experience of demonic possession and the power of elemental forces to unleash harm even on the innocent make healing a central religious practice. Consequently, the environment is familiar with healing experts and visionaries. The emergence of Pentecostal and charismatic movements, with emphasis on the healing power of the Holy Spirit, reinterprets indigenous traditional healing approaches by affirming the supreme authority of God in the healing process. Uzukwu recognizes this authority for healing in the African Initiated Churches (AICs) and Pentecostal movements since integral healing involves the whole person and not just pathology. He welcomes the adaptation of ancestral healing in the Christian movement in Africa.

Ecclesiology

Uzukwu's book, The *Listening Church: Autonomy and Communion in local Church*, expresses his vision for the church in Africa, and indeed, for a true catholicity of the church. He argues for the autonomy of the local church, which would not, however, insulate them from other local churches. The bond of communion and reciprocity in exchange of gifts must be preserved. Differently put, one can see his argument as deconstructing the myth of ontological priority, or the understanding of the universal church as located in a particular local church. His thinking about the church also involves how the church celebrates its sacraments through its liturgies. A decentralization of governance is reflected in a liturgy that incorporates the anthropologies and cosmologies of its particular locales. So, the possibility of the local

---

55. Uzukwu, "Body and Belief," 214.

church correlates with the possibility of unique liturgical celebrations and the sacraments that belong to the celebrating church.

Sacrament, Source and Summit of Ecclesial Life

Uzukwu highlights a deep connection between sacraments and ecclesiology since the sacraments belong to the church as ecclesial realities. As was demonstrated in chapter 3, Uzukwu prioritizes the ecclesiological over the Christological dimension of the sacraments, although the link between the two in sacramental celebration is not ruptured. Differently stated, his assent on the ecclesiality of the sacraments does not neglect or detract from their Christological aspect. Nonetheless, he emphasizes the role and interpretative power of the community to celebrate what Christ has already bequeathed to it, expressed in the elements and dimensions of the sacraments, and informed by ecclesial community's imagination. Since this community is essential in determining certain sacramental aspects, we can discuss the sacraments as ecclesial realities on which Uzukwu lays great emphasis.

The sacraments cannot be discussed without the church. In fact, the mystery of the church and the mystery of the Eucharist are inseparably bound together since they originate from the personal mystery of Jesus the Christ. Through the action of the church, the glorified Christ is made present for the community that is already gathered in his name. Hence, in the two mysteries there is a reciprocal causative relationship. The Second Vatican Council defined this relationship when it stated,

> Liturgical services are not private functions but are celebrations of the Church which is "the sacrament of unity," the holy people united and arranged under their bishops. Therefore, liturgical services pertain to the whole Body of the Church. They manifest it and have effects upon it. But they also touch the individual members of the Church in different ways, depending on their orders, their role in the liturgical services, and their active participation in them.[56]

The council continued this thinking by insisting that sacramentality is the very nature of the church.[57] The sacraments, especially the Eucharist, are foundational to the church, as it is the source of the communion with the Trinity and with the members of the church. In this sense, we can state that the Eucharist predates the church or, differently put, the church is made

---

56. SC 26.
57. LG 1.

by the Eucharist, just as the church makes the Eucharist. The sacraments mediate holy things among the people of God.

Reimagining the sacraments and their liturgical celebration inevitably involves rethinking the model of the church that celebrates the sacraments. Uzukwu envisages the emergence of a local church that is autonomous and yet in communion with other churches, appealing to the authority of Saint Cyprian, the bishop of Carthage. He insists on a church that will be self-reliant in most of its needs. African churches, then, to have a churchly dignity and to think for themselves, must retract from the logic of extroversion. Theological maturity should also resonate in other facets of ecclesial life and ministry. Uzukwu insists, however, not on a church that will be insulated and closed on itself, but a church that would look inwardly to utilize its spiritual and material resources for development. In fact, his ecclesiology follows his theological methodology anchored in relationality. A concrete demonstration of this ecclesiology is found in the *First National Pastoral Plan of the Church in Nigeria*, which identifies self-propagating, self-supporting and self-ministering as basic components of being a local church.[58] These attributes enhance development and are, indeed, indicators of the maturation of the local church. A self-propagating church must be open to other missionaries and become missionaries to sister churches as well. Similarly, a self-supporting church, while enjoying the dignity of independence, must be open to giving and receiving support from other ecclesial communities. *The Lineaments of First National Pastoral Plan* stresses this idea: "Africans are becoming missionaries unto themselves and in the area of personnel, some Nigerian Dioceses are self-reliant without closing themselves to receiving missionaries."[59] Yet, for Uzukwu, the local church must be open to and in communion with other churches. Also important is the exchange of charity in the local church. Uzukwu argues for a local church that is disposed to undertake the responsibility of providing for her basic needs. Perhaps Okoh expresses this idea well,

> It is of the highest importance to the welfare of the work that wherever local Christians are formed they should be trained to contribute towards the support of the ministry they enjoy. A missionary society may confer inestimable blessings in commencing a work in any country, but when a flock is gathered, it should

---

58. See Catholic Bishops' Conference of Nigeria, *The Church in Nigeria*, 19.

59. *Lineaments for the First National Congress*, no. 193, cited in Igwegbe, "Exchange of Charity," 48.

supply its wants and not leave them to be provided by strangers.... Grants-in-aid should always be considered supplementary to the local initiatives that are already in existence. As long as the local Church regards subsidies from overseas as sufficient for its survival, there will never be any hope of local independence in terms of self-sufficiency.[60]

Hence, the emergence of a true local church involves a revision of not only strictly theological aspects but also the understanding of charity, which must be recognized as charity, unexpected in the budgetary plans, but accepted as the exchange of charity. When a large percentage of the budget is covered by grants expected in charity, the budget must be seen as intrinsically flawed. Proper pastoral planning must take the availability of resources into consideration. In this way, the idea of a *receiving* church versus a *giving* church, if not completely obliterated, will be greatly blurred.

Reconsidering the Question of the Local Church

Discussions in chapters 4 and 5 show that Uzukwu is interested in the emergence of a robust local church, where the Eucharist is celebrated involving the members of the communities in the presence of the Holy Spirit. John Zizioulas's thinking on the significance of the local church is crucial in this regard. He argues that not every gathering of Christians constitutes a church, and not every church qualifies for the designation of local. To this seeming dilemma, he points out that,

> The church is local when the saving event of Christ takes root in a particular local situation with all its natural, social, cultural and other characteristics which make up the life and thought of the people living in that place. Just as it happens in the Eucharist where the people offer to God as the Body of Christ all that is "his own."... [T]he same must apply to the Church's life, if it is to be truly local: it must absorb and use all the characteristics of a given local situation and not impose an alien culture on it.[61]

This description perfectly captures Uzukwu's main theological understanding of the church, which must take on local characteristics and modes, becoming, indeed, a true incarnation of the church. The emergence of an authentic local church that celebrates the sacraments liturgically so as to capture the

---

60. Okoh, *The Maintenance of Priests*, 28.
61. Zizioulas, *Being as Communion*, 254.

wisdom of the situation remains a task for which Uzukwu offers solutions in the West African region. In *A Listening Church,* Uzukwu articulates the questions of identity and self-awareness of the African church, which must be in communion with other sister churches. The question of authority is discussed primarily as service, following the indigenous authority models, where leadership is bestowed and remains under the ancestors' watchful gaze. In fact, Charles Nyamiti, commenting on Uzukwu, remarks, "Perhaps what is most important in his book is the emphasis on the exercise of church authority as a listening process."[62] For Uzukwu, ecclesial authorities should be gifted with large ears and listen to every member of the community who are also endowed with the spirit. Authority is not for domination. One may recall the timeless statement of Jesus the Christ: "whoever wants to be first among you must be the servant of all" (Mark 10:44).

The current teaching of the church on *sensus fidelium*[63] gives credence to Uzukwu's position. If every baptized member of the church is recognized as gifted with the Holy Spirit and has a charism to contribute for the ongoing growth of the ecclesial community, then no voice becomes marginalized or reduced to inconsequential importance. In summary, dialogue should characterize the relationship among the local churches. Uzukwu sees the whole Christian community as a communion of local churches, with the Church of Rome presiding only over charity, as a prerogative accruable to the Petrine See, and not with the authority to dominate the other local churches.

Toward an Appropriate Model for African Ecclesiology

Contemporary studies use ecclesiological models to offer insights into the mystery of the church.[64] According to Louis Luzebetak, if a model has "a common core of meaning; invariably it refers to a particular perspective from which the real world is being examined and described."[65] This idea is expressed in the opening section of Avery Dulles's *Models of the Church,* in which he states,

> In selecting the term "models" rather than "aspects" or "dimensions," I wish to indicate my conviction that the Church, like other

62. Nyamiti, *Some Contemporary Models of African Ecclesiology,* 77.
63. LG 12.
64. See Dulles, *Models of the Church.*
65. Luzebetak, *The Church and Cultures,* 135.

theological realities, is a mystery. Mysteries are realities of which we cannot speak directly. If we wish to talk about them at all we must draw analogies afforded by our experience of the world. These analogies provide models.[66]

Precursors to the ecclesiology of Vatican II, like *Mystici Corporis,* had begun to shift attention from the emphasis on the institutional model of the church, to the activity of the Holy Spirit in the church. It may be appropriate to recall, according to Yves Congar, that pre-Vatican II theology created "substitutes" for the Holy Spirit, such as the pope, the Eucharist, and Mary,[67] under the hierarchical model of the church. So Vatican II's revision reinstates the church to its early roots.

The Second Vatican Council declined to define the church with a particular model, like the institutional model. Its basic document on the church, *Lumen Gentium,* indeed marks a watershed in the ecclesiology of contemporary Catholicism. According to Veli-Matti Karkkainen, "Perhaps the most important development of Vatican II was the replacement of the old *societas perfecta*, institutional-hierarchic ecclesiology, with the dynamic 'people of God' notion, in which the church is seen first of all as a pilgrim people on the way to [a] heavenly city."[68] The theme of the church as the people of God, reminiscent of the dominant description of Israel in the Old Testament, shifts attention from the hierarchy to the essential dignity of every member of the church, a dignity conferred by the sacrament of baptism. What is paramount under this consideration is the focus on communion ecclesiology. *Lumen Gentium* further gives a vivid description of this communion ecclesiology when it states that God "has, however, willed to make men holy and save them, not as individuals without any bond or link between them, but rather to make them into a people who might acknowledge him and serve him in holiness."[69] We can therefore see this communion with the Trinitarian community as a result of the sacraments and membership in the church. To this effect, the Council used various imageries and expressions such as sacrament, mystery, people of God, and body of Christ to give expression to the reality of the church.[70]

---

66. Dulles, *Models of the Church*, 9.
67. Congar, *I Believe in the Holy Spirit*, 1:154.
68. Karkkainen, *An Introduction to Ecclesiology*, 28.
69. LG 9.
70. Chapter 2 discussed the church as sacrament.

IMPLICATIONS OF REIMAGINING THE SACRAMENTS

Theology in Africa as an exercise of dialogue between the Gospel and indigenous cultures has been engaged in searching for appropriate ecclesiological models. Expressing the church using indigenous models has been a mission that makes the church more relevant to cultures outside the dominant centers of Christianity. Hans Kung made a precise case for the contextualization of the church when he asserted,

> Following the example of Paul, the Church became Greek with the Greek world and Barbarian with the barbarian world. However, it has not become Arabic with the Arabs, Black with the Blacks, Indian with the Indians, or Chinese with the Chinese. Viewed as a whole, the Church of Jesus Christ has remained a European-American affair.[71]

The effort toward inculturation, responds to this challenge. Pope Francis expressed a similar sentiment when he wrote, "We would not do justice to the logic of the incarnation if we thought of Christianity as monocultural and monotonous. While it is true that some cultures have been strongly associated with the preaching of the Gospel and the development of Christian thought, the revealed message is not identified with any of them; its content is transcultural."[72]

The openness of Vatican II enabled reformulations of ecclesial communities. Development in one area of theology has a direct bearing on other areas:

> Liturgical adaptation cannot be an isolated task. It has to be framed within the broader outlines of adaptation in the Church. The liturgy is not an independent unit of ecclesial life. The faith celebrated in the liturgy is the same faith formulated by theology. Progress in one area necessarily involves changes in the other.[73]

Various African theologians, have consequently, tried to reimagine the church from African models in a way that resonates with aspects of the African worldview. For instance, inspired by the council's concept of the *communion* and *people of God*, the 1994 African Synod adopted a model of the church as family.[74] This model, deeply rooted in an African worldview, resonates with the relationality that undergirds Uzukwu's theology;

---

71. Kung, *Concile et Retour a L'unite*, 14–15.
72. Francis, *The Joy of the Gospel*, 117.
73. Chupungco, *Cultural Adaptation of the Liturgy*, 79.
74. John Paul II, *Ecclesia in Africa*, 43.

however, Agbonkhianmeghe Orobator's reaction to this model is quite instructive. According to him, "To say that the church is family of God commits us to the very important task of transforming the prevailing images and practices of our church in a way that embodies the positive values of the family."[75] Family values like warmth, ready-welcome, and hospitality deserve emphasis, while negative family practices like male domination and a high level of patriarchy—traditions that often dehumanize—stand in need of evangelization.[76] Hence, this section examines the paths to appropriate ecclesiology for the church in Africa.

Uzukwu in his essay in the 1980s articulated a hospitality model for the church in Africa,[77] arguing that a basic African attribute is a sense of hospitality: "Despite the destabilization of traditional life by colonialism, foreign world views, technology and modern living.... African hospitality has held rather well to the extent that it could be described as a way of being an African."[78] He therefore proposed a theological model based on hospitality. In Africa, strangers are ideally treated with warm welcome, affection, and friendliness. This accounts for the ready welcome with which Christian and Muslim missionaries were received by the people adhering to ancestral religions. One can see this attitude of quick acceptance as consistent with a culture that celebrates differences, seen as part of nature and showcasing the beauty of the galaxy.

This traditional openness accounts for the favorable disposition that helps the bearer of the Gospel and the content of his message. It guarantees dialogue and an exchange of ideas in an atmosphere of encounter, reducing the tension that may surround the meeting of unknown parties. According to Uzukwu, "The demonstration in dialogue reduces the aggression of the hosts who would regard the guest's contribution as more of a threat than a good fortune."[79] Consequently, Uzukwu seems to anchor hospitality in the stranger's good disposition. This tends to introduce dualism in a value that should be found across the board. The logical stretch of this syllogism would place conditions on the value of hospitality. A "blind" hospitality,

---

75. Orobator, *Theology Brewed in an African Pot*, 89.

76. Widowhood experienced across most parts of Africa, is in need of reform and renewal in the light of the Gospel of Christ. It defeats the idea of family if some of its members are made to feel subordinate to others. There is also over-clericalism.

77. Uzukwu, "Missiology Today."

78. Uzukwu, "Missiology Today," 158.

79. Uzukwu, "Missiology Today," 169.

to my mind, isolates the African uniqueness as a hospitable people. In the process of receiving of the Gospel, hospitality remains pivotal as an instrument of welcome. The goodness in hospitality encounters another goodness in the Gospel, so that the latter is reflected in the former.

Commenting on Uzukwu's position, Francis Njoku, a Nigerian theologian, argues that hospitality must not be paraded as a sole African attribute or value, since it is found in other cultures. He buttresses his position by giving instances of brutality and hostility between various clans in Africa.[80] Beyond this critique, however, he appreciates the value in hospitality as an ideal: "On the whole, I adopt hospitality as a Gospel attitude of acceptance and communal fraternity. It is very enriching; it has infinite merits in terms of creating a solid foundation for dialogue and Christian growth."[81]

Inspired by Uzukwu's seminal work, Gregory Olikenyi, a Nigerian theologian, takes hospitality as a model of the Gospel further in his doctoral dissertation, *African Hospitality: A Model for the Communication of the Gospel in the African Cultural Context*. After acclaiming Uzukwu's work and the significance of African hospitality as a social and religious phenomenon, he notes,

> Unfortunately, Uzukwu, in his article, probably for reasons of scope, and space, did not go wide and deep enough to analyze African hospitality; for a wider and deeper attempt would reveal other important features and many more symbolic elements (and their meanings) that perhaps would be very relevant in constructing a more adequate articulation of the gospel message not only for first evangelization but also for other missionary situations in Africa and even within any manifestation of the Church's life.[82]

Against this backdrop, Olikenyi argues for the transition of the Gospel through African cultural matrices, as a way of building an authentic local church. He therefore discusses the symbols and symbolisms in African hospitality to demonstrate the value of hospitality. He notes the fact of reciprocity between host and stranger, and an unconditional readiness to share as the condition of hospitality: "The principle of reciprocity that underlie[s] African hospitality is usually direct, but it can also be indirect. The hospitality which one expects from his kith and kin, neighbors, or friends is directly reciprocated."[83] Besides

---

80. Njoku, *Essays in African Philosophy*, 246.
81. Njoku, *Essays in African Philosophy*, 246.
82. Olikenyi, *African Hospitality*, 27.
83. Olikenyi, *African Hospitality*, 107–8.

this, he creates a model that represents the African Church family that would see itself as *guest, host,* and *gift.* This theological insight resonates which the identification of the church as sacrament of Christ, who is the host, the guest, and the gift to the ecclesial community.[84]

Charles Nyamiti, a Kenyan theologian, identifies two respective trends in African ecclesiology: inculturation and liberation.[85] Inculturation models stress the interaction between the Gospel and indigenous African cultural practices. According to Nyamiti, this model is generally non-speculative: instead, it adopts the anthropological cultural research model.[86] The liberation trend, in contrast, focuses on existential African issues of justice, such as oppression in South Africa and African feminist theology. On the inculturation of ecclesiology, Nyamiti notes that a few African theologians have attempted to use elements of African culture to express an enhanced ecclesiology for the region. One example is the clan model of John Waliggo, a Ugandan theologian. This model emphasizes the African traditional clan system, where the clan head ensures fraternal communion and charity and clansmen's participation in the decision-making process. The ecclesiology of Benezet Bujo, a Congolese theologian, focuses on Christ as proto-ancestor. Without romanticizing the African tradition, Bujo argues that a retrieval of the traditional African values is an important step toward the emergence of African theology. Two major contributions are discernible in his work. First is a correlational theory that attempts to develop an African Christology. Appropriating the ancestor model, Bujo endows Jesus with the mediational and communicative role of the cult of African ancestorship. In describing him as a proto-ancestor, Bujo underscores the fact that Jesus transcends traditional African ancestors. Second, Bujo creates a new vision for African ecclesiology that will be more community-oriented, devoid of over-clericalism and an overarching hierarchical structure. Thus, he argues for an ecclesiology that will take

84. Olikenyi, *African Hospitality*, 215.

85. Nyamiti, *Some Contemporary Models of African Ecclesiology*, 71–72. The theme of inculturation as the basic challenge of the church in Africa was articulated by the Synod Fathers of the Special Assembly for Africa. See John Paul II, *Ecclesia in Africa*. For other authors who identify inculturation and liberation as basic models of theology in Africa see Eugene Hillman, *Inculturation Applied*. In fact, Hillman, a one-time missionary in East Africa, argues for the imperative of inculturation for the emergence of authentic African Christianity.

86. It may be necessary to state that Nyamiti's dissatisfaction with the inculturation model stems from what he describes as lack of a strong "systematic or philosophical foundation," which for him should be modeled on the Western philosophical tradition.

the laity seriously in every aspect of the church's life.[87] His position here resonates with that of other African theologians.

Jean Marc Ela, a Cameroonian theologian, upholding a similar thought, argues that belief in Christianity does not imply severing relationships with the living dead. Communion with the dead reflects the African belief that abhors annihilation; and sees death as a transition, highlights such expressions as "passing away" and "joining the ancestors." Ela points out that, "if the relationship with the ancestors consists of the belief that the deep communion established among the members of the family is not broken by death, but is maintained despite and beyond death, then nothing in this relationship is contrary to the Christian faith"[88] That the invisible is as real as the visible is the philosophy that undergirds the relationship with the ancestors. This invisible relationship with the dead gives rise to the mediation role of ancestors and the "sacrifices" offered to them. Given immense importance of the ancestors, Ela explains the condition for assigning an ancestor to the dead: "For an African to be clothed with the dignity of an ancestor implies that one has constantly excelled in the practice of virtue," and he recasts this condition into the Vatican II position on those "who through no fault of their own, do not know the Gospel of Christ or his church, but who nevertheless seek God with a sincere heart, and, moved by grace, strive in their actions to do his will as they know it through the dictates of their conscience."[89]

Kwesi Dickson, a Ghanaian biblical theologian, on his part, appreciates the sources of theology—scripture, tradition, experience, and culture to propose a theology that reflects African contexts. He argues against the lingering influence of Western theological methodology in contemporary Africa. For him, the African religious-cultural worldview cannot be dismissed with a wave of the hand; because of insensitivity to things African, the Christian faith has remained an alien on the African soil. According to him: "The faith can be meaningful only when Christ is encountered as speaking and acting authentically, when he is heard in the African languages, when culture 'shapes the human voice that answers the voice of Christ.'"[90] Specifically, he calls for decolonizing the prevailing theological

---

87. Bujo, *African Theology in Its Social Context*.
88. Ela, *My Faith as an African*, 20.
89. Ela, *My Faith as an African*, 20; LG 16.
90. Dickson, *Theology in Africa*, 5.

and liturgical orientations in Africa so that they can respond to the cultural context of African Christians.

The approach that may be closest to what Uzukwu is attempting in ecclesiology is that of Laurenti Magesa, for whom, "Inculturation is a prism through which the whole personal and communal life can be understood, including one's relationship to church laws and practice."[91] Proceeding from this conceptual framework, he argues for the evolution of a mature Christianity in Africa which would imply that the liturgy, church organization, and pastoral life, become truly African. He concludes that inculturating these aspects of the Church's life would overcome the liminality of Christianity in Africa. The community would then be dependent on the subject of the liturgy, namely Jesus Christ, and the events of the paschal mystery.

John Wangbu, a Nigerian theologian, in recent work offers a model of ecclesiology for the incarnation of the Gospel in Nigeria. He uses a concept that serves as the fulcrum of community existence in Ikwerre of Nigeria, namely, Ogbaknor, to express a community-oriented model of the church. As a concept, "Ogbaknor refers to the gathering of villagers, brought together by a—common necessity to discuss in [a] public forum the problems of the community."[92] This discussion in an atmosphere of equality and fair listening to all enables the leader to make decisions that respond to everyone's concerns. This process complements Uzukwu's model of a leader with large ears.

Pneumatology

A balanced theology of the sacraments recognizes the inextricable unity of ecclesiology, sacramentology, and pneumatology. The church is not just a sociological reality; it is a community endowed by the Holy Spirit and realizes presence through the words of Christ and the action of the Holy Spirit. The Council of Constantinople (AD 381) articulated the third article of the creed, "I believe in the Holy Spirit, the Lord and giver of life." This addition, which sought to balance the Christological emphasis in the church, was to be fully realized in Vatican II, yet one cannot deny the work of the Spirit during the intervening time.

In the Nicene-Constantinopolitan creed, the identification of the church as One, Holy, Catholic, and apostolic is guaranteed by the Holy

91. Magesa, *Anatomy of Inculturation*, 61.
92. Wangbu, *Laity in Nigeria*, 276.

Spirit. "The church is one because of the indwelling of the one Holy Spirit in all the baptized; it is holy because it is set apart by God's graciousness for the reception of a mysterious love of predilection; it is catholic in the original sense of the word, meaning that it is whole and entire, possessing all the parts needed to make it integral; and it is apostolic because it remains in continuity in essentials with the original witnessing of the first—century apostles."[93] Contemporary theology highlights the Trinitarian origin of the sacraments and, indeed, of the Church. Consequently, Uzukwu perceives the Spirit as a viable point of entry into the Trinitarian community. The relational world vision of West African indigenous cultures and religions squares with the relational communion of the Trinitarian mode of existence. The dynamism and relational characters of the Holy Spirit and its life-giving ministry resonates with experience of the Spirit in African Traditional Religion (ATR). Uzukwu remarks, "While all Christians reject ATR cult, its deities and rituals, they recognize the creative, active and healing presence of the Holy Spirit. This recognition is, in my view, a successful retrieval and transformation of the dynamic dimension of Spirit in West African ATR."[94] By engaging the Trinitarian theology of Origen, Uzukwu articulates the evolving merging of the familiar West African notion of Spirit (through their ancestral religion), and the Holy Spirit in the Judeo-Christian tradition.

Retrieving the Pneumatology of Origen of Alexandria

Uzukwu finds in Origen an interesting template on which to construct an African theology of pneumatology. Through this pneumatology, he identifies correlations between the ATR personal spirits and the AIC's emphasis on the Holy Spirit and healings as consistent with Origen's position. He thus articulates an African Christian experience that resonates with the ancestral or inherited religion of African Christians. In a seeming rebuttal to insinuations of syncretism, he argues, "But since the air that West African Christians breathe is suffused with ATR and Biblical cosmology, Christians must come to terms with and make sense of the new faith in their context."[95] This context is one that is loaded with the

---

93. Michael Farley, "Church," in Fiorenza and Calvin, *Systematic Theology*, 43.
94. Uzukwu, *God, Spirit, and Human Wholeness*, 137.
95. Uzukwu, *God, Spirit, and Human Wholeness*, 163.

awareness of spirits and the Holy Spirit as one that distributes gifts under the predetermined destiny of each individual.

Origen of Alexandria (AD 185–254) was a source of inspiration to many of the Fathers. His works, numbering about a thousand titles,[96] were a source of further theological reflection, in agreement or not. Focusing interpretation and commentary on the scripture, his theological exploration was consistent with the Spiritism of the Alexandrian Church. According to Rene Cadiou, "The Alexandrians easily sacrificed history in their desire to impose symbolism, even though Christian revelation is, in the first place, a historical event."[97] It is understandable, then, why Origen's systematic theology makes enormous use of symbolism and focuses on the Spirit, including the interaction between anthropology and pneumatology in human holiness. Such ascent is constructed on the strong foundation of anthropology, which probably makes his teaching attractive to Uzukwu, for the West African encounter of the spirit centers on human flourishing.

Origen's anthropology focuses on the pre-existence of the soul and on the three-parts of the human constitution (spirit, intellect, body), with their components in a relational communion. The main role of *pneuma, which* pre-existed the intellect (*nous*) and the body (*soma*), is the grounding of the human spirit in divine life and finds expression in the West African religious traditions. This convergence provides moments of engagement with Origen's anthropology of human ascent. Appropriating this understanding, Uzukwu argues, "Many West African narratives have a corresponding spirit bestowed on each human by the creator, embodying the individual's destiny—a providential indwelling spirit testifying to the accompaniment of the individual by God."[98] The highly spiritualized world vision of the West African universe has antecedents in Christian pneumatology. The spirit as the agent of God's relationship with humans serves as the principle of dynamism in the Trinitarian community and in human life. In this way, Uzukwu understands the *pneuma* as the principal relationship in the divine and human modes of existence. Anticipating the Constantinopolitan addition to the creed, Origen speaks of the high dignity of the Holy Spirit: "We believe, however, that there are three Persons, the Father and the Son and the Holy Spirit; and we believe none to be unbegotten except the Father. We admit, as more pious and truer, that all things were produced through the

96. Lubac, *History and Spirit*, 42.
97. Rene Cadiou, *La Jeunesse d' Origene*, 54, cited in Lubac, *History and Spirit*, 9.
98. Uzukwu, *God, Spirit, and Human Wholeness*, 142.

Word, and that the Holy Spirit is the most excellent and the first in order of all that was produced by the Father through Christ."[99] Even though the Spirit appears as the principle of divine communion with humans, Origen underscores that the Father is also relational, endowed with the qualities of mercy and compassion. Here, one observes a nuanced understanding of transcendence. Considering this, Uzukwu says, "Transcendence is affirmed in extraordinarily strong terms by Origen. But transcendence is not the 'departure' or 'eclipse' of God. Rather transcendence of the relational Trinity paradoxically entrenches divine pity and presence."[100] The relationality guaranteed by the spirit mitigates absolute transcendence.

Uzukwu retrieves the religious anthropology of Origen, which in many ways resonates and overlaps with West African anthropology, to construct a Christian appropriation of indigenous West African anthropology and cosmology. In doing this, he demonstrates how Origen's pre-existence of the soul is integral to numerous indigenous West African views of the person. Thus, the person, in this worldview, is considered as a reincarnation. This phenomenon is expressed in the concept of *chi* among the Igbo (Nigeria), *ori* (Yoruba, Nigeria), *kra or okra* (Asante, Ghana), *se* (Adja-Fon), *aklama or kla* (Ewe, Ghana).[101] Individual destinies in these traditions are regarded as predetermined before birth through the agency of the personal spirit in collaboration with the great God. Personal spirits are identified as emanations or sparks of God, which are similar to the small-scale manifestations of God already discussed. It is this spirit manifestation that links the individual to pre-existence and life in the world. Uzukwu equates the individual human spirit to the Greek *pneuma*. Accordingly,

> The description of the human *pneuma* by Origen as life coming from God puts the West African principle on the same pedestal as the Greek *pneuma*—both are humanizing principles that come from and return to God: God is Spirit, "breath of Life." The ontological truth about this reality expressed in the language of myth is that each person is a unique creation, a unique concern of God, and an intimate of God the creator.[102]

---

99. See Origen, "Commentary on John 479," in Jurgens, *The Faith of the Early Fathers*, 1:202.

100. Uzukwu, *God, Spirit, and Human Wholeness*, 147.

101. Uzukwu, *God, Spirit, and Human Wholeness*, 152.

102. Uzukwu, *God, Spirit, and Human Wholeness*, 153.

The concept of *chi*, from the Igbo perspective, gives a deep insight into the person; in it, one can discern much of Igbo philosophy and religion. According to Christopher Nwodo, author of *Philosophical Perspective on Chinua Achebe*, "What Achebe has done in this study of *chi* is to set in motion a study of Igbo philosophy, particularly Igbo metaphysics as well as Igbo religion, including their philosophy of religion, as these are contained in Igbo oral literature, especially folk-tales."[103] In his analysis of *chi*, Uzukwu relies heavily on the work of Chinua Achebe, who describes the concept of *chi* as "so elusive and enigmatic." According to Achebe, "There are two clearly distinct meanings of the word chi in Igbo. The first is translated as god, guardian angel, personal spirit, soul, spirit-double, etc. The second is day or daylight but is commonly used for those transitional periods between day and night or night and day.... I am chiefly concerned here with the first meaning of chi, a concept so central in Igbo psychology and yet so elusive and enigmatic."[104] Achebe associates the second meaning of *chi* as daylight to the first, in the sense that *chi* resides with the Sun, and the Igbo see the Sun as an agent of *Chukwu* who has extraterrestrial existence.[105] In this way, personal *chi* is inextricably tied to the Supreme God (*Chukwu*) in the Igbo worldview. In the spiritual universe of the Igbo, the concept of *chi* serves as the rallying point and basic worldview of the people. We can establish the theological implications of *chi* as an emanation of the Supreme God in the distribution of gifts, talents, and destinies. Appropriating Origen's *pneuma*, Uzukwu sees *chi* as personal spirit emanating from God, which determines each human being's goals and destinies. It is a spiritual reality that accompanies the process of humanization, endowing everyone with peculiar characteristics. Consequently, Uzukwu points out, "Diversity or multiplicity is the rule; yet all humans are at equal distance from God no matter the differences in parentage or genealogy."[106] The unity of the Holy Spirit with the personal spirit makes pneumatology a high point of entry into the Trinitarian God as experienced in religious traditions and AICs and charismatic movements. The gifts and work of the Holy Spirit are for the common good. One difference between Origen's and the AIC's concept of the Spirit's relationship with humans lies in how Origen's belief that the Spirit draws Christians upward to a life of

---

103. Nwodo, *Philosophical Perspective on Chinua Achebe*, 239.
104. Achebe, *Morning Yet on Creation Day*, 93.
105. Achebe, *Morning Yet on Creation Day*, 243.
106. Uzukwu, *God, Spirit, and Human Wholeness*, 154.

holiness, while for the AICs the Spirit descends and empowers the elect for the work of ministry within the human community. Differently put, the difference lies in the ascent and descent characteristics of the One Holy Spirit. According to Yves Congar, "The Spirit supports the pastoral hierarchy of the Church and through it guides Christian communities, but he does much more than this. He does not bring about unity by using pressure or by reducing the whole of the Church's life to a uniform pattern. He does it by the more delicate way of communion."[107]

Spirit in Biblical and West African Cosmology

In chapter 4, we presented Uzukwu's theological method and the similarities he establishes between West African and Hebraic cosmology. What was prominent in this connection was the relationship between the pre-exilic concept of Yahweh and how God is experienced in West African cosmology. In that section, Uzukwu distanced himself from the militancy and intolerance of the post-exilic or Deuteronomistic Yahweh. This section does not repeat the already stated fact but focuses instead on how this similarity is experienced in the area of pneumatology. Uzukwu discusses the plurality (multiplicity) of spirits and spirit manifestations in the West African worldview, which resonates with the experience of the God of Hebrew scripture as a creative entry point into Trinitarian theology. It is the communion within the Trinity and outward communion with humankind that spirit guarantees. "A participation of the human spirit in the life of the divine spirit brings one in union with God and with other creatures in whom God's spirit is immanent."[108] The African worldview is heavily laden with transcendental spiritism. The spirit is constitutive of the African ontology, epistemology, and cosmology, much as in the biblical world. It is designated with varying functions in the scriptures, *ruah*, *nishamah*, commonly translated in the Septuagint and the New Testament as "wind," "breath," "soul," source and seat of insight," and "will."[109] The Old Testament was apparently dominated by the divine formative act attributed to the Father, yet the prophets spoke of the coming of the messiah. The Holy Spirit that was part of the creative act (Gen 1:1–3) was the instrument of

---

107. Congar, *I Believe in the Holy Spirit*, 2:3, 17.

108. Odoemene, "African Worldview and the Understanding of the Holy Spirit," 83.

109. Arndt and Gingrich, *A Greek English Lexicon of the Old Testament*, 674–78; see also Dufour-Leon, *Dictionary of Biblical Theology*, 570.

the conception of Jesus, his baptism, and his ministry, and Jesus promised to send the Holy Spirit to continue his ministry (Acts 1:4–5). So, the Holy Spirit is clearly a point of entry into the Trinity.

As an undergirding principle, Uzukwu states, "My basic assumption is that the West African is not utterly dissimilar from the Jewish-Christian experience of God. Because [a] plurality of active deities that do not threaten the transcendent One God dominates the West African universe, I opt for a perception of hierarchy in divinity that is flexible and dynamic to explore aspects of the history of God in the Jewish-Christian tradition."[110] He bases his argument on the fact that the Hebrew concept of the *One* and *only* God Yahweh is a later historical development, whereas the understanding of God prior to the campaigns of the Deuteronomy reformers was more tolerant, and head of a divine council. The idea of flexibility and the dynamic relationality of the Hebrew God is also expressed in a nuanced fashion by Benjamin Sommer, whose book, *The Bodies of God and the World of Ancient Israel* discusses the fluidity of gods in ancient Israel as a phenomenon that concurrently maintains monotheism and accounts for divine epiphanic visitations and theophanies. By divine fluidity, Sommer means the kind of body that gods have, which is radically different from human bodies.[111] Yahweh's apparitions at several places and in several forms suggest fluidity.[112] Although our focus is not on objects of divine apparition, it is important to note that they began to be associated with sacred presence. Sommer describes these presences (through messenger angels), as "a small-scale manifestation of God's own presence, and the distinction between the messenger and God is murky."[113] The angels or messengers (or in Sommer's illustration, the avatar) had something of God, which, however, did not exhaust or completely reveal God.[114] Arguably, Sommer demonstrates that, while ancient Israel was not totally

---

110. Uzukwu, *God, Spirit, and Human Wholeness*, 105.

111. Sommer, *The Bodies of God and the World of Ancient Israel*, 12.

112. Sommer, *The Bodies of God and the World of Ancient Israel*, 39.

113. Sommer, *The Bodies of God and the World of Ancient Israel*, 40.

114. An instance of this thinking occurs when ambiguity occurs in the manifestation or presence of God, like the angel-of-the-Lord episode in Genesis 18:1–2: "Yahweh manifested Himself to Abraham . . . amidst the trees of Mamre while Abraham was sitting at the entrance of his tent, at the heat of the day. He lifted up his eyes and saw three men coming toward him." Sommer deduces from the above quotation that Yahweh appears in the form of three men, or at least in the form of one of the three men, which we may identify as the angel of the Lord.

polytheistic in its religious devotion, the understanding of its monotheism is the recognition of a supreme God, which accommodates other divine existential beings. He makes a subtle distinction between this understanding of monotheism and polytheism, which recognizes multiple gods of equal status and powers.[115] Jewish monotheism, therefore, is not an absolute, or strict monotheism without qualification.

Another instance that offers credence to Uzukwu's position on the pre-exilic notion of God is *The Messenger of the Lord in Early Jewish Interpretations of Genesis*, a detailed work by Camilla Heijne, who in it argues for the unique identity of the being identified as the angel of the Lord, focusing on the question of the ontological and functional status of the angel of the Lord in relation to YHWH. Heijne gives a critical analysis of the various "angel-of-the-Lord" texts in the Hebrew Bible, which tell of encounters that present the feeling of an interaction with YHWH. Such occurrences as alternate changes between the first person and third person, the presence of concrete human activities (like eating and drinking), and the angel's refusal to give its name, suggest a direct dialogue between man and God. The Hebrew Bible resonates with these merged identities. Specifically, the episodes of Abraham and Jacob present a clear identification between the divine being and YHWH, so that the author endorses the opinion of Hamori as realistic anthropomorphism.[116] In these encounters, the ambiguity of identity serves to preserve the mystery of God.[117] Besides, the Jewish belief that "no one who sees God will live" makes it imperative on God to shield himself for the sake of man. Conversely, it could be argued that God was preserving his full epiphany in the various epiphanies until the appropriate time of the Incarnation. The interpolation theory and the unresolved identity of God and the angels allow for the paradox that should surround human knowledge of the divine, given human finitude and God's utter incomprehensibility.

After a thorough analysis of the theme from various Jewish writings and *Targums*, Heijne concludes,

> The conclusion must be drawn that there is no unambiguous or homogenous interpretation of "the angel of the Lord" and his identity in our sources. He is sometimes depicted as a divine emissary separate from God, while in other cases he appears to be seen

---

115. Sommer, *The Bodies of God and the World of Ancient Israel*, 147.

116. Heijne, *The Messenger of the Lord*, 87.

117. Heijne, *The Messenger of the Lord*, 62.

as a manifestation or hypostasis of God Himself. The ambivalence in the relationship between God and His angel remains in many of the interpretations of the texts, and in relation to "ordinary" angels 'the angel of Lord' is generally awarded a special high status.[118]

Consequently, we can establish that the angel of the Lord mitigates the absolute monotheism that militates against God's flexibility and dynamism.

Associated with West African spiritual cosmology is the Second Vatican Council's emphasis on the Bible, which stresses the centrality and use of the text.[119] The Council effectively restored the Bible to the center of Catholic life and practice. Hence, for Uzukwu, an important area of inculturation is the translation of the Bible into indigenous languages. Translation mediates cross-cultural dialogue[120] and enables various peoples to possess the Bible in some sense. Writing on the centrality of the Bible to (African) theology, the Pan African Conference of Third World Theologians echoes Vatican II's *Dei Verbum*,

> The Bible is the basic source of African Theology, because it is the primary witness of God's revelation in Jesus Christ. No theology can retain its Christian identity apart from Scripture. The Bible is not simply a historical book about the people of Israel; through rereading of this scripture in the social context of our struggle for our humanity, God speaks to us in the midst of our troublesome situation. This Divine Word is not an abstract proposition but an event in our lives, empowering us to continue in the fight for our full humanity.[121]

The difference in hermeneutical or contextual understanding of the Bible has been taken seriously by the AICs.[122] For Uzukwu, the context deter-

118. Heijne, *The Messenger of the Lord*, 377.

119. Vatican II rediscovered the centrality of the Bible and called for not only *Lectio Divina* but a celebration of the Word of God. Consequent upon this declaration, the post-Synodal Exhortation Ecclesia in Africa endorsed translations of the Bible into the vernacular in order to provide easy access to the Sacred Scripture. See John Paul II, *Ecclesia in Africa*, 58.

120. Uzukwu, "Bible and Christian Worship in Africa," 18.

121. Appiah-Kubi and Torres, *African Theology en Route*, 193.

122. The African Instituted or Initiated Churches adopted a Biblical hermeneutic that takes seriously the context of Biblical interpretation in such a way that the Bible speaks to the people in their concrete situations and is able to give life. This approach to the Bible can also be described as postcolonial reconfiguration. It holds the exegesis of the colonial era in abeyance, while offering an alternative Biblical hermeneutic. Sugirtharajah captures postcolonialsim as "an active confrontation with the dominant system of thought,

mines the applicability of the Bible and hermeneutics. Undergirding interpretation for Uzukwu, are issues of life, liberation, and in a broader sense human flourishing. A rationalist or abstract exegesis as a model of interpretation avails nothing in African cultural contexts. Indeed, we can state that inculturation of Biblical studies in such contexts has gained more currency in contemporary times. This is perceived as a part of the mission of liberation and making the Gospel at home in Africa.

The emphasis on the Bible in the AICs, in a way, circumvents missionary Christianity, especially by searching for resonances in the Old Testament. As already stated, this is overwhelmingly found in Jewish and African cosmologies. Indeed, we can say that, "The similarities and commonalities between African and Bible peoples make the stories address life today, and expand the life and the story."[123] Philip Jenkins, corroborates Uzukwu's position in arguing that the churches of the global South are more biblically based and draw inspiration from the Bible. The daily experience of life resonates with the Biblical world: "For the growing churches of the global South, the Bible speaks to everyday, real-world issues of poverty, and debt, famine and urban crisis, racial and gender oppression, state brutality and persecution."[124] The importance of context in Biblical interpretation must then predominate an inflexibility that is consistent with a rationalist model. In this way, Jenkins underscores the role of context in Biblical interpretation. Theology and interpretation are culturally, historically, and socially conditioned.[125]

Historically speaking, Uzukwu locates the early encounter between the African world and the Biblical world to the 3rd century BCE translation of the Hebrew Bible into Greek at Alexandria (Africa), which provided the meeting point of Hebrew Biblical faith and Greek culture. The second

its lopsidedness and inadequacies, and underlines its unsuitability for us. Hence, it is a process of cultural and discursive emancipation from all dominant structures, whether they be political, linguistic or ideological" (Sugirtharajah, *Postcolonial Reconfigurations*, 15). This is precisely how a particular Biblical hermeneutic and Negro spirituals serve as a medium of articulating the people's experience and an expression of faith and hope in the liberation. Armed with the critical postcolonial tool, the AICs read the Bible through a decolonizing prism, which gives expression to their immediate concerns. Linda Smith describes how indigenous peoples can overcome the totalizing and universalizing understanding of history through a decolonizing strategy, which provides expression for indigenous concerns. See Smith, *Decolonizing Methodologies*, 20–34.

123. Uzukwu, "Bible and Christian Worship in Africa," 9.
124. Jenkins, *The New Faces of Christianity*, 5.
125. See Schreiter, *Constructing Local Theology*, 3–4.

FAITH AND CULTURE

translation of the Septuagint into Latin was also realized in Africa at Carthage.[126] These translations on African soil provide a solid foundation to the argument that Christianity is no stranger to Africa. There has always been an interchange of values and cultures, which is, perhaps, another major reason that African Christians find the Bible inspiring and relevant to their context. Consequently, Uzukwu argues that, "The historical roots that link Africa with the Bible are relevant to the theological enterprise and discourse in Africa."[127] He points out that the survival of Coptic and Ethiopian Christianity from antiquity to the present despite the assaults of Islam, is traceable to the translation of the Bible into their indigenous languages, unlike the resident Latin and Greek churches, which were easily wiped out. Much the same Biblical spirituality is identified in the manuals of the era of slavery in the resilience of African slaves forcefully and violently uprooted from their homeland. This substantiates the discovery of modern scholarship that language is a basis of culture.[128]

Translatability as a quality of the Word of God gives the translated sacred word a new life in various contexts. For the AICs, interpretation and hermeneutics show continuity with African culture. The Bible was the major fact for the emergence of these churches and their continuing relevance, and practices; such practices as visions, dreams, prophecy, healing, and polygamy all draw inspiration from their biblical foundations. These religious activities are consistent with the Old Testament biblical experience, where prophetic ministry was not limited to the proclamation of the word of God, as current Catholic thinking posits. Rather, prophetic ministry in the AICs integrates the aspects of visions, dreams, and revelations, as was found in the Old Testament and the Pauline churches.[129] Uzukwu's theology, then, would be incomplete without underscoring the inculturation of biblical studies as a means of liberation and maturity of the Christian message in the region.

---

126. Uzukwu, "Bible and Christian Worship in Africa," 10–11.
127. Uzukwu, "Bible and Christian Worship in Africa," 10–11.
128. See Thion'o, *Decolonizing the Mind.*
129. Paul identifies various gifts of the Holy Spirit, which include speaking in tongues, prophecy, teaching, and so forth. Scripture scholars agree that Paul's list is not exhaustive. See 1 Cor 12; Eph 4. Probably Paul's injunction, "Pursue love and strive for the Spiritual gifts, and especially that you may prophesy," more forcefully justifies the AIC orientation to prophetism. See 1 Cor 14:1.

IMPLICATIONS OF REIMAGINING THE SACRAMENTS

The Holy Spirit and the Sacraments

Probably no council has stated the relationship between the sacraments and the Holy Spirit as clearly as the Second Vatican Council. It stated that the Holy Spirit joins believers in the body of Christ since, "through the sacraments, [they] are united in a hidden way to Christ."[130] The sacraments express the nature, structure, and operation of the church,[131] and affirm that they are sacraments of faith.[132] The Holy Spirit is God's gift to believers, and sanctifies the people of God, residing not only in the clergy, or through the sacraments, but also in every believer who is endowed with charism for the good of the Church and for humanity generally.[133] It is thus appropriate to highlight the various senses of Christ's presence in the community—in the Word (Vatican II states that "Christ is liturgically present in his Word"),[134] in the Preacher, and especially in the fact of *sensus fidelium* (present in all the faithful who have been sealed by the Holy Spirit through baptism), further justifying this claim.[135]

John McKenna,[136] a sacramental theologian, gives an interesting interpretation of the Holy Spirit in the sacraments, especially the sacrament of the Eucharist, discussing the understanding of the eucharistic presence from the early patristic fathers to the contemporary period. He focuses particularly on the presence and influence of the Holy Spirit in the eucharistic consecration of the early times. For the Fathers of the church, the Holy Spirit not only acted in transforming the bread and wine but was also the source of the disciples' witnessing and the participant's transformation. Pneumatic ecclesiology and Eucharistic theology were eclipsed in posterior ecclesiology, with the subsuming of a spirit epiclesis to the Christological epiclesis. The emphasis of the Scholastic era on the somatic presence, realized under the formula of the institutional narrative, demeaned the interpersonal presence toward which the Eucharist is geared according to McKenna.

Hence, McKenna argues for a *personalistic* approach to eucharistic presence, grounded in interpersonal presence. From this perspective,

130. LG 7.
131. LG 11.
132. LG 21.
133. A.A 3.
134. SC 7.
135. "Vatican II affirms that the 'body of the faithful as a whole, anointed as they are by the Holy One, cannot err in matters of belief'" (LG 12).
136. McKenna, *The Eucharist and Holy Spirit*.

the somatic presence is understood as a higher, deeper form of interpersonal presence, going beyond the Scholastic framework of real presence through transubstantiation.[137] The eucharistic presence becomes only the starting point and a means for a deeper level of presence. Conversely, consecration implies not only change in the elements of bread and wine but change in those partaking of the Eucharist. McKenna anchors his argument in the patristic understanding of epiclesis, which offered prayers for the transformation of the partakers of the Eucharist, and not just of the gifts of bread and wine. Hence, the current force and emphasis on transformation of elements appear as narrow, except when seen as only instrumental to the transformation of those partaking of the Eucharist. In the same vein, the moment of consecration, which the Scholastics consider an instantaneous moment, becomes problematic. The personalist approach, therefore, de-emphasizes the moment of consecration, since such a moment seems to determine and force God's sovereign action.[138] This understanding corroborates the position of the early church, which saw the whole eucharistic prayer as consecrating.

The Second Vatican Council's retrieval of the theology of the Holy Spirit plays a crucial role in the development of Uzukwu's theology. To be precise, Catholic theological tradition has always ascribed sacramental efficacy to the action and agency of Christ. Thus, the Christological dimension of the sacraments became the sole agency of sacramental mediation.[139] This tradition, probably, beginning from Augustine and enhanced by Aquinas, continues to resonate with sacramental understanding even in post-Vatican II theology. Vatican II states, "By his power, Christ is present in the sacraments so that when anybody baptizes, it is really Christ himself who baptizes."[140] While this statement refers to the Christological dimension of the sacraments, post-Vatican II theology has focused on the ecclesial and pneumatological dimensions of the sacrament more profoundly. Incorporating the ecclesial and pneumatological aspects of the sacraments replaces

---

137. McKenna, *The Eucharist and Holy Spirit*, 176–77.

138. McKenna, *The Eucharist and Holy Spirit*, 185–89.

139. In chapter 2, we discussed the implications of the emphasis of the Christological dimension of the sacrament and the revision that Vatican II brought about. The Council incorporated the ecclesial and pneumatological aspects of the sacraments, which enrich sacramental theology. A comprehensive articulation and understanding of sacraments remains elusive; the act of praise and thanksgiving for God's free self-giving in them is the most adequate response.

140. SC 7.

the mechanical and magical posture of the sacraments engendered by Christological dimension alone. It broadens the notion of presence as the givenness of the Holy Spirit.[141] The agency of the sacrament in this consideration is broadened to incorporate Christological, pneumatic, and ecclesial identities. Whereas in chapter 3 we indicated the power of symbols and language to mediate reality through rituals, in sacramental celebration the rituals become efficacious through the action of Christ and the work of the Holy Spirit in the community of faith. Emphasizing the power of language to bring about reality must give full expression to the indispensable role of the Holy Spirit, for sacraments have an indelible Trinitarian dimension. Reflecting on sacramental presence Madathummuriyil cautions that focusing on the power of language and symbols to bring about efficacy could simply become a fitting replacement of causality unless the action of the Holy Spirit is highlighted in sacramental presence. He points out that, "Even in postmodern sacramental thinking, sufficient attention has not been paid to correlate sacramental presence to the role of the Holy Spirit in a consistent manner. In other words, they somehow fail in situating the role of the Spirit in the sacramental event."[142] A more balanced understanding of sacraments in contemporary times focuses on the role of the Holy Spirit and, more properly speaking, the Trinity in sacramental mediation. The rethinking in ecclesiology also involved a reassessment of sacramental theology and a pneumatological reinstatement of the role of the Holy Spirit in the sacramental process, reinforced further in the West African worldview suffused with the Spirit. The agency of the Spirit in transforming and realizing the good is integral to West African spiritism. The epiclesis of the consecration finds similarity in the epiclesis of the prayer of consecration over those chosen (ordinarily through a revelation by the Holy Spirit) to serve in the various ministries in the AICs.

---

141. Madathummuriyil suggests that the Christological view of sacramental presence, originating from the cause and effect syllogism, leads to mechanical or magical understanding of the sacrament. In effect, this process does not accentuate the givenness of the sacrament through the Holy Spirit. To overcome this narrow understanding of presence requires a return to the understanding of the sacrament as basically a gift, a given. Madathummuriyil, *Sacrament as Gift*, 253–55.

142. Madathummuriyil, *Sacrament as Gift*, 257.

Pneumatology as the Entry Point to the Trinity: Toward an African Christian Pneumatology

The foregoing discussion shows the convergence of Christian experiences of the Holy Spirit and indigenous African experiences of spirits; the Christian unity of the Holy Spirit resonates profoundly with personal spirits in the African universe. Paul's pneumatology is a case in point:

> For all who are led by the Spirit of God are children of God. For you did not receive a spirit of slavery to fall back into fear, but you have received a spirit of adoption. When we cry, "Abba! Father!" it is that very *Spirit* bearing witness with *our spirit* that we are children of God, and if children, then heirs, heirs of God and joint heirs with Christ—if, in fact, we suffer with him so that we may also be glorified with him. (Rom 8:14–17)

The unity of the Holy Spirit and the human personal spirit, which Uzukwu describes differently in various West African languages as *chi*, *okra*, and *ori*, is underscored in the above citation. The personal spirit is the humanizing agent and God's protective gift to everyone, which ensures communion with God.[143] One could think of a personal spirit as the agent or outlet of the Spirit; the gifts of the Spirit find expression through personal spirits, or in the words of Origen, human *pneumata*.

While the African Christian experience remains an integral part of the inherited culture, with openness to negative spirits that do not always bring about the good, a central challenge for a Christian becomes the issue of syncretism. It would be naïve to transpose uncritically the qualities and functions of the Holy Spirit to the plurality of spirits that inhabit the West African universe. The task of inculturation can be tricky and delicate. Uzukwu is aware of this problem. He asks, "Can we justify AICs' reinterpretation and integration of deities as dimensions of God's Holy Spirit, while eliminating the ambivalent and evil aspects associated with the deities?"[144] His answer relies on the history of religion and, more precisely, on the development of sacramental theology. First, following the Jewish appropriation and identification of the attributes of the Canaanite deities to the One and Only Yahweh, Uzukwu sees an interesting antecedent in the reinterpretation of religion according to contexts and worldviews.[145] The West African context

---

143. Uzukwu, *God, Spirit, and Human Wholeness*, 165.

144. Uzukwu, *God, Spirit, and Human Wholeness*, 169.

145. In writing about the Celestial Church of Christ, which demonizes the *vodhun*

IMPLICATIONS OF REIMAGINING THE SACRAMENTS

of a plurality of spirits and deities, therefore, is not discontinuous with the Biblical experience and naming of Yahweh. Second, in the development of sacramental theology, the fathers of the Church assimilated and appropriated the language and rituals of the mystery cults to give expression to their nascent faith in Christ.[146] Put differently, they engaged a narrative familiar to them to give vent to the new reality of the Christ-event. The AICs, in Uzukwu's opinion, exemplify this inculturation of the ancestral religion and the Christian experience. Consequently, he sees the Spirit focus of the AICs as the basic point of entry into the community of persons in the Trinity. The flexibility and relationality of the West African worldview serves the purpose of accommodating or assuming the plurality of spirits in the One Holy Spirit. Therefore, he states, "The solution of the One Holy Spirit recognized in multiple gifts or charisms, a melody or harmony of epithets, for the good of the community and humanity, is the contribution West African insight makes to the pneumatology of the Great Christian tradition."[147] This is a logical conclusion to the prevalence of the Holy Spirit in the Christian tradition and the West African universe.

In terms of the relationship between the Spirit and personal spirits, Uzukwu believes "Christian faith introduces a qualitative modification of the traditional beliefs and anthropology instead of introducing quantitatively something totally new." He recognizes the Christ event as the fundamental difference between these theologies. Nonetheless, he does not see a discontinuity in the differing cosmologies; rather, he argues for consistency based on the salvation-history approach. From this perspective, one sees continuity with the indigenous religions, but up to a point. The radical difference instituted by the Christ event remains to be fully developed. Perhaps the development in African Christology attends to this query.[148] The challenge may not

---

and yet adopts some of their ritual practices, he states, "The advantage Celestials have in being rooted in the Bible is that only one Holy Spirit descends on the elect and endows the community with gifts or charisms hitherto in individualized *vodhun* or deities" (Uzukwu, *God, Spirit, and Human Wholeness*, 170–71). However, it becomes difficult or complex to identify the boundaries with ancestral religious practices. He sees this problem when he avers, "There is no doubt that Christians, by the nature of constituting an alternative community with an alternative narrative, must set boundaries with the ATR cult" (Uzukwu, *God, Spirit, and Human Wholeness*, 170–71).

146. Uzukwu, *God, Spirit, and Human Wholeness*, 173.

147. Uzukwu, *God, Spirit, and Human Wholeness*, 178.

148. Justin Ukpong, "Christology and Inculturation: A New Testament Perspective," in Gibellini, *Paths to African Theology*, 41–43, discusses five approaches adopted in the development of African Christology. First, the incarnational approach insists on

lie so much in the existence of deities or spirits, which serve the purpose of easy inculturation by Christian theology, as in the understanding of the ontological status and functionality of these spiritual beings. For Christian theology, the West African narrative of spirits would require the further examination of the original purpose. Clothing the Holy Spirit with the qualities and attributes of the ancestral deities would be too simplistic; on the contrary, an understanding of the plural spirits as emanations or sparks of God poses another burden of how some spirits serve evil purposes. It stands to reason that missionary Christianity and neo-Pentecostal movements may have taken the easy route of discounting these spirits, thereby avoiding the rigor of intense theological process required to distil an authentic and theologically valid African Christian pneumatology.

The power of God visible in the work of the Holy Spirit assumes all the expressions of the spirits in a unified vision of One God so that Spirit provides insight into the activity of the Father, the Son (Word), and the Holy Spirit. Pope Francis expresses this idea thus, "The Holy Spirit, sent by the Father and the Son, transforms our hearts and enables us to enter into the perfect communion of the blessed Trinity, where all things find their unity."[149]

Consequently, Uzukwu holds, "The multiple deities, in their variety of operations in favor of the community, are transformed into the operations and denominations of the Holy Spirit of God. They are aspects of the Holy Spirit or charisms through which the Holy Spirit is operative within the Christian community."[150] This methodology is consistent with his approach of continuity in revelation, as already established. Uzukwu thus creates an African Christian pneumatology that responds to the African context and the Christian teaching on the Holy Spirit. Probably what remains to be done in this regard is accounting for the negative spirits that also populate the West African universe. Uzukwu distances himself from the position of

---

inculturation of the Word in every culture; the expression of the identity of Christ with various African figures instantiates this approach. Second, the logos *spermatikos* (seeds of the Word) is diffused in every culture. Third, the functional analogy approach seeks to express the redemptive acts of Christ through analogous African categories, like the Ancestor. Fourth, the paschal mystery approach sees the Christ event as cosmic and consistent with pre-Christian cultures. Fifth, the biblical approach sees the oneness of Jesus and the Father. Consequently, the status and worship of the Father in traditional religions is indirectly a recognition and worship of Christ.

149. Francis, *The Joy of the Gospel*, 117.

150. Uzukwu, *God, Spirit, and Human Wholeness*, 211–12.

the African Pentecostal movement, which upholds a contrary position of disdain for all spirits associated with the ancestral religion because of the possibility of evil spirits. He considers this position as introducing duality in African cosmology and therefore, inconsistent with African epistemology. Conclusively, he cautions and projects a hermeneutic of taking a second look at everything, instead of a radical and premature discounting of everything ancestral as pagan. The Christian God must be freed from the apron strings and vestiges of Greek gods and its dynamism recognized.

Conclusion

The controlling metaphor in Uzukwu's theology as analyzed in this chapter is the cultural appropriation of Christianity. This principle surfaces in his understanding of liturgy, ecclesiology, and pneumatology, from his theological constituency. A proper incarnation of the Gospel, therefore, requires a review of the received ecclesiology and its sacramental celebrations in the liturgy of the church. These three aspects occupied our focus in this chapter. Uzukwu's model of the church is one that is locally grounded, yet in communion with other local churches. This opinion finds strong support in Vatican II theology. Indeed, the incarnation of the church is an approach well supported by a host of African theologians.[151] The overall import of this chapter rests in the fact that a reinterpretation of ecclesiology with resources from the African region involves a review of liturgy under the guarantee of the Holy Spirit, which has acquired more prominence in the Vatican II Church. This is a contribution that African Christianity, from its unique cosmology, makes to the universal church.

---

151. Onwubiko, *The Church in Africa*. Appropriating the East African concept of *ujamaa*, Onwubiko constructs a theology of the family that reflects the mind of *Ecclesia in Africa*. The concept of *ujamaa* designates a communality that eschews discrimination, meaning, according to the Onwubiko, "togetherness, familyhood, brotherhood" (Onwubiko, *The Church in Africa*, 34). Therefore, the community and extended family system, which *ujamaa* undergirds aptly describes the church as family. Under this consideration, the African family and community become ideal theological models for church. See also Laurenti Magesa's position on incarnational theology. Arguing from the perspective of the incarnational theology and the culture that is integral to the Gospel, Magesa insists that Christian mission is inevitably cultural. Hence, inculturation, for him, implies conversion: "Subverting Western cultural possessiveness of the Gospel and faith is crucial for the process of evangelization in Africa" (Magesa, *Anatomy of Inculturation*, 148).

Chapter 7

Uzukwu's Contributions to African Theology and Christianity

Introduction

ROMAN CATHOLIC SACRAMENTAL THEOLOGY experienced a great renewal at the Second Vatican council. The main impact of the council is probably experienced in its profound adaptation of liturgical celebrations. For the average Catholic, perhaps, it's greatest accomplishment lies in the basic renewal and change in sacramental celebrations. This new openness marks a major watershed, with its true globalization of the church and its recognition of the beauty of plurality and difference. Hence the contribution from an African Christian perspective is an important addition to Christian tradition and, indeed, to the catholicity of the church. It is under this consideration that the work of Elochukwu Uzukwu, the leading African sacramental and liturgical theologian, finds a favorable context. This book has thus focused on his contributions to sacramental theology by drawing on the resources from the African cultural context.

Following the provisions of the Second Vatican Council, which allows a profound adaptation in every aspect of the Christian life, we took as the thesis of this book that appropriating sacraments is a practical mission of the church that resonates in every aspect of Christian life. In this work, we have tried to remain faithful to this thesis by drawing implications of the sacramental reinterpretation to theology and practical Christian living, since liturgy gives rise to ethics.

Summary

To evaluate Uzukwu's contributions to African theology and Christianity a brief recapture of the central points of our work is necessary before we present a general conclusion. Chapter 1 discussed the development of African theology establishing the need for serious theological engagement. We underscored the need for a theological engagement that takes the African collective experience seriously. Chapter 2 established pertinent theological and historical context of our work, noting the uniqueness of the Christ event and the need for a terminology to give insight into the reality of the Christian initiation into the mystery of Christ. The term *sacrament*, although non-Christian in origin, was readily adopted and adapted by the Fathers of the Church to give expression to a reality beyond human naming. The use of this terminology and elements of Greek philosophy to express the sacramental experience indicate the divine acquiescence to human anthropology and sociology. From this perspective, we presented the sequential development of the sacraments from their Jewish roots to the Vatican II reform and its renewal of the sacraments. In the major epochs treated, we underscored the interplay of sociology, philosophy, and theology, revealing the power of the divine to respond to human imagination and give itself freely to humankind. The accent on the genius of sacramentality then lies more with God's work than with any human contribution or imagination. God's continued gift of himself continues through the Church and her sacraments. It is in this light that Vatican II's understanding of Christ as the primordial sacrament and the church as the sacrament of Christ opens new vistas for reflecting on the phenomenological dimensions of the sacraments. This renewal in the post-Vatican II Church and its openness to various cultures ushered the era of plurality in theological and liturgical expressions.

Chapter 3 looked at the anthropological and sociological dimensions of sacraments thereby establishing sacraments divine—human realities. This chapter also highlighted the contemporary ritual studies and the significance of language in symbolization. These developments help to further contextualize our work, especially with reference to the Second Vatican Council's renewal and reformation of sacramental and liturgical theology.

By focusing on Uzukwu's work, this work seeks to further the call of Vatican II for a profound "adaptation" of Christian life.

Chapter 4 demonstrated the major influences and Uzukwu's theological development. We identified his upbringing in a traditional village and its rituals as the starting point of his interest in a theology that responds simultaneously to the culture and the Gospel as proclaimed by the church. The Vatican II church, in which he was trained, provided an atmosphere conducive for dialogue with indigenous cultures. Its recovery of the validity and theological significance of the local church, and the postcolonial status of the African nations, offer great opportunities for rethinking the version of Christianity received in Africa, especially its western region. In fact, the re-emergence of the theological validity and authenticity of the local church makes it possible even to think of an African Christianity. Thus, it is through Uzukwu's understanding of the legitimacy of the local church that he champions unique sacramental and liturgical celebrations. In a sense, this practice involves both autonomy and communion of churches. To realize the local church further implies a theology and methodology taken from indigenous cosmology, which has become Uzukwu's distinctive contribution to global Christianity.

This chapter also presented the African epistemology and cosmology that undergird the development of Uzukwu's theological methodology. It is derived from West African traditional wisdom as encouraged by Vatican II and is characterized by a dynamic flexibility that abhors exclusivism, absoluteness, and universalism. Thus, everything exists in relation to everything else. This orientation has wide implications for theology and could lead to a revision of some long-held theological assumptions. The chapter concluded by presenting Uzukwu's retrieval of Hebraic and patristic theological experiences, reinforcing his theological orientation.

Chapter 5, we demonstrated Uzukwu's understanding of sacraments as an intersection between a foundational event and community rituals. Here we focused on indigenous rites of passage, which re-enact foundation stories of the groups that correlate with Christian rituals. The power of rituals to relive the events they commemorate made it necessary to retrieve culturally and philosophically the historical development of ritual studies, indicating the plausibility of Uzukwu's reinterpretation. We further presented areas of convergence between the indigenous rites of passage and sacraments of initiation. Since Uzukwu accentuates the ecclesiological dimension of the sacraments without disregarding the

Christological foundation, we underscored the community's role in sacramental imagination. His doctoral thesis, which we analyzed in the previous chapter, is a sustained rigorous study of the Judeo-Christian Eucharist from the Jewish ritual meal to the elements of the Greco-Roman worldview that are integral to the sacrament. Consequently, Uzukwu, in engaging the spirituality and cosmology of the Igbo of Nigeria, developed *Eucharistia Africana*, a work of first impression.

In response to theological necessity and as a sequel to the sacraments, chapter 6 focused on the implications of reimagining the sacraments in three pivotal theological areas of ecclesiology, liturgy, and pneumatology, which we described as the trilogy of Uzukwu's theology. A balanced discussion on the sacraments inevitably involves a reflection on these areas, since it is the Church that celebrates the sacraments under the agency of the Holy Spirit, and more broadly speaking, the Trinity. Uzukwu's theological works, from my perspective, mainly explore these aspects of theology, constituting the trilogy from which his overall theology can be seen. Incidentally, these areas of theology underwent renewal at the Second Vatican Council and are essential for the emergence of the true local church that Uzukwu envisages. Liturgically, Uzukwu argues for more expressive worship, which involves the African understanding of the body, as the gateway to the whole person. In this regard, he identifies major differences between the African and the Greco-Roman understanding of the body. The immobility of the Roman worship pattern contrasts significantly with the African proclivity for expressive worship. This view is consistent with the African principle of relationality which negates various dualisms, especially between body and Spirit. The chapter further expressed the relationship between sacraments and church as emerging from the same mystery of Christ. Hence sacramental celebration in liturgy necessarily affects the model of the celebrating church. This chapter examined the question of the local church and the representative models of the church in Africa, as well as Uzukwu's model of hospitality to highlight the model of the church as communion and community. This model, reflective of African family ecclesiology as endorsed by the 1994 African Synod, responds to the dominant ecclesiological motif of Vatican II—of the church as the people of God. A proper understanding of this designation highlights the community and its rituals as basic to the sacrament.

The last section of the chapter focused on pneumatology, which was emphasized by Vatican II. The convergence in the understanding of the

Holy Spirit in biblical and West African cosmology with Origen's pneumatology serves to establish Uzukwu's emphasis on Spirit as the point of entry into the Trinity. This convergence enhances the functionality of the African Initiated Churches (AICs) and various charismatic movements, both Catholic and Protestant. The overwhelming experience of the Spirit and Spirit manifestations in the West African universe offers insight into a retrieval of the ATR experience of spirits. The African Christian's approach, then, becomes a retrieval of ancestral experiences. The emphasis on Spirit serves as the unique contribution of the West African region to the universal church, through Uzukwu. The emphasis on the Spirit reminds everyone that the Spirit is always the agent of mission. What is necessary is the proper discernment of the work of the Spirit. This appropriation remains consistent with the organic and incipient development of Christian practice; however, questions will continue to arise as this approach becomes further clarified and crystalized.

This work does not claim to have exhausted all the contributions of Elochukwu Uzukwu. I have tried to study him through the limited lens of sacramental theology, and obviously numerous other perspectives of his theology could be studied. The present work is, rather, a modest contribution to the numerous works that could and would be done in the future on Uzukwu's theology.

An Appraisal of Uzukwu's theological Efforts

So far, we have analyzed the work of Uzukwu in demonstrating the intersections between Christian sacramental celebration and indigenous rituals. The continuity in his work is demonstrated by the credibility that Jewish and Greco-Roman anthropology give to his work. As a historical theologian from the point of view of liturgy, Uzukwu accesses the liturgy from its anthropological and phenomenological perspectives, thereby underlining the significance of divine sacramental *self-giving* through various anthropologies and sociologies.

My interest in Uzukwu's work was informed by two factors: Vatican II's call for a profound adaptation of the liturgy, and Uzukwu's avid effort at realizing this directive in a way that is consistent with that teaching and responsive to the needs of the local church. He therefore works within the provision of the church, although he is sometimes critical of her. He can thus be described as a critical orthodox theologian, beholden to the church, to academia, and to society; to the church, he focuses on liturgy through the current disposition of the church; to academia, his scholarly research is responsive to the rigors and demands of academics; and to society, his firm belief in contextual theology makes necessary the West African Christian experience in the pool of Christian thought. Since theology responds to concrete human questions and the deep concerns of people of faith, answers cannot be limited to contexts, but are open to wherever similar questions of faith arise. His contribution in this sense springs from the openness of Vatican II and the possibility of exchange of theological insights.

Incarnating the Gospel in the local church is a delicate activity that must always keep guard over syncretism, which involves discernment. Consequently, Uzukwu argues for the emergence of an authentic local church, one that would imply autonomy and communion of local churches. For instance, the local church of Nigeria, which is Uzukwu's immediate context, has attained a maturity that is demonstrable in the quality of theological production, the economic affluence of major sees, and the goodly number of Catholic faithful. To Uzukwu, the continued reliance on *Propaganda Fide* keeps the church in Africa in the status of liminality despite its maturity in years and resources, both material and human. Incarnating Christianity through cultures is a sign of the maturity of the faith and the time-tested way of transmitting the faith. Uzukwu often undertakes the challenge of identifying the historical development of Christian practices through their Jewish roots and the Greco-Roman world, which provided the first culture for the transmission of the Christian faith in a non-Jewish environment.

Consistency with this practice requires the same incarnation of the faith in non-Western cultures as was heroically discerned and approved by Vatican II. Uzukwu's theological enterprise responds to this important mission of the church. He has often engaged indigenous cosmology and ATR generally to express this incarnation. In so doing, he has remained faithful to the salvation-history approach, which he adopted in his doctoral dissertation. This approach has received a major boost in his adoption of a basic West African dynamic of being, which includes more than it excludes as an approach to the Trinitarian God who is relational and communion.

Uzukwu deserves credit for distilling a theological method created from African traditional wisdom and the works of literary icons from the region. He declares this indebtedness,

> Drawing my inspiration from the works of African [West] African literary guides, principally Chinua Achebe and Wole Soyinka

> ..., my concern is to engage the questions of theology framed from my West African epistemic location, without ceasing to be in conversation with diverse geographical, cultural or provincial locations.[1]

Acknowledging his indebtedness to the epistemology of the region, Uzukwu gives a theological reinterpretation that articulates the African Christian theological appropriation of indigenous cosmology.

In the contemporary age of plurality and recognition of differences as legitimate, Uzukwu's contribution furthers theological discussions in various disciplines, and provides necessary foundation for interdisciplinary collaboration. His non-absolutist approach makes listening an important theological component, listening to the various voices, especially voices that have not been prominent in theology, like the feminist theological insights. These insights are made possible in the contemporary dispensation. The age of Vatican II marks a major shift. In the words of Massimo Faggioli, "The shift here is from disavowal to recognition."[2] This recognition overcomes the danger of exclusivism and the mono-cultural expression of Christian patrimony. It overcomes the binaries and dualities often associated with Greek metaphysics, as well as some Christian practices informed by this logic. One can well appreciate the recognition of difference and plurality that Vatican initiated. Upon this recognition stands the genius of relationality as an interpretive prism of a new theology.

The wider implication of this methodology, far from relativism, is a novel contribution to the concept of globalization, enriching the depository of the Catholic faith. According to David Power, "The preaching of the Gospel today has to be postcolonial, freed from alien dominance, but it has to address multiple sufferings of the people in their present situation."[3] This is exactly what Uzukwu champions in his theological enterprise, which this book seeks to highlight. Our current awareness of the demographic shifts and the current growth of theological exploration makes it difficult to ignore contributions from locales outside the dominant centers

---

1. Uzukwu, "The Imperative of Location," 3.

2. Faggioli, "Reading the Signs," 332–50. By engaging *Gaudium et spes*, Faggioli, with the prism of the hermeneutics of recognition, itemizes various shifts in Vatican II, including a recognition of differences in contexts and culture, recognition of culture as constitutive of theology, and a recognition of the critical mindset of the current age, which requires new validation of knowledge. These shifts make a new way of doing theology imperative.

3. Power, "The Word in the Liturgy," 49.

of Christianity. Hence, the apparent question of Christianity today requires a remapping the contours of Christianity.

Put differently, Uzukwu's contribution from the West African theological and cosmological perspectives enriches the catholicity of the church. This sacramental theology deserves interaction with the postmodern sacramental theologians, especially the thoughts of Jean-Luc Marion and Louis-Marie Chauvet. I see strong overlaps in how these authors engage the sacraments and the sacramentology that Uzukwu's theology relates. In a concrete sense, the postmodern emphasis on pneumatology and the experience of Spirit in the West African universe calls for further investigation. The Spirit and the community are indispensable agents of sacramental celebration in re-enacting the foundational narrative of the Christian community. These aspects in the various traditions are indicators of a great overlap and serve as points of deepened catechesis in sacraments and liturgy. This approach, in some sense, restores and returns the sacraments to the faithful, with the challenge of the daily living of the sacraments in concrete lives. From this perspective, my future work will seek to identify ways in which the postmodern sacramental theology might reinforce and benefit from Uzukwu's sacramental reflection. Again, the aspects of *givenness* and pneumatology, which appear to overlap with the West African perspective that Uzukwu develops, deserve further theological reflection.

Uzukwu's phenomenological approach has the support of Vatican II theology, which refers to the history of sacramentology and theology, broadly speaking. These anthropological elements remain essential aspects of our Christian tradition. How else is revelation given without the adoption of the human condition? This is a truth which existential phenomenology imposes upon scholarship beyond the essentialism and rigidity of ontotheological thinking. This is the genius of Vatican II, in a broader sense, which goes beyond the narrow juridical and institutional understanding of the church to describe it as a mystery, the people of God, the body of Christ. These descriptions situate the reality of the church in its cultural and existential contexts. Consequently, we can truly say that, "The joys and the hopes, the griefs and the anxieties of the men of this age, especially those who are poor or in any way afflicted, these are the joys and hopes, the griefs and anxieties of the followers of Christ. Indeed, nothing genuinely human fails to raise an echo in their hearts. For theirs is a community composed of men."[4] As a sociological reality, the concrete situation of the church is one that the

4. GS 2.

document recognizes because the Church is not an abstract reality. This further presents the need for a thorough contextualization of the Gospel within concrete society. Uzukwu's penchant for a profound anthropological appropriation of the faith beyond intellectual theological methodology is a service in response to theological necessity and the existential concerns of the contemporary theology. Put differently, it is a duty to the provincial concerns that contributes to the entire Christian experience.

Difference in contextual issues makes it imperative to search for appropriate theological methods. Uzukwu acknowledges correlational theological method as his starting point:

> Early in my career, I adopted the correlational method developed by Paul Tillich. At that point in time I found convincing Tillich's argument that philosophical-theological reflection should take off from the framing of questions of existence (estrangement) that predisposes already the theological answers.[5]

The correlational method inevitably gives rise to adaptation of indigenous values and models. Uzukwu acknowledges the use of this method early in this theological career, which later evolved in the inculturation. Perhaps, the aspects that remains to be emphasized is the need for more profound theological exchange in the age of globalization and compression of distances.

By adopting a theological methodology that is developed from an African context, Uzukwu gives a Christian interpretation to contextual issues that are outside the purview of the dominant theology. His task in this sense has some affinity with that of Juan Segundo,[6] a Peruvian theologian, who uses the expression "hermeneutic circle" as a guiding tool in theological reflection because he believes that every theology follows some ideological pattern: "Anything and everything involving ideas, including theology, is intimately bound up with the existing social situation in at least an unconscious way."[7] Thus the interplay of past and present reality is experienced in a continuous reinterpretation that leads to the hermeneutic circle. More precisely, Segundo defines the hermeneutic circle as: "the continuing change in our interpretation of the Bible which is dictated by the continuing changes in our present-day reality, both individual and societal."[8] Hence a monolithic interpretation guided by a

5. Uzukwu, "The Imperative of Location," 1.
6. Segundo, *The Liberation of Theology*.
7. Segundo, *The Liberation of Theology*, 8.
8. Segundo, *The Liberation of Theology*.

mono-theological methodology would not be faithful to the scripture and to diverse human and cultural experiences. Uzukwu eloquently demonstrates this fact in his novel theological methodology.

His approach represents a development in Catholic tradition that marks not a radical departure from tradition, but a development in continuity. The fact that history attests to this approach is traceable to Catholic practice. John Thiel gives us the various senses of tradition, and discusses how development of tradition can be contiguous with tradition's inner logic:

> The development that this sense of tradition appreciates is not one that anticipates rupture with the past, with what the tradition has represented as indispensably true. And it is not one in which development issues from ecclesial experience de novo, in a manner discontinuous with the past. Rather the sense of development-in-continuity fathoms the truth of tradition as a growth that occurs in a consistent way throughout an ecclesial time and space, a growth that preserves tradition's truth as it develops it.[9]

This is an acknowledgement of the organic development that has been consistent with the history of the church. We identify this development as characteristic of the church in the epithet *"ecclesia simper reformanda,"* the Church must always be reformed. The changes in the awareness and experiences of the faithful enlarge the sources of doctrine beyond scripture, tradition and magisterium. This is an idea expressed in the contextuality of the faith, and therefore makes renewal an important aspect of the church. This sense of tradition overcomes that constancy and dogmatism that are often associated with a literal sense of tradition.

However, just as Herbert Vorgrimler, a former student and colleague of Karl Rahner would say of the latter, "Naturally Karl Rahner's theology, like any theology, is the work of a fallible and inadequate human being,"[10] Uzukwu's work, as product of an imperfect man has areas that could be reinforced, following his approach of always taking "a second look at everything." His retrieval of indigenous cultural practices remains salutary, yet the existence of these practices either in memory or practical functionality in an age of reflexivity and hybridity requires further examination. Put differently, the mutating nature of culture would make it necessary for theology to be an ongoing negotiation with current practices and lived experience. This claim justifies the fact that theology is not a finished product.

---

9. Thiel, *Senses of Tradition*, 57.
10. Vorgrimler, *Understanding Karl Rahner*, 121.

Inculturation would require a further re-contextualization, since theology involves a constant interaction between the faith and changing culture. Again, just as Stephen Bevans remarks, theology that takes culture seriously can easily become a cultural theology, yet theology has to inevitably engage human cultures and lived experience.

Conclusion

UZUKWU IS WITHOUT DOUBT one of the most important and well-known African theologian. His contribution is a great service to the region and indeed to Christian theology generally. This work has demonstrated how sacraments could become more meaningful and relevant through inculturated liturgical celebrations. In the historical analysis of the basic function of the church, the liturgy, Uzukwu reminds readers of the often-forgotten issue that every theology, and specifically sacramental practice, begins with a context, and has an underlining anthropological basis. This recognition inevitably opens wide latitude for anthropological reinterpretation of the sacraments. Consequently, a proper understanding of the sacraments requires a border-crossing to acquiesce with various anthropologies, a practice that has characterized the history of sacramentology.

The anthropological appropriation of Christianity, consequently, serves two purposes: it responds to various contexts, and it enriches the church, demonstrating its true catholicity and formation of new hybridities.[1] Here lies the uniqueness of Uzukwu's theology. He restores the sacraments to their original liturgical domain, retrieving the indispensable anthropology that is integral to every liturgical celebration. He has highlighted how the inherited Roman liturgy can be appropriated through traditional anthropology and cosmology. His emphasis on the Spirit and its action is of great importance to contemporary theology; particularly concerning sacramental reality, it

---

1. See Schreiter, *The New Catholicity*.

restates the indispensability of the Spirit, beyond every other possible human articulation, in the sacramental process. Sacraments are then better understood as gifts made possible through the transforming work of the Holy Spirit. An investigation into the Nicene-Constantinopolitan creed, already seen in chapter 3, points to the Holy Spirit as the "Lord and giver of life," demonstrating this fact. The principle of relationality anchored in a flexible dynamism challenges a rigid and static view of sacraments. Hence, this principle, prominent in Uzukwu's theology, beckons toward an important revision of theological construction with exclusionary and absolute models. This revision calls for humility in negotiating the interception between faith and culture, an idea that finds succinct expression in the opinion of Third World Theologians: "We recognize also as part of the reality of the Third world the influence of religions and cultures and the need for Christianity to enter in humility into a dialogue with them. We believe that these religions and cultures have a place in God's universal plan and the Holy Spirit is actively at work in them."[2] The salvation-history model Uzukwu adopts in his evaluation of the salvific value of non-Christian religions highlights the activity of the Spirit, which is consistent with the role of the Spirit in the sacraments. The West African cosmology that makes ample reference to the Spirit opens new vistas in reflecting on the Spirit as the basic agency of sacraments. This emphasis reinforces the pneumatological dimension of sacraments, which relativizes and repositions the overarching Christological emphasis of sacraments. A revision of this kind resonates in the ecclesial structure and liturgy of the Church. Under this consideration, the liturgy becomes a continuation of divine manifestation in creation. A sacramental rethinking of this kind challenges any strict distinction between the mundane and the divine, and further justifies Uzukwu's principle of relationality.

Beyond this estimation, Uzukwu identifies human flourishing as an essential element of religion in African cosmology. Hence, one sees an interconnection between anthropology and the cosmic order in a relationship that is the ground of divine manifestation. Under this consideration, the universe becomes a locus of the divine in the ongoing incarnation and sacramentality that culminates in the Parousia. We can therefore agree with Kwame Bediako's position: that religion in this cultural perspective provides a matrix in which men and women experience and respond to the sacred in

---

2. Torres and Fabella, *The Emergent Gospel*, 270.

the human existence.[3] This interconnectivity and relationality further highlights the need for dynamic flexibility in theological methodology.

Much of the theology on African issues applies generic ecclesiological and sacramental models to the African context, with methods taken from other existential and ecclesiological contexts. They remain burdened by the circumstances of their emergence and do not actually capture the specificities of the region. Perhaps this is a truth Uzukwu amply demonstrates—that is, the constituent nature of every theology, content, and method. Notwithstanding, theology can always benefit from the experience and methods of other Christian contexts; in this case, dialogue with multiple contexts and methods should undergird the theological exercise. Uzukwu's theological enterprise is therefore a necessary addition to the pool of Catholic sacramental celebration. One may disagree with some of his assumptions, like the less critical attitude to indigenous cultures, yet academic honesty will make it difficult to ignore his contribution as an important prolegomen onto any future Christian sacramental reinterpretation.

---

3. Bediako, *Jesus and the Gospel in Africa*, 40–41.

Appendix

Interview with Professor Elochukwu Uzukwu held January 20, 2015

Emmanuel: Prof, what would you say has influenced your theological thinking over the years?

Prof: Do you mean in a sense of from the beginning and something that has been continued, and something perhaps I would never abandon, is it?

Emmanuel: Yes Prof! Something that has been there from the beginning?

Prof: Ok, yeah, now if that is what you mean, right from my childhood, up to this point I'm talking to you, it is the village. You won't understand it when I say the village, because many young people today, do not know the village. So, the village, the indigenous Igbo rituals, my village rituals. And when I talk about rituals, since I come from Nnewi, even my own clan, we have our calendar. That's the indigenous calendar. How you portion off the year, ok? Now, and I loved the big traditional celebrations. Ok, uh even when I started going to primary school, the annual celebration of the New Year is not the regular calendar, Julian calendar New Year, but the indigenous traditional New Year, *Ichu afo*. You know, we always took delight in it because we loved to go and eat the coconut. You know the way you celebrate the New Year is you clean out everything and then the heads of household who are still not Christian, they bring the coconut and put them at the crossroads and the children run out from the primary school and rush at the coconut and eat the coconut. We are *umu aro*, we are the children of the year. Now people forget that the year (*aro*) in itself is a deity. Now we don't remember that at all. These are the researches I want to do. I was talking with someone here the other day . . . yes, I was talking with Marinus. He is trying to present a paper on indigenous religion, and it may be interesting to converse with him because he didn't grow up in the village, he grew up in northern Nigeria. So, he does not really understand, he comes frequently to talk about indigenous religion with me. I'm not an expert in indigenous religion, but I grew up reading it, and this is interesting—he was telling me that he was going to present a paper on peacemaking, from the perspective of indigenous religion. I say, oh I am working on something like that already. I'm already working on that—I have two papers now, I have that I want to develop the whole area of indigenous religion and peacemaking, but people who didn't know indigenous religion don't even bother to study the history of its impact on Christianity. But then, when I look back, when I was talking with him, I said look at the various calendars that we have, like the kind of thing I'm saying now. People don't really understand them, but I grew up in that. I grew up in that and they stick with me and it's true that in my village, in 1914, my grandfather, it was said, established the church. Moved the church from another king's compound, you know, to the *ajo ofia*, evil forest. The place that was called evil forest. They cleared ground there and started gathering from 1914. And since I am from Catholic family, I missed being initiated into the *mmo*, because my father was a Catholic and my father refused to allow us to go to the compound to be initiated. And it pained me that I missed out on that, because I became inferior immediately the following day with all my age grade, I was inferior. The others were initiated except myself and my younger brother. So, these things remain still, the values that I find in the traditional culture; they remain engrained in my mind. I don't think that I'm going to throw them away. They carry me up to this day. That's basically the way I grew up in my childhood and it's so difficult to throw that away.

Emmanuel—So Prof, cultural and traditional upbringing has made this lasting impact on you- Community, village, and the rituals. Did you have any relationship with your catechist or indigenous teachers when you were growing up?

Prof: Ok, well, that is interesting. You are asking me now, the way my theology, as a child, was formed?

Emmanuel: Exactly!

Prof: Well, that is interesting! It goes two interesting ways. It's good you're asking me because it's making me think. You are asking me the way my theology was formed as a child. In summary, I will tell you that my ecclesiology is radically rooted in my own father's ecclesiology. My father, the person that gave birth to me. And I can talk about, I can do a book on that, you know; the influence of my father's ecclesiology on me, because I thought my father was wrong, but later on I realized that my father was right in his understanding of the local church, what the local church should look like. Because my grandfather established the church, my father followed suit, I followed as well and all those working in the church. And everybody going to the primary school has to, all of us going to the primary school we have to learn the catechism, you know. So, you have to pass not only in religion class, but also you have to pass the various grades of going to communion, and so on and so forth. But that's one thing, the other one is a practical one. But every one of us in the early 50's not only do we go to Sunday Mass, if there is one, but also we go the Benediction, if there is one. But there was no Benediction. The Benediction was catechism. Now what we loved as children, then, was to watch the elders debate their faith with their catechist. All of them assemble, and they are debating the elements of the catechism, it was phenomenal, what they call *nkwusi nke okwukwe*. It was phenomenal. And we watched them, and we took delight in that. Even when they are trying to drive us away to go and learn the catechism of children, we wanted to stay with the elders to know what they were doing. You know, to know the way that they were understanding it, because my father learned different kind of catechism than we learned, you know. Ok, so that's the first level. The second level is my father's understanding of the local church. As soon as you start going to communion, you must go to Mass where the Reverend Father is celebrating Mass on a Sunday, even if it means traveling three miles, four miles. And our teachers used their bicycles, and they are there, and they give numbers to every child. And Monday morning, the Monday assembly, first of all is "what was your number?" So, if you did not get a number, you know what follows. You get a beating. And then we have to get a number. My father understood that we are going to get a beating if we didn't get a number, so he allowed us to keep going. But my father totally disagreed with that ecclesiology. As far as he was concerned, the church building that was there is where we should gather every Sunday. He literary says, if all of us are pursing the priests, who is there then to collect and the old women and the children and the elders to pray on a Sunday? We are pursuing the priests; we want to go to where the priest is. You know, we have a catechist here, let him set up a service for us here. So, my father never, I never saw him once, leave our own station to go elsewhere for Mass, never! And I still think his ecclesiology is better than mine about the local church. And my cousin was a teacher as well, I lived with him, as of standard three. He was an ex-seminarian himself, he wanted to go to the seminary, but they didn't allow him to go. He started, but he was stopped from going because of his family background. There will be nobody in the family to take on the family, that's why he didn't continue the seminary. So that's basically the influences, teachers, and stuff like that.

Emmanuel—Thank you, Prof! That's very helpful. Prof, going to your academic and intellectual formation, where do you think your theology began? Was it in the seminary, or when you began graduate studies? When did you really begin the academic theological orientation?

Prof: Yes, let me tell you this, you won't see it written in anywhere, but I will still look for the edition, the early edition of the Bigard Torch magazine. One, during the war, with a colleague of mine, we were very interested in oracles, very interested in oracles. So, seminarians then, we had what we called the theological society and the liturgical society. So, in the liturgical circle, both of us produced a report on our visit to two shrines in Okija. One shrine was *igba afa*, you know, like an oracle that will tell you whatever you've done, you know whatever you have in mind. Okija was noted so much for those oracles. So, both of us, myself and Boniface Asouzu spent a whole day in 1968 or 69. No, wait a minute, it was in 1969, because soon the war was over. In 1969 we spent the whole day researching on this particular phenomenon. And the oracle is there, the talking bird, or oracle. The bird would talk and then somebody would interpret the speech of this bird. Ok, so that's one. The other oracle that we visited the same day was more expansive because it is called *ita nzu* you know, oracle, that they give you portions of chalk, and if you stole something, it would be manifest. If you didn't steal, it would be manifest. So, we were there until 5pm with a group of people. So, I think, we presented the paper of course, but we were highly skeptical about the workings of the oracle. I think we went there to disprove, that the oracle spoke the truth. And our people, in the community, were saying oh you people are really biased, prejudiced, and you are not very good researchers. That's one thing we did as seminaries. But second thing I did as a seminarian, is something that was published in the Torch magazine, Bigard Torch magazine. And someone told me that it could still be there because I wasn't interested in finding out what I wrote. The title of that paper published was *Wedding Bells*, because I was very interested in marriage then, and I wanted to find out some of the rites that surrounded marriage within the Nnewi village group. And I got most of the information from my father himself. My father was amused when I was asking him the questions about the kind of things, why our people do certain things. What is the movement from being agboo, new married to *ibia ache*. But he said *ache* is a rope, that's the first time I heard it. It's a rope that you pick from the shrine of *edoo*. *Edoo* is a deity of Nnewi. And then, as soon as a woman gives birth to the first child, then she is *ibia ache*. She will take it and tie it around her waist. I could not believe this I just could not believe this. And the other one is *isi nkpo*. Now, once a young lady has come out of *ibi*. Ibi is a ceremony of initiation of the young women. Once they come out, they do their hair in such a way, we call it *isi nkpo*. The hair is made in such a way that it goes up, and she will never carry water again, until she goes to the husband's house. She won't carry water. So, they are practically sacred women, they are moving towards marriage. So, I was honored to find out the meaning of those ceremonies. Those were the issues that interested me. That was before I ever got ordained as a priest. And I was continuing that way after ordination. I have put a bit of it in my journey as a theologian. But what changed me, the trajectory, was pastoral experience. My pastoral experience brought me face to face with the limitations of what you can permissibly do in the Roman Church. My professor of moral theology was Albert Obiefuna, the late bishop of Onitsha. And in the field, I was meeting this young man and women leaving with their partners, married according to Igbo traditional marriage. But not married in the Church. I was annoyed with them, I said why seat around here, why not take the marriage? And one of them challenged me one day, one young man challenged me. He said listen, Reverend father, "If it were not for the mother of this woman, the woman was asking me, pushing me, pushing me, telling me, go and get married. If it just because of the mother of this woman that I'm going to get married in church, but as far as I am concerned, I am married. As far as I'm concerned, I'm married." I said, is that? He said yes! So, I wrote up a paper and sent it to my professor of moral theology, asking him what the difference is? I mean, these people have concluded their marriage ceremonies. Why is it that they must wait another lengthy time in order to get married in the Church? Why can't we do it all together? And he laughed and sent it back to me. He said Rome would not permit that. That's why I moved away from moral theology. I said there's no place for me there, I cannot work there. And I moved into liturgical animation, and I was already taking up the choral society for years, when I was a seminarian. And I led the choral society quite often. So, when I moved from the Novitiate to the Umu owa seminary, I developed the liturgy there, it was pretty good. The young boys really loved the liturgy there. From there, it was everything. I think I mentioned this as well, the development of my theological and liturgical thinking did not start in abstract, and it started with a pastoral problem, especially about the Eucharist.

Not until I read then, the book of Fr. Ifeanyi Anozie. Thanks to him because he came back from Rome and was teaching us. He decided to teach us liturgy. That's very good and that's the first time I read the book of Don Gregory Dix, *The Shape of The Liturgy*, published in 1945. Now that book saved my life. At least it helped me go ahead and take ordination. Because I wasn't sure I was going to take ordination without addressing the issue of the Eucharist and real presence. It was then I realized that the Eucharist is not magic. Transubstantiation, all these words, are just words. They did not touch me profoundly; I did not know what it meant. But when I realized the Eucharist was in the setting of a meal, a meal with a tradition, you see. Meal, tradition—from one thing to the other, it was easy. The Jews have their tradition, they have their meals, tradition. Their prayers are ritual prayers. So also, the Igbo people have their meals, their tradition. They have their prayers, their ritual prayers. From one to the other, it was very easy for me to open that channel, a research area, and a life area.

Emmanuel: Prof, from then, you now went on to your graduate studies on the Eucharist and all of that. This is the foundation.

Prof: Yes, well this is already founded me. As a matter of fact, I did a Bachelor of Divinity (B.D.), paper which I carried on my way to Toronto, I don't know where it is now. My B.D. paper was on the Eucharistic prayer. It was on the prayer of Hippolytus, Eucharistic prayer number two. There's a Jewish background to that prayer. So that's what my B.D. paper began. I took it to Toronto when I was going to study and I gave it to Prof. Mitloshazzi, who was my moderate, who guided all through my time in Toronto and he was fascinated by that and thought I should continue in that area. Yes, I did!

Emmanuel: Ok, I can now see why you are interested in developing African Eucharist theology, from our conversation of on Igbo rituals.

Prof: Yes, but that's not all, because developing in Eucharistic theology, I was very interested in historical theology. And I wanted to know where, what's the narrative of all the practices we have in Christianity. And the best part of the narrative of all of the practices we have in Christianity are in the liturgy. Because they always take shape in the liturgy. And since the liturgy kind of sums up my personal quest in Christian life, why not? It was easy for me to channel my work towards the liturgy. And the first thing I did of course was the *Memory and Tradition*. How would memory and tradition within the Jewish set up, how did it translate into anamnesis in Christian liturgy. So, from one thing to the other, yeah. I think that's it, so you can see the connection with liturgical studies. But that doesn't mean I marginalized other aspects of theology. But its kind of interrupted, because you must do, just as you do here, you must do other aspects of theology, like ethics, before you make your choice.

Emmanuel: Prof, before I go to the next question, I would like to know something about your ordination, and if ever you had a pastoral responsibility, because you said that changed your thinking about marriage.

Prof: The pastoral did change a lot. I was telling my friend Brian Cronny last night, that after my ordination my superior said now get ready you are going to Louvain. I said ok. You are going to study philosophy we need people to teach philosophy. I said that's alright, I'll go to Louvain. But then, after that, I was assigned to the Novitiate in Awo mamma, as the bursar and the assistant novice master. So, then we had pastoral responsibilities, and I was bored in the Novitiate, honestly, and I did not know what I was doing there. But the pastoral work was interesting. Where we had the pastoral work was far away from the Novitiate, but then in the village itself, I was always taking a walk into the village to talk with young people and ask them about their life and so on and so forth. So, in that way, the pastoral work, the contact, the one-to-one contact with young people, did change my viewpoint. But then the following year, from 1973 to 1975, I was the director of the seminary in Umu owa, our first and second year, with about 120 students and the parish as well, I was the parish priest. So, there is absolutely no way you will not get into problems about the parish, and about sickness. In fact, I even studied praying—prayer ministry. I was in the prayer ministry because people were going, you know, moving away from the parish and going elsewhere and talking about moving into some of the churches and talking about all this fantastic stuff that happened to them. So, we just gathered, and we prayed. We didn't get any healings, of course, because I wasn't a magician, you know, but at least it helped the people who were sick to come together to pray. The pastoral work in 1973. I was ordained in 1972. 1975, I was in Umuowa seminary and parish.

Interview held October 15, 2016

Emmanuel: We now go to your teaching experience when you finished your doctorate. Where are the places you taught, and what subjects did you teach?

Prof: Ok, now first, the first place I never wanted to work in was Nigeria. That was clear to me. As soon as I was finishing, I had almost like a trauma. What am I going to do with my doctorate? First, I didn't want to do a doctorate. I didn't want to do a doctorate. I wanted to do just a master's and then finish it and to move into master's in education. And then go home and work with our formation house. I didn't want to do a doctorate, this is true. And so, the directors at the University of Toronto were worried, especially the dean. Why don't you want to do it? One of my professors- Joann Juwer, she was my professor in patristics. And she was mad at me when I told her I was going to Ontario to register for master's in education. And she said, "education is not a science, what are you doing?" I said listen, there are so many people in Nigeria with doctorates, I don't know what they're doing with it. There's a shocking list of people with PhD's. What are they doing with it? It made no sense to me. And my friend, Banabas Okolo, was doing a second doctorate in Toronto there, in the same school, and he looked at me and said you must be a mad person. People are dying to come and do a doctorate. You have the opportunity to do it and you are refusing. If I ever get into this, I'm not coming out of it. That was it that was the commitment. So, when I applied, now, I applied to Ontario's for education, and my application was turned down. Why? Because I claimed I did philosophy, but there were no transcripts. All the transcripts were lost during the war. So, there was nothing, I could provide no evidence that I had studied philosophy. Not even an iota of evidence. That's why I didn't go to Ontario. Otherwise, I would not be here, talking theology. I said ok, I picked up the phone, I called the dean and said, is it possible for me to apply for the PhD now? He said, O yeah, sure, let me check. He checked the results, and the thesis have not yet been evaluated, but the results are good. So, I applied for the doctorate. But I made up my mind, if I get into this, I'm not coming out of it. If I am going to do a doctorate, then I have to use it. So, I have to use it. Now, when I was finishing there, going back to Nigeria, I realized I wasn't going to use it, because it means a church orientation in Nigeria is not open to new theological research and I already sent the Eucharistic prayer I did to Arinze when I finished, I sent it to him. I gave the thesis to two people to read before the defense, to Obiefuna and Metuh. They sent their comments that I filed to my thesis director and that consoled him that it was in the right direction, because he did not know much our traditional rituals and the like. But Arinze, himself said oh that's wonderful, but our people are not yet ready for this. So, because of that, I said I am not sure I will go back to Nigeria to work. A friend of mine, an Irish- Canadian was asking me why not talk to our superior general so that you go to East Africa. He had hardly finished talking when I got the word that I was going to work in the Congo. That's why I when to the Congo. Others were pitying me in Nigeria, they don't allow you to come back. They did not even realize that I did not want to come back to Nigeria, to teach. So, the Congo was very good for me. Now, the Congo was another kind of place. I reorganized my theology. I completely reorganized my theology in the Congo. And yes, studying in Canada was good, but the Congo recreated my theology completely, because I have to teach theology in French, I had to throw away all the English books that I had, I have to go to the library during the vacation to prepare my lectures. I had to redo my theology in French. And the philosophical component of French theology is basically excessive here. What people take for granted philosophically in all the systems, from Kant to Descartes down, to existentialism. What they take for granted in French high schools. So, before the last grade in French, in high school, in the Congo, they have already done a good chunk of philosophy. What we take for granted at doing in philosophy schools and things like that. So that helped me. I started teaching, first of all, Approaches to African Theology, Method in African Theology that was the very first course I taught in Brazzaville. But when I taught it, the students didn't understand what I was talking about, because I was translating from English to French. So that's why I had to sit down and learn French properly. I learn French before going to Congo, but it wasn't a French I could use in the classroom. So, I had to relearn, I never used any English textbook anymore, it was all French. I had to redo my theology. From there, to teaching the sacraments, and approaches to the liturgy. I taught one year in Brazzaville, and the next year I was teaching in Kinshasa, and the next year I was teaching in faculty Theologie Katholieke.

Emmanuel: So, you taught in many other schools in the Congo?

Prof: Yeah, I was in the Congo, Congo Brazzaville is the French Congo. And on the other bank of the Nile, is Kinshasa. Congo Kinshasa really made my life as a teacher. I taught full time in Brazzaville. But in Kinshasa is the best colleges and the best universities we have in Africa, theological colleges. And Kinshasa meant meeting cardinal Malula. Cardinal Malula was practically a father to me. Kinshasa also meant a Zaire liturgy. Not only that I participated it in, but I presided over the Zaire liturgy in the Congo, Brazzaville itself. Kinshasa was fascinating for me. It meant people, it meant the academy, it meant people like Ngindu Mushete, people like Sese Mulago. You know, like the older people. So, all these people that made theology in Kinshasa great. I was sitting with them. Ikwesi was the secretary general of the conference of bishops. Ngindu Mushete was the theologian for cardinal Malula. Vincent Mulago was in charge of the university seminary. So, all these early people like Mulago were classmates with Stephen Ezeanya, and Stephen Ezeanya with Bishop Sarpong were friends, and so on that level I was meeting with them, and it was amazing. An awesome experience. I mean, I was privileged.

Emmanuel: The father, did you ever work with the Zaire bishops Conference in production of the Zairean rite?

Prof: No! What I did was this . . . . If you got that sense that is my mistake and I am misleading, you. No! What I did was this, in the Congo, the advisor that they had as a liturgist was a monk that relocated to South America. The advisor that they had in the production of the liturgy, because the work on the Zairean rite started in 1969, and the book was complete in 1973. So, in 1973 I was still in Nigeria, so I could not have inspired it. That's clear, Ok? In 1973 there was talk about giving permission to utilize this *ad experimentum*. From 73 already, ok? And there are so many things developing in Zaire then, by 1973, Malula himself had already started the Bagandi pastoral practice. That is whereby a layperson is in charge of the parish, not a priest. The layperson, an elder that has 3 years training in theology is working as the pastor of the parish, in Kinshasa itself in 1973. And I arrived Brazzaville in 1979. Ok, but by 1979, there was no liturgist. No liturgist! That's amazing, that we are producing a liturgy, but there was no liturgist in Kinshasa. So, it was then, by 1979, or 80, that the pressures were coming from the Sacred Congregation for the sacraments. And Kinshasa wanted approval, because they'd been using this rite *ad experimentum*.

Emmanuel: You mean the Zairean rite?

Prof: Yeah, they had been using it *ad experimentum*. They were allowed to use it. They wanted it to be officially approved. So, the liturgists in Rome and the people in the sacred congregation for divine worship and the Discipline of the sacraments were sending queries. And these queries came to my table. Because there was no body who would respond to that. So, when the queries came to my table, I started writing then and responding. My writing and responses that was this, *Liturgy Truly Christian, Truly African*. So, I was writing and responding to them, and I said let us situate liturgy historically. What they are asking you in Rome is not wrong. Because you are calling it a Zairean rite. But the rite is not simply the Eucharist. The rite is too big to be simply called the Eucharist. The rite includes all the discipline of the sacraments, Religious life, and theology. So, the rite is wider than that. So, the Roman rite for example, includes so many things, not just the Roman Eucharist, not the canon, not the mass. So, for them, it was interesting, because they want to stick to the rite, but the Romans want to change the title. So finally, I ask them, what do you want? Isn't it to celebrate what you have? Let them call it whatever they like. Let them call it whatever they like. But it has to be, known that it's not Zairean as such. It has to be Romano-Zairean. And I plotted out to them the structure of the Eucharistic families and rites. You are within the Latin family; you cannot say you are not within it. No matter how you struggle. Logically, it is within it. That was the conservative element in me, you know, the tradition, we are within the Roman tradition, within the Latin tradition. We are not within the orthodox tradition. Because the zaireans were saying, ok that's the way the Ethiopian liturgy developed and so. But I say, the Ethiopian liturgy is within the Coptic tradition. When you plot it out, you see it's within the Coptic. And the Ethiopians borrowed a lot from Alexandria, whether you like it or not. Just as you are borrowing. So that's the conservative element in any liturgist, is the history part of liturgy. I didn't create the Zairean rite. I did not!

Emmanuel: But Prof, you certainly helped in finalizing the Zairean rite.

Prof: Yes, in the sense of giving them ideas about how to respond. I didn't change a word in the text. The text was already there, their work. It is and was never my work, never! Rather, I advised, that's all. I gained more from it, maybe than they gained, because for me it means I have to study their liturgical text. I have to study the minutes of the meetings, and they made it all available to me. God only knows where these texts, all these things are now, I don't know.

Emmanuel: Let me digress a little bit. What do you think is responsible for the fast theological development in the East African church compared to the west? Why do they have Zairean rite and there is no rite for the whole of West Africa that could even be under the Roman rite, so to speak? Why is the East more theologically developed than the west?

Prof: And I'm just doing my class in Christianity in Africa. I wish you could come to my class—Approaches to African and African American theology. I just finished doing Ethiopia, and Africa in 1500. You know, Islam, Christianity, and so on in Africa, sub-saharhan Africa. The next thing we are doing now, is the Congo itself, the Congo before the 15th century, the big flourishing of the Church in the Congo in the 15th Century. Amazing flourishing of the Church, for 300 years the Church flourished in the Congo.

Fr. Emmanuel—From the 15th Century?

Prof: Yeah, from the 15th century, you know the conversion of the Congo, and so on, up until the fizzling out of this Church because of so many political and violent military conquest by the Portuguese and so on and so forth. Ok, so you cannot underestimate the fact that when a place called Mbanza Congo and Central African region was already Christian in the 15th century. Ok, you cannot underestimate that. Because it goes, whether I like it or not, it has penetrated, and the Congo *cross*, which I don't have it here, I used to have the Congo cross. When I go home, I'll see if I have my Congo cross in Nigeria. The Congo cross is a certain kind of, let me see what I can show, I can show it to you, let me see . . . Ok, now, look at that. It dates to 17th century, but it started before then, but 17th / 18th century is the flourishing. The demographics of Congo covered 250 miles expanse inside and southwards. It was not a small kingdom, including the place they call Zaire, Brazzaville area and parts of Angola then.

The kingdom of the Congo. And the Church flourished, flourished in those places. So, we are going to do that again on Tuesday because we could not finish. And the whole idea of the propaganda fide, the establishment, propaganda fide was inspired by progress in the Congo. What you call today propaganda fide, established in 1622, was from the issues that arose in the Congo. You know, because the king of the Congo for years has been asking Rome, we want a direct link with you. But because of the patronage in existence, now this is mission history. The Roman pope gave Portugal and Spain the powers all over the place where they ruled, like the nomination of bishops, movement of missionaries are in your hands. The popes did it, but they regretted it. They did it in the 15th century, but they regretted it. And the big thing that they did in 1622 was to put together a document, not only now for Africa, but also for the East, for Asia. You know because things were happening in Africa before it got to China. But people don't take this history seriously. Why? Because you don't have literacy in Africa, yes? But there are documentations of the letters between the king of Portugal and the king of the Congo in the 15th century. So, this is important. I mean, where you try to do the historical background to theology in Africa and why the Congo is the Congo it is today. You cannot ignore that. And secondly, I must have written somewhere, I think it is there somewhere, the history of the development of Congolese church art in the 1920's. And then, in the fifties as well, the exposition, both in Rome and the Congo, but in Rome and the Congo in the fifties, 1951 or so. Both Rome and the Congo, on the Congolese religious art. Ok, now Congo suffered a lot, one of the worst experiences of colonialism in Africa.

Emmanuel: Was Congo under colonial rule in the 15th century? Or Congo was free of colonialism.

Prof: No, they were not! These are independent kingdoms. You know, that is the king of Portugal and the king of Spain. Sorry, the king of Portugal and the king of the Congo were corresponding. It is of course, true that the king and the court, they took Portuguese names. And they were able to learn

Portuguese. The prince of Soyo in the Congo was chanting the gospel in Latin, you will not believe it. I mean they read, and they wrote and stuff like that. The first catechism was a catechism in Ki Congo, but they never really translated the Bible into Congo because it was not Catholic to do so. It was the Dollards that translated the Bible in England in the 16th, 17th century, were being pursued for heresy because they translated the Bible into English. We are not allowed to do that. A person like Theresa of Avila, she didn't read Latin, she didn't read Latin. So, what she got was only the fallout from whatever in Spanish language. She didn't read Latin, so she wouldn't quote scripture direct, you know, it would be an indirect quotation of scripture. So, these are issues, and this is true. So, you are asking me, let me go back to your question, why. Because they took the measures, ok. And their reaction to colonialism was only different as our reaction. Our colonialism wasn't as horrendous as the Congo colonialism. That's the first point. The second point would be the liturgical movement. The liturgical movement! We were evangelized by the Irish, and there was not a clear impact on the liturgical, 19-20th century liturgical movement in Ireland. There was not a clear impact. When the liturgical movement in Mombe, participated a lot in the liturgical movement. These are all inspirations of the liturgical movement. What would be happened in Belgium would be happening in the Congo. And secondly then, the appointment of local bishops and pioneer priests. The establishment of the facultie Theologie Katholicke in 1957 was called Louvanium. Louvanium was established in Kinshasa.

Emmanuel: If I may ask, why was it called Louvanium?

Prof: Louvanium that is transplanting to Kinshasa. It was called Louvanium, and I did not know whether they still call it Louvanium today, but the professors from Louvain in Belgium, they were all working hand-in-hand. And then the establishment within the Louvanium itself, of the center for African studies. It was called the Center for the study of African Religions, established in 1957. So, there you are! So 57, 65 it was done and they were publishing everything about African religions. So, you did not have a comparable inspiration in Nigeria or in Ghana. You didn't have it. So, you have an extraordinarily strong developed thing. And then you have a bishop, you know, who may not have had superior education, but who was a spiritual man, he was ordained in 1959, Joseph Malula and whose book, in the field of his ordination, that he's dreaming of a Church that is African, in an independent African nation. In 1959, before Congo was independent. So you have that kind of energy moving and unfortunately, Patrick Mumba's revolution did not work out, you know, and he was killed and there are so many people involved in that. But the dynamics of the liturgy and the theology was very strong. Very, very strong. So as soon as the Vatican council II was called, the only African there in the commission, for preparatory commission, for the Vatican council II, was Malula. He was in the commission for liturgy. And Malula was asked by the secretary of the commission on liturgy, to give us an indication of what this new liturgy we are working at would be like. And what did Malula do? Malula sang the Our Father in Lingala.

1962! 1962, he sang the Our Father in Lingala. Ok, now, 1962 in Nigeria, all the things were still in Latin, ok? So, there you are. I know that Monsignor Nwanegbo translated the book that is called *Nafa Nna*? (In the Name of the Father). The translation did not mean that liturgy moved forward, it didn't move forward. This gives an explanation and indication of different trajectories in liturgical experimentation.

Emmanuel: Father, let me take you back to the Congo church again. From the 15th century to the 18th century you have strong Catholic presence.

Prof: 300 years of presence.

Emmanuel: So, what happened the time in between, from 18th century to 20th century?

Prof: Ok, what happened—it was all political, military, you know, political, military and then, the structure of the Catholic Church. Structurally, the Catholic Church is a church that is hierarchical and is guided by this so much. Now, in Banza Congo, in fact, one of the most destructive things happened here. You know, the battle from ambilla in the 18th century. That battle was terrible!

Emmanuel: Battle between which groups?

Prof: The Portuguese, the Portuguese and the Congo king. You know, because everything was destroyed, including the archives. This guy went to war with, carried all his archives with him, a lot of his things were destroyed. So, you can check this history, of course. It's very easy to check the history. Very easy to check the history. I can even send it to you. I can send it to you, or I can copy it out. See the book by Adrian Hastings. This history is very good, very good history of this. So, it is partly destroyed by the battle of Ambilla. There was a movement, African feminist movement. They the first theologian Karbitha who was burned as first feminist theologian. Because she challenged the Capuchins.

Emmanuel: Ok, I've read about that.

Prof: So that war destroyed everything. The kingdom was destroyed. Now unfortunately that is the story of the connection between church and state. So, the state ensured the survival of the church. When the state was destroyed, you know, the church frittered away and disappeared. And that is true. Because the members of the not just the royal family, but of the aristocracy, they are all church people. ALL of them.

Fr. Emmanuel—In Congo?

Prof: All of them were church people, from the emperor down, all are church people. The common people didn't really follow. There are very few peopled that followed. So, outside the capital, you have few participating. But within the capital, you have cannons regular, cannons, chanting the offices in the cathedral. Cannons, you know. So, if the seminary had worked, there was an establishment of the seminary, but it did not work. They moved down to Angola and then to South Tomey. South Tomeys was the first seminary, it was established, the first seminary. The Portuguese, the bishops could send people to the seminary there, they sent people to work in the Congo. If they continued it, sending priests from South Tomey, the Congo church would have survived, but it didn't survive.

Emmanuel: So, the battle basically had political reasons and were there theological reasons that stopped the missionaries from coming to Congo.

Prof: Political reason was the major thing, because it is a top down church. It doesn't have a future. A bottom up church, like the kind of church I tell you my grandfather moved the church over there, the people liked it, so whether a priest came or not, the church was there. Or what happened in Japan, you have the church, but for 100, 200 years there was no priest, and still people came back and recognized the church in Japan. So, the bottom-up church is better than the top-down church. But the 15th, 16th century method was king, royal court that was all. It was an elite church. Just as you have in Ethiopia, it was emperor talk to emperor, but Ethiopia was stronger,

APPENDIX

because it was based on monastic life. Monasticism made sure that no matter what happened to the king, the church was there. And the Ethiopian church is still strongly monastical today.

Emmanuel: Father you talked about your teaching experiencing in Congo Brazzaville, Kinshasa. Can we move now to your teaching experience in Nigeria? Your teaching and leadership positions in Nigeria and beyond. When did that start and what where the specific courses you taught?

Prof: 1982, I was back to Nigeria, in 1982. I was still going to Congo to teach; I was teaching in the Congo until 1984. 1982 I was back to Nigeria, teaching in the Bigard seminary. It was tough again, beginning to teach in English, because I had to learn English all over again. And I was sorry for my students, because it was almost like speaking French to them. And people were not very familiar with the use of sociology in theology. So, students were complaining, yes, what you are saying is interesting, but there is a textbook to read, to be able to answer all the questions you are asking us. And Bigard had not had a liturgy teacher for a long time, I think at least since Ogwu left they didn't have a liturgy teacher. So, I was having a classroom that had over 200 students at the same time. It was terrible, it was a terrible kind of teaching. But I enjoyed it, by then things were changing. I was not just teaching, but I was in charge of our formation house at the same time. And I was dissatisfied with the systematic theology taught in the Bigard. I was dissatisfied. I was watching the people teaching these things and they are still using the same books that were being used when I was studying there myself, so that was painful. And then I wanted to introduce some courses. The advantageous thing was the dean then, was a friend of mine and another Spiritan. So, I was pushing this, that there is no missiology in this place. Why can you stay here, you don't do anything on evangelization, liberation, inculturation, you don't do anything like that. They say you talk about missiology, but we study missiology in church history. I said it's not the same thing. So finally, after two years their missiology came to the curriculum, but on the condition that I would teach it. So, I was teaching that, I was teaching missiology, and that is the place where some of the students were able to hear about liberation theology and stuff like, maybe for the first time. It was an interesting experience, but because of the dissatisfaction I had with the curriculum, and that you cannot change it because of the affiliation with the Propaganda Fide, we were saying no, we are going to move away from Bigard. So, in my second year there, we were already talking about finding land and by 1985 we were ready to start building. In 1987, the Spiritan International School of Theology (SIST) was established, and I moved away from Bigard. I was teaching in the Bigard, of course, until 1991. But I completely revised the program in SIST, for 16 years.

Emmanuel: You began at SIST in 1985?

Prof: In 1987. It's now 25 years since SIST was established. I was there for the celebration of the silver jubilee. Prof. George was there; he was the chair when we signed the agreement with Duquesne in 1989. The agreement was signed in 1989. It may be interesting to look at it because when I was thinking up stuff, I asked them about the program that we sent to them, because the curriculum, whether they still have it? They gave me, they have the curriculum here (in Duquesne) that we sent to them in 1989 to get the approval for the affiliation. The affiliated us, but I was just telling him the other day, that they are doing affiliations now and are permitting people to write M.A. dissertations. But they affiliated and refused to allow us to do M.A dissertations, because our library is not sufficiently equipped, and, therefore we do additional courses to make up for the M.A requirements and, then, before doing the comprehensive exams. So, we do courses. But others, like the people now in Ibadan, the Dominicans entered later. But no doubt Ibadan has a better library. And they are close to the university library. But it is interesting, I was just asking them whether we would reapply to do the M.A. dissertation, instead of taking one full year course. Because it just gives them the habit of writing the thesis.

Emmanuel: Father thank you so much, I learned the things I couldn't read in any book from you. I have one more question for you. How would you summarize your theological career and why did you choose the theological methodology you have used in your work. Or, what is the basic primary methodology you have used all along?

Prof: Let me say that I have a very powerful, two people in Toronto, who were really mentoring me. One of them ended up being a bishop, he is from Hungary. And another one that really my guided my thinking on systematics and method was Tipot Hollervard. Now one of his books, I still have here. He was somebody who was writing a thesis on apologetics and wanted to defend the thesis here and I looked at the structure of the thesis and it was near defense, and I told the chair, I would fail this person. I would certainly fail this person. Because you cannot talk about apologetics with

Vatican Council II without looking at the history of apologetics as such. But they wanted to get the person out of this place, so they have to change the examiner. So, I said, do not put me in it, because I will fail the person. Because my principal formator in method Hollervard, his first major book was faith understood as apologetics. How do you start thinking, asking the questions on the faith? How do you defend the faith? And one of the great things I learned from Tipot was if you are beginning something; when you are beginning something and you want to write, always on the very first page tell us, what you want to do and your conclusion, so that at the end we will not be disappointed. I want to know what your conclusion is going to be. And let it be as modest as possible. Don't arouse the hope of everybody that I'm going to break a new, new area. But just say, this is what I'm going do, this is how I'm going to do it, and this is how I'm going to conclude. That's it! Walk away, let it be as modest as that. So, my formator was very good in structuring my way of thinking. Therefore, he said, you want to work on African theology, I will help you, but the first thing is you must know African history, you must know African language. You must! Anyone who doesn't know the history or the language, traditions, forget about. And then you must know African anthropology. So, I spent most of the time learning African anthropology, learning African history and studying the languages that make up Africa, you know, the languages of Africa. These are initiatory things. And then secondly, you must do theological method. So, one of the courses I did, and one of the first things I published in 1978 was notes on methodology. I've not completely moved away from that method, because I did, I decided to use Paul Tillich's method of correlation. It would be foolish to think you are asking questions you have already not predicted the answer. When you are asking a question, you are already predicted the answer. Because the question is correlated to the answer. Because when you ask the question then you are thinking where the biblical areas are; this is an old method. But then, it is still interesting. I know my friend, Boodoo, would not want a correlation method, but rather would like a contextual method. But even contextual and correlation are still related. But in the contextual method the questions arise from the context, clarify the answers you have in the bible. So, the context throws light on the issues and on the answers and challenges. Context might be richer than the correlation method in the sense that it throws light and raises further questions, and keeps on changing as you move on, in the contextual methodology. But the correlation method is that to ensure you are consistent, the questions you are asking already predisposes you to say where do I find the answers to my questions. So that's the way I have already worked. So that's why when I was asking the questions about the *Blessing and Thanksgiving*, already I started, but where am I going to find the answers? I find the answers among the Igbo. But they are the only people who have blessing in their tradition. Since we are Christian, I must find the answers in the Jewish and the Christian. And therefore, it's connected. His criticism of my thesis, in the defense is, are you sure this is inculturation? Or simply adaptation? And I said, well, you can have adaptation as adaptation. If you call it adaptation, then I'll call it radical adaptation. Because truth to tell, give that prayer that I did to the Roman, they said no, that's not the Roman prayer. Therefore, if it is adaptation, it is radical adaptation. My questions are correlating. And that's why I still insisted I'm going to use the prayer. And as an anecdote, I was in the Holy Rosary Convent, in Ethiopia, Addis Ababa. I don't know what year. And on October 7th, they have their celebration of the Holy Rosary. And the sister superior was saying please Father, will you please use this particular text for presiding at the Eucharist? I said, anything you want me to do, I will do. And the text, they called it African Eucharistic prayer. And I was looking at this and that was the Eucharistic I composed. But that's interesting, that at least people are using it. I know in Germany they are using it for the youth liturgies. So that's it. That's the issue of my method.

Emmanuel: So basically, you combined sociology, anthropology in your theological method?

Prof: Yes, it is impossible to study theology without anthropology because they are related, and, Rahner does the same thing as well. The human question? So, every theological question is an anthropological question. And every anthropological question deals with the human condition. But then, Rahner will move from here to philosophical anthropology. Ok, but that's not just anthropology. Anthropology is what comes from the culture, you need to use the cultural materials. That's my preference!

Emmanuel—Prof, thank you so much for your time.

Prof—You are welcome!

Bibliography

Works of Elochukwu Uzukwu

Books

Uzukwu, Elochukwu. "Blessing and Thanksgiving among the Igbo (Towards a Eucharistia Africana)." ThD diss., University of St. Michael's College, 1978.
———. *God, Spirit, and Human Wholeness: Appropriating Faith and Culture in West African Style*. Eugene, OR: Pickwick, 2012.
———. *A Listening Church: Autonomy and Communion in African Churches*. Maryknoll, NY: Orbis, 1996.
———. *Liturgy: Truly Christian, Truly African*. Eldoret, Kenya: Gaba, 1982.
———, ed. *Inculturation: A Nigerian Perspective*. Enugu, Nigeria: Snaap, 1988.
———. *Worship as Body Language: Introduction to Christian Worship: An African Orientation*. Collegeville, MN: Liturgical, 1997.

Journal Essays and Presentations

Uzukwu, Elochukwu. "African Personality and the Christian Liturgy." *The Journal of the Faculty of Theology of the Catholic Higher Institute of Eastern Africa* 3.2 (1987) 61–74.
———. "African Symbols and Christian Liturgical Celebration." *Worship* 65.2 (1991) 98–112.
———. "The All-Africa Eucharistic Prayer: A Critique." *African Ecclesial Review* 21 (1979) 338–47.
———. "Bible and Christian Worship in Africa: African Christianity and Labor of Contextualization." *Chakana* 1.2 (2004) 7–32.
———. "The Birth and Development of a Local Church: Difficulties and Signs of Hope." *Concilium* 1 (1992) 17–23.

———. "Body and Belief: Explorations in Africa Ritology—the Magic of Body Language." *Jaarboek voor liturgie—onderzoek* 24 (2008) 199–218.

———. "Body and Memory in African Liturgy." *Concilium* 3 (1995) 71–78.

———. "Endless Worlds, Creative Memories: Indigenous (West) African Eschatologies Exploding the Future of Christianities." Unpublished Lecture delivered at the University of Geneva. 'Game Over'—Good or Bad News? Making Sense of Eschatology International Conference, October 22–24, 2015.

———. "Food and Drink in Africa and the Christian Eucharist: An Inquiry into the Use of African Symbols in the Eucharistic Celebration." *Bulletin of African Theology* 2.4 (1980) 171–87.

———. "Igbo Spirituality as Revealed through Igbo Prayers. *Cahiers Religions Africaines* 17.33/34 (1983) 155–72.

———. "The Imperative of Location in Developing Contextual Theological Method in Africa." Unpublished paper presented at the Catholic University of Eastern Africa, AMECEA, Faculty of Theology, International Colloquium, May 12–13, 2016.

———. "Inculturation and the Liturgy (Eucharist)." In *Paths to African Theology*, edited by Rosino Gibellini, 95–114. Maryknoll, NY: Orbis, 1994.

———. "Liturgy, Culture and the Postmodern World: Echoes from Africa." In *City Limits: Mission Issues in Postmodern Times*, edited by Joe Egan and Thomas Whelan, 160–83. Dublin: Milltown Institute of Theology and Philosophy, 2004.

———. "Missiology Today: The African Situation." In *Inculturation: A Nigerian Perspective*, edited by Elochukwu Eugene Uzukwu, 146–73. Enugu, Nigeria: Spiritan, 1988.

———. "Notes on Methodology for an African Theology." *African Ecclesial Review* 19 (1977) 155–64.

———. "Re-Evaluating God Talk from an African Perspective." In *Thinking the Divine in Interreligious Encounter*, edited by N. Hintersteiner and F. Bousquet, 55–71. Amsterdam: Rodopi, 2021.

———. "The Sacramental Imagination: African Appropriation of Catholicism before and after Vatican II." *Questions Liturgiques/Studies in Liturgy* 94 (2013) 299–329.

———. "Traditioning and the Emerging Shape of a Local Church: A Nigerian Example." In *The Shape of Tradition: Context and Normativity*, edited by Colby Dickinson, 215–30. Leuven: Peeters, 2013.

Uzukwu, Elochukwu, and Gerald Boodoo. "Globalization, Politics and Religion in Postcolonial Africa." *Bulletin of Ecumenical Theology* 25 (2013) 80–98.

Other Sources

Achebe, Chinua. *Morning Yet on Creation Day: Essays*. New York: Anchor, 1976.

Akpunonu, Peter. "The Universal Church and the Local Churches of Africa." In *Proceedings of the First Theology Week of the Catholic Institute of West Africa*, edited by Justin Ukpong et al., 27–36. Port Harcourt, Nigeria: CIWA, 1990.

Alberigo, Giuseppe, et al., eds. *The Reception of Vatican II*. Washington, DC: Catholic University of America Press, 1987.

Allen, John. *The Future Church: How Ten Trends Are Revolutionizing the Catholic Church*. New York: Image, 2009.

BIBLIOGRAPHY

Appiah-Kubi, Kofi, and Sergio Torres, eds. *African Theology en Route: Papers from the Pan African Conference of Third World Theologians, December 17-23, 1977, Accra, Ghana.* Maryknoll, NY: Orbis, 1979.

Aquinas, Thomas. *Summa Theologiae.* Translated by Laurence Shapcote. Edited by John Mortensen and Enrique Alarcón. Lander, WY: Aquinas Institute for the Study of Sacred Doctrine, 2012.

Arndt W. F., and Gingrich F. W. *A Greek English Lexicon of the Old Testament and Early Christian Literature.* 2nd ed. Chicago: University of Chicago Press, 1979.

Asouzu, Innocent. "The Heuristic Principle of African Ethics and the Ontological Objectivist Dichotomy." *West African Journal of Philosophical Studies* 1.1 (1998) 120-25.

Barfield, Thomas. *The Dictionary of Anthropology.* Oxford: Blackwell Publishers, 1990.

Barnard, Alan, et al., eds. *Encyclopedia of Social and Cultural Anthropology.* London: Routledge, 1998.

Bediako, Kwame. *Jesus and the Gospel in Africa: History and Experience.* Maryknoll, NY: Orbis, 2004.

Benedict XVI, Pope. *Holiness is Always in Season.* San Francisco: Ignatius, 2009.

Bevans, Stephen. *Models of Contextual Theology: Faith and Cultures.* Maryknoll, NY: Orbis, 1992.

Bevans, Stephen, and Jeffrey Gros. *Rediscovering Vatican II: Evangelization and Religious Freedom.* New York: Paulist, 2009.

Bisong, Kekong. "The Eucharistic Mystery: From Sign to Symbol." *Koinonia* 2.1 (2004) 137-54.

Bordeyne, Philippe, and Morrill Bruce, eds. *Sacraments: Revelation of the Humanity of God: Engaging the Fundamental Theology of Louis-Marie Chauvet.* Collegeville, MN: Liturgical, 2008.

Bosch, David. *Transforming Mission: Paradigm Shift in Theology of Mission.* Maryknoll, NY: Orbis, 1991.

Boyarin, David. *The Jewish Gospels: The Story of the Jewish Christ.* New York: New, 2012.

Buhlmann, Walbert. *The Coming of the Third Church: An Analysis of the Present and Future of the Church.* Maryknoll, NY: Orbis, 1976.

Bujo, Benezet. *African Theology in Its Social Context.* Maryknoll, NY: Orbis, 1992.

Catechism of the Catholic Church. 2nd ed. Rome: Libreria Editrice Vaticana, 1997.

Catholic Bishops' Conference of Nigeria. *Called to Love: Ethical Standards for Clergy and Seminarians in Nigeria.* Revised ed. Abuja, Nigeria: Catholic Secretariat of Nigeria, 2012.

———. *I Chose You: The Nigerian Priest in the Third Millennium.* Abuja, Nigeria: Catholic Secretariat of Nigeria, 2004.

———. *The Church in Nigeria: Family of God on Mission: Instrumentum Laboris for the First National Pastoral Congress.* Lagos, Nigeria: Catholic Secretariat of Nigeria, 2002.

———. *Formation and Collaboration in Communion: On Mutual Relations between Religious Institutes and Dioceses in Nigeria.* Abuja, Nigeria: Catholic Secretariat of Nigeria, 2009.

———. *Ratio Fundamentalis Institutionis Sacerdotalis.* Abuja, Nigeria: Catholic Secretariat of Nigeria, 2005.

———. *Salt of the Earth and Light of the World (Matthew 5:13-16): Manual of the Laity.* Abuja, Nigeria: Catholic Secretariat of Nigeria, 2009.

BIBLIOGRAPHY

Chapp, Carmina. *Encounter with the Triune God: An Introduction to the Theology of Edward Kilmartin*. San Francisco: Catholic Scholars, 1998.

Chauvet, Louis-Marie. *The Sacraments: The Word of God at the Mercy of the Body*. Collegeville, MN: Liturgical, 2001.

———. *Symbol and Sacrament: A Sacramental Reinterpretation of Christian Existence*. Translated by Patrick Madigan and Madeleine Beaumont. Collegeville, MN: Pueblo, 1995.

Chibuko, Patrick. "New Prefaces for the Liturgical Season of Advent." *African Ecclesial Review* 39.5/6 (1997) 320–33.

Chike, Chigor. "Proudly African, Proudly Christian: The Roots of Christologies in the African Worldview." *Bigard Times* 6.2 (2008) 221–40.

Childs, Brevard. *Memory and Tradition in Israel*. Naperville, IL: Allenson, 1962.

Chupungco, Anscar. *Cultural Adaptation of the Liturgy*. New York: Paulist, 1982.

Code of Canon Law. https://www.vatican.va/archive/cod-iuris-canonici/cic_index_en.html.

Congar, Yves. *I Believe in the Holy Spirit*. 3 vols. Translated by David Smith. New York: Crossroad, 1997.

———. *The Mystery of the Church*. Translated by A. V. Littledale. Baltimore: Helicon, 1960.

Congregation for the Divine Worship and the Discipline of the Sacraments. *The Roman Liturgy and Inculturation: Fourth Instruction for the Right Application of the Conciliar Constitution on the Liturgy*. Vatican City: Libreria Editrice Vaticana, 1994.

Conway, Pierre. *Metaphysics of Aquinas: A Summary of Aquinas' Exposition of Aristotle's Metaphysics*. Lanham, MD: University Press of America, 1996.

Crichton, J. D. "The Sacraments and Human Life." In *Sacraments: Readings in Contemporary Sacramental Theology*, edited by Michael Taylor. New York: Alba, 1981.

Crim, Keith, ed. *Abingdon Dictionary of Living Religions*. Nashville: Aubrey, 1981.

D' Costa, Gavin. "Extra Ecclesiam Nulla Salus Revisited: Religious Pluralism and Unbelief." In *Religious Pluralism and Unbelief*, edited by Ian Hamnette, 130–47. London: Routledge, 1990.

Dickson, Kwesi. *Theology in Africa*. Maryknoll, NY: Orbis, 1984.

Dogmatic Canons and Decrees: Authorized Translations of the Dogmatic Decrees of the Council of Trent, the Decree on the Immaculate Conception, the Syllabus of Pope Pius IX, and the Decrees of the Vatican Council. New York: Devin-Addair, 1912.

Donders, Joseph. *Non-Bourgeois Theology: An African Experience of Jesus*. Maryknoll, NY: Orbis, 1986.

Douglas, Mary. *Natural Symbols: Explorations in Cosmology*. London: Routledge, 2003.

Dufour-Leon, Xavier. *Dictionary of Biblical Theology*. Updated 2nd ed. Harrisburg, PA: Word Among Us, 1995.

Dulles, Avery. *Models of the Church*. New York: Image, 1987.

———. *The Priestly Office: A Theological Reflection*. New York: Paulist, 1997.

Echema, Austin. "Liturgy: A Teaching in Action." *Journal of Inculturation Theology* 5.2 (2003) 141–55.

Edwards, Paul, ed. *The Encyclopedia of Philosophy*. Vol. 5. New York: Macmillan, 1967.

Ela, Jean-Marc. *My Faith as an African*. London: Chapman, 1989.

Eliade, Mircea. *Rites and Symbols of Initiation*. New York: Harper Torchbooks, 1965.

———. *The Sacred and the Profane*. New York: Harcourt Brace, 1959.

Espin, Orlando, et al. *Futuring Our Past: Explorations in the Theology of Tradition.* Maryknoll, NY: Orbis, 2006.
Faggioli, Massimo. *Vatican II: The Battle for Meaning.* New York: Paulist, 2012.
———. "Reading the Signs of the Times through a Hermeneutics of Recognition: Gaudium et spes and Its meaning for a Learning Church." *Horizons* 43.2 (2016) 332–50.
Ferrara, Dennis. "In Persona Christi: Toward a Second Naivete." *Theological Studies* 57.1 (1996) 66–88.
———. "Representation or Self-Effacement? The Axiom in Person Christi in St. Thomas Aquinas and the Magisterium." *Theological Studies* 55.2 (1994) 195–224.
Fiorenza F. S, and J. P. Calvin, eds. *Systematic Theology: Roman Catholic Perspectives.* Minneapolis: Fortress, 1992.
Flannery, Austin. ed. *Vatican Council II: The Conciliar and Post Conciliar Documents.* New revised ed. Northport, NY: Castello, 1984.
Fourez, Gérard. *Sacraments and Passages: Celebrating the Tensions of Modern Life.* Notre Dame: Ave Maria, 1983.
Francis, Pope. *The Joy of the Gospel: Apostolic Exhortation: Evangelii Gaudium.* Vatican City: Libreria Editrice Vaticana, 2013.
Gachiri, Ephigenia. *Rite of Passage for Christian Boys.* Nairobi: Paulines Africa, 2006.
Gaillardetz, Richard. *Ecclesiology for a Global Church: A People Called and Sent.* Maryknoll, NY: Orbis, 2008.
Gaillardetz, Richard, and Catherine Clifford. *Keys to the Council: Unlocking the Teaching of Vatican II.* Collegeville, MN: Liturgical, 2002.
Gavin, F. *The Jewish Antecedents of the Christian Sacraments.* New York: Ktav, 1969.
Gennep, Arnold van. *The Rites of Passage.* Translated by Monika Vizedom. Chicago: University of Chicago Press, 1960.
Gibellini, Rosino, ed. *Paths to African Theology.* Maryknoll, NY: Orbis, 1994.
Gonzales, Justo. *The Story of Christianity, Volume 1: The Early Church to the Dawn of Reformation.* New York: HarperCollins, 2010.
Gorman, C. *The Book of Ceremony.* Cambridge: Whole Earth Tools, 1972.
Grainger, Roger. *Bridging the Gap: The Christian Sacraments and Human Belonging.* Brighton, Toronto: Sussex Academic, 2012.
———. "Sacraments as Passage Rites." *Worship* 58.3 (1984) 214–22.
Gray, Richard. *Christianity, the Papacy, and Mission in Africa.* Maryknoll, NY: Orbis, 2012.
Grenz, Stanley, and John Franke. *Beyond Foundationalism: Shaping Theology in a Postmodern Context.* Louisville: Westminster John Knox, 2001.
Grimes, Ronald. *Beginnings in Ritual Studies.* New York: University Press of America, 1982.
Guarino, Thomas. *Foundations of Systematic Theology.* New York: T&T Clark, 2005.
Haight, Roger. *Christian Community in History, Volume 1: Historical Ecclesiology.* New York: Continuum, 2004.
———. *Dynamics of Theology.* New York: Paulist, 1990.
Healey, Joseph, and Donald Sybertz. *Towards an African Narrative Theology.* Maryknoll, NY: Orbis, 2004.
Hearne, Brian. "Conciliar Fellowship and the Local Church: A Catholic View from Africa." *Ecumenical Review* 29.2 (1977) 129–40.
Hector, Kevin. *Theology without Metaphysics: God, Language, and the Spirit Reconciliation.* Cambridge: Cambridge University Press, 2011.

Heidegger, Martin. *On the Way to Language*. Translated by Peter D. Hertz. New York: Harper and Row, 1971.
Heijne, Camilla. *The Messenger of the Lord in Early Jewish Interpretations of Genesis*. Berlin: de Gruyter, 2010.
Hengel, Martin. *The Son of God: The Origin of Christology and the History of Jewish Hellenistic Religion*. Eugene, OR: Wipf & Stock, 2007.
Hickey, Raymond, ed. *Modern Missionary Documents and Africa: Issued by Popes and Synods*. Dublin: Domincan, 1982.
Hillman, Eugene. *Inculturation Applied: Toward an African Christianity*. New York: Paulist, 1993.
Hitchcock, James. *History of the Catholic Church: From the Apostolic Age to the Third Millennium*. San Francisco: Ignatius, 2012.
Horton, Robin. *Patterns of Thought in Africa and the West: Essays on Magic, Religion and Science*. Cambridge: Cambridge University Press, 1993.
Hurtado, Larry. *Lord Jesus Christ: Devotion to Jesus in Earliest Christianity*. Grand Rapids: Eerdmans, 2003.
Idowu, Bolaji. "Introduction." In *Biblical Revelation and African Beliefs*, edited by Kwesi A. Dickson and Paul Ellingworth, 9–16. London: Lutterworth, 1969.
Igwegbe, Isidore. "Exchange of Charity: A Critique of Self-Reliance Ecclesiology." *Nigerian Journal of Theology* 16 (2002) 43–58.
Irenaeus of Lyons. *On the Apostolic Preaching*. Translated by John Behr. Crestwood, NY: St. Vladimir's Seminary Press, 1997.
Isichei, Elizabeth. *A History of Christianity in Africa: From Antiquity to the Present*. Lawrenceville, NJ: Africa World, 1995.
Iwuchukwu, Marinus. *Media Ecology and Religious Pluralism: Engaging Walter Ong and Jacques Dupuis toward Effective Interreligious Dialogue*. Köln, Germany: Lambert Academic, 2010.
Jacob, Louis. *A Jewish Theology*. New York: Behrman, 1973.
Jenkins, Philip. *The New Faces of Christianity: Believing the Bible in the Global South*. Oxford: Oxford University Press, 2006.
Jeremias, Joachim. *The Eucharistic Words of Jesus*. Philadelphia: Trinity Press International, 1990.
John Paul II, Pope. "Address of John Paul II to the Bishops of Kenya." https://www.vatican.va/content/john-paul-ii/en/speeches/1980/may/documents/hf_jp-ii_spe_19800507_vescovi-kenya.html.
———. *The Apostolic Exhortation, Catechesi Tradendae*. http://w2.vatican.va/content/john-paul-ii/en/apost_exhortations/documents/hf_jp-ii_exh_16101979 9_catechesi-tradendae.html.
———. *Ecclesia in Africa*. https://www.vatican.va/content/john-paul-ii/en/apost_exhortations/documents/hf_jp-ii_exh_14091995_ecclesia-in-africa.html.
———. "Letter of the Holy Father Pope John Paul II to all the Bishops of the Church on the Mystery and Worship of the Eucharist: *Dominicae Cenae*." In *Letters to My Brother Priests*, edited by James Socias, 26–54. Chicago: Midwest Theological Forum, 1992.
———. "Celebration of the World Day of Peace 1 January 2001". https://www.vatican.va/content/john-paul-ii/en/messages/peace/documents/hf_jp-ii_mes_20001208_xxxiv-world-day-for-peace.html.

John, John St. "The Sacred Meal: The Roots of Christian Ritual." *Dialogue and Alliance* 6.3 (1992) 52–69.
Jurgens, William. *The Faith of the Early Father*. 3 vols. Collegeville, MN: Liturgical, 1979.
Jungmann, Joseph. *The Mass of the Roman Rite: Its Origins and Development*. Translated by Francis Brunner. Allen, TX: Christian Classics, 1949.
Justin Martyr. *Dialogue with Trypho*. Translated by Thomas Falls. Edited by Michael Slusser. Washington, DC: Catholic University of America Press, 2003.
Karkkainen, Matti-Vetti. *An Introduction to Ecclesiology: Ecumenical, Historical and Global Perspectives*. Downers Grove, IL: InterVarsity, 2002.
Keller, Catherine, et al., eds. *Postcolonial Theologies: Divinity and Empire*. St. Louis, MO: Chalice, 2004.
Kilmartin, Edward. *The Eucharist in the West: History and Theology*. Edited by Robert J. Daly. Collegeville, MN: Pueblo, 1998.
———. "Sacraments as Liturgy of the Church." *Theological Studies* 50.3 (1989) 527–47.
Kung, Hans. *Concile et Retour a L'unite*. Paris: Cerf, 1961.
———. *On Being a Christian*. New York: Image, 1968.
Lane, Dermot. "Theology in Transition." In *Catholic Theology Facing the Future: Historical Perspectives*, edited by Dermot Lane, 3–23. New York: Paulist, 2003.
Lonergan, Bernard. "Theology in Its New Context." In *A Second Collection*, edited by William F. J Ryan and Bernard Tyrrell, 55–68. Philadelphia: Westminster, 1975.
Lubac, Henri de. *History and Spirit: The Understanding of Scripture according to Origen*. Translated by Anne Englund Nash. San Francisco: Ignatius, 2007.
Lussier, Ernest. *The Eucharist: Bread of Life*. New York: Alba, 1977.
Luzebetak, Louis. *The Church and Cultures: New Perspectives in Missiological Anthropology*. Maryknoll, NY: Orbis, 1988.
Madathummuriyil, Sebastian. *Sacrament as Gift: A Pneumatological and Phenomenological Approach*. Leuven: Peeters, 2012.
Magesa, Laurenti. *African Religion: The Moral Traditions of Abundant Life*. Maryknoll, NY: Orbis, 1997.
———. *Anatomy of Inculturation: Transforming the Church in Africa*. Maryknoll, NY: Orbis, 2004.
Maldonado, Luis. "Liturgy as Communal Enterprise." In *The Reception of Vatican II*, edited by Giuseppe Alberigo et al., 309–21. Washington, DC: Catholic University of America Press, 1987.
Marion, Jean-Luc. *God without Being*. Translated by Thomas Carlson. Chicago: University of Chicago Press, 1991.
Martey, Emmanuel. *African Theology: Inculturation and Liberation*. Maryknoll, NY: Orbis, 1993.
Martos, Joseph. *Deconstructing Sacramental Theology and Reconstructing Catholic Ritual*. Eugene, OR: Resource, 2015.
———. *Doors to the Sacred: A Historical Introduction to the Sacraments in the Catholic Church*. Liguori, MI: Liguori, 2001.
Mbiti, John. *African Philosophy and Religions*. London: Heinemann, 1990.
McBrien, Richard. *Catholicism*. Study ed. San Francisco: Harper and Row, 1981.
McDonnell, Kilian, and George T. Montague. *Christian Initiation and Baptism in the Holy Spirit: Evidence from the First Eight Centuries*. Collegeville, MN: Liturgical, 1991.
McKenna, John. *The Eucharist and the Holy Spirit: The Eucharistic Epiclesis in 20th Century Theology*. London: SPCK, 1975.

McKeon, Richard, ed. *Introduction to Aristotle*. New York: Modern Library, 1947.
Metuh, Ikenga. *God and Man in African Religion: A Case Study of the Igbo of Nigeria*. Enugu, Nigeria: Snaap, 1999.
———. "Inculturating Christianity in African Worldviews." In *The Church in Africa and the Special African Synod*, edited by Justin Ukpong, 9–23. Port Harcourt, Nigeria: CIWA, 1993.
Mignolo, Walter. *Local Histories / Global Designs*. Princeton: Princeton University Press, 2008.
Monika, Hellwig. "Christian Eucharist in Relation to Jewish Worship." *Journal of Ecumenical Studies* 13.2 (1976) 322–28.
Mueller, J. J. *What Are They Saying about Theological Method?* New York: Paulist, 1984.
"Mustérion." http://biblehub.com/greek/3466.htm.
Ngugi, Thion'o. *Decolonizing the Mind: The Politics of Language in African Literature*. Portsmith, NH: Heinemann, 1986.
Njoku, Francis. *Essays in African Philosophy, Thought and Theology*. Enugu, Nigeria: Snaap, 1986.
Nwigwe, Boniface, and Christian Emedolu. *Emergent and Contentious Issues in African Philosophy: The Debate Revisited*. Port Harcourt, Nigeria: University of Port Harcourt Press, 2004.
Nwodo, Christopher. *Philosophical Perspectives on Chinua Achebe*. Port Harcourt, Nigeria: University of Port Harcourt Press, 2004.
Nyamiti, Charles. *Some Contemporary Models of African Ecclesiology: An Assessment in the Light of Biblical and Church Teaching*. Studies in African Christian Theology 3. Nairobi, Kenya: CUEA, 2007.
Okoh, I. E. *The Maintenance of Diocesan Priests: In the Light of the Code of Canon Law and the Norms of the Catholic Bishops' Conference of Nigeria*. Lagos, Nigeria: Mbeyi & Assoc., 1995.
O'Malley, John. *Tradition and Transition: Historical Perspectives on Vatican II*. Wilmington, DE: Glazier, 1988.
O'Malley, William. *Sacraments: Rites of Passage*. Allen, TX: More, 1995.
Odoemene, F. N. "African Worldview and the Understanding of the Holy Spirit." In *Proceedings of the Fourth Theology Week of the Catholic Institute of West Africa*, edited by Augustine Nebechukwu, 71–88. Port Harcourt, Nigeria: CIWA, 1993.
Odozor, Paulinus. *Morality Truly Christian, Truly African: Foundational, Methodological, and Theological Considerations*. Notre Dame: University of Notre Dame Press, 2014.
Olikenyi, Gregory. *African Hospitality: A Model for the Communication of the Gospel in the African Cultural Context*. Enugu, Nigeria: Snaap, 2001.
Onwubiko, Oliver. *The Church in Africa in the Light of Ecclesia in Africa*. Nairobi, Kenya: Pauline Africa, 2001.
Orobator, Agbonkhianmegbe. *Theology Brewed in an African Pot*. Maryknoll, NY: Orbis, 2008.
Osborne, Kenan. "Methodology and the Christian Sacraments." In *The Sacraments: Readings in Contemporary Sacramental Theology*, edited by Michael Taylor, 46–47. New York: Alba, 1981.
———. *Sacramental Theology: A Critical Introduction*. New York: Paulist, 1988.
———. *Sacramental Theology: 50 Years after Vatican II*. Cincinnati: Lectio, 2014.

BIBLIOGRAPHY

Osigwe, Emmanuel. "Ikwerre Rites of Passage and Sacraments of Initiation: A Framework for Inculturation in Port Harcourt Diocese of Nigeria." *International Journal of African Catholicism* 8.1 (2016) 72–89.

Paterson, James, and Edwin George MacNaughon. *The Approach to Latin: First Part*. Edinburgh: Oliver and Boyd, 1964.

Paul VI, Pope. "Africae Terrarum." *African Ecclesiastical Review* 10.1 (1968).

———. *Apostolic Exhortation on Evangelization in the Modern World: Evangelii Nuntiandi*. London: Catholic Truth Society, 1975.

———. *Apostolicam Actuositatem*. https://www.vatican.va/archive/hist_councils/ii_vatican_council/documents/vat-ii_decree_19651118_apostolicam-actuositatem_en.html

———. *Lumen Gentium*. https://www.vatican.va/archive/hist_councils/ii_vatican_council/documents/vat-ii_const_19641121_lumen-gentium_en.html.

———. *Nostra Aetate*. https://www.vatican.va/archive/hist_councils/ii_vatican_council/documents/vat-ii_decl_19651028_nostra-aetate_en.html.

———. *Presbyterorum Ordinis*. https://www.vatican.va/archive/hist_councils/ii_vatican_council/documents/vat-ii_decree_19651207_presbyterorum-ordinis_en.html.

———. *Sacrosanctum Concilium*. https://www.vatican.va/archive/hist_councils/ii_vatican_council/documents/vat-ii_const_19631204_sacrosanctum-concilium_en.html.

Pius XI, Pope. *Quas Primas*. https://www.vatican.va/content/pius-xi/en/encyclicals/documents/hf_p-xi_enc_11121925_quas-primas.html.

Power, David. *Sacraments: The Language of God's Giving*. New York: Crossroad, 1999.

———. "The Word in the Liturgy: Incarnating the Gospel in Cultures." In *Sacraments: Revelation of the Humanity of God: Engaging the Fundamental Theology of Louis-Marie Chauvet*, edited by Philippe Bordeyne and Bruce Morrill, 47–62. Collegeville, MN: Liturgical, 2008.

Rahner, Karl. *The Christian of the Future*. New York: Herder and Herder, 1967.

———. *The Church and the Sacraments*. New York: Herder and Herder, 1963.

———. *Inquiries*. New York: Herder and Herder, 1964.

———. *The Shape of the Church to Come*. Translated by Edward Quinn. New York: Seabury, 1974.

Rahner, Karl, and William Dych. *Foundations of Christian Faith: An Introduction to the Idea of Christianity*. New York: Seabury, 1978.

Rasing, Thera. *Passing on the Rites of Passage: Girls Initiation Rites in the Context of an Urban Roman Catholic Community on the Zambian Copperbelt*. African Studies Center Research Series 6. Amsterdam: African Studies Centre, 1995.

Ratzinger, Joseph. *Called to Communion: Understanding the Church Today*. Translated by Adrian Walker. San Francisco: Ignatius, 1991.

———. *Introduction to Christianity*. Translated by J. R. Foster. San Francisco: Ignatius, 1990.

Ratzinger, Joseph, and Vittorio Messori. *The Ratzinger Report: An Exclusive Interview on the State of the Church*. Translated by Salvator Attanasio and Graham Harrison. San Francisco: Ignatius, 1986.

Rausch, Thomas. *Towards a Truly Catholic Church: An Ecclesiology for the Third Millennium*. Collegeville, MN: Liturgical, 2005.

The Rites of the Catholic Church. New York: Pueblo, 1976.

Rites of Christian Initiation of Adults. Strathfield, NSW: St. Paul's, 2003.

Rordorf, Willy, et al. *The Eucharist of the Early Church*. Translated by Matthew J. O'Connell. New York: Pueblo, 1978.
Schillebeeckx, Edward. *Christ the Sacrament of Encounter with God*. New York: Sheed & Ward, 1963.
———. *The Church with a Human Face: A New and Expanded Theology of Ministry*. London: SCM, 1985.
Schreiter, Robert. *Constructing Local Theologies*. Maryknoll, NY: Orbis, 1985.
———. *The New Catholicity: Theology between the Global and the Local*. Maryknoll, NY: Orbis, 1997.
Second Vatican Council. *Ad Gentes*. https://www.vatican.va/archive/hist_councils/ii_vatican_council/documents/vat-ii_decree_19651207_ad-gentes_en.html.
———. *Unitatis Redintegratio*. https://www.vatican.va/archive/hist_councils/ii_vatican_council/documents/vat-ii_decree_19641121_unitatis-redintegratio_en.html.
Sedmak, Clemens. *Doing Local Theology: A Guide for Artisans of New Humanity*. Maryknoll, NY: Orbis, 2002.
Segundo, Juan. *The Liberation of Theology*. Eugene, OR: Wipf & Stock, 2002.
Shorter, Aylward. *African Christian Spirituality*. London: Chapman, 1978.
———. "Liturgical Creativity in East Africa." *Afer* 19 (1977) 258–67.
Sluga, Hans et al., eds. *The Cambridge Companion to Wittgenstein*. Cambridge: Cambridge University Press, 2007.
Smith, Linda. *Decolonizing Methodologies: Research and Indigenous Peoples*. London: Zed, 1999.
Sobrino, Jon. *A True Church for the Poor*. Maryknoll, NY: Orbis, 1985.
Sommer, Benjamin. *Bodies of God and the World of Ancient Israel*. Cambridge: Cambridge University Press, 2009.
Sugirtharajah, R. S. *Postcolonial Reconfigurations: An Alternative Way of Reading the Bible and Doing Theology*. St. Louis, MO: Chalice, 2003.
Terrien, Samuel. *The Elusive Presence: Toward a New Biblical Theology*. Eugene, OR: Wipf & Stock, 2000.
Theisen, Jerome. *The Ultimate Church and the Promise of Salvation*. Collegeville, MN: St. John's University Press, 1976.
Thiel, John. *Senses of Tradition: Continuity and Development in Catholic Faith*. Oxford: Oxford University Press, 2000.
Tilley, Terrence. *Inventing Catholic Tradition*. Maryknoll, NY: Orbis, 2001.
Torres, Sergio, and Fabella Virginia, eds. *The Emergent Gospel: Theology from the Underside of History*. Maryknoll, NY: Orbis, 1976.
Tracy, David. *Blessed Rage for Order: The New Pluralism in Theology*. New York: Seabury, 1975.
Turner, Victor. *Dramas, Fields and Metaphors: Symbolic Action in Human Society*. Ithaca: Cornell University Press, 1974.
———. *The Drums of Affliction: A Study of Religious Processes among the Ndembu of Zambia*. Oxford: Clarendon, 1968.
———. "Liminality and Communitas." In *Readings in Ritual Studies*, edited by Ronald L. Grimes, 358–74. Upper Saddle River, NJ: Prentice Hall, 1996.
———. *The Ritual Process: Structure and Anti-Structure*. Chicago: Aldine, 1969.
Vanderwilt, Jeffrey. "Rites of Passage: Ludic Recombination and the Formation of Ecclesial Being." *Worship* 66.5 (1992) 398–416.

Vorgrimler, Herbert. *Sacramental Theology*. Translated by Linda Maloney. Collegeville, MN: Liturgical, 1992.

———. *Understanding Karl Rahner: An Introduction to His Life and Thought*. New York: Crossroad, 1986.

Wangbu, John. *Laity in Nigeria: Post Vatican II Experience*. Enugu, Nigeria: Snaap, 2013.

White, James. *Introduction to Christian Worship*. 3rd ed. Nashville: Abingdon, 2000.

———. *Roman Catholic Worship: Trent to Today*. New York: Paulist, 1995.

Wickeri, Philip. "Mission from the Margins: The Missio Dei in the Crisis of World Christianity." *International Review of Mission* 93.369 (2004) 182–98.

Wicks, Jared. "Sacraments: A Catechism for Today." In *The Sacraments: Readings in Contemporary Sacramental Theology*, edited by Michael Taylor, 19–30. New York: Alba, 1981.

Wittgenstein, Ludwig. *Philosophical Investigations*. Translated by G. E. M Ascombe. Malden: Blackwell, 2001.

———. *Tractatus Logico-Philosophicus*. Translated by C. K. Ogden. New York: Routledge, 2005.

Worgul, George. *From Magic to Metaphor: A Validation of Christian Sacraments*. New York: Paulist, 1980.

Wright, Ernest. *Biblical Archeology*. Philadelphia: Westminster, 1960.

Zizioulas, John. *Being as Communion: Studies in Personhood and the Church*. Crestwood, NY: St. Vladimir's Seminary Press, 1985.

Index

Aaron, 21n41
Abraham, 18n33, 24n54, 65, 156n114, 157
Achebe, Chinua, 154, 154nn104–5, 173
Akpunonu, Peter, 75n56
Allen, John, 87n99
Anozie, Ifeanyi, 60, 187
Appiah-Kubi, Kofi, 158n121
Aquinas, Thomas, 27, 28n66, 34n80, 42, 42n108, 45, 49n5, 63n15, 113, 113n63, 162
Arinze, 190
Aristotle, 27, 27n63, 28, 28n64, 32, 52, 54
Arndt, W. F., 20n37, 155n109
Asouzu, Boniface, 185
Asouzu, Innocent, 63n14
Augustine of Hippo, 14, 14n13, 25, 26, 26nn59–60, 53, 63, 67, 113, 132, 162

Barfield, Thomas, 50n9
Barnard, Alan, 50n9
Bediako, Kwame, 9, 9n27, 180, 181n3
Pope Benedict XV, 71
Pope Benedict XVI, 24n51, 38. *See also* Ratzinger, Joseph
Bevans, Stephen, 71nn40–41, 85, 85n, 86nn95–96, 87n97, 178

Bisong, Kedong, 14n15
Bonaventure, 112
Boodoo, Gerald, 79n73, 200
Bosch, David, 70n38
Boyarin, Daniel, 16, 16nn19–22
Buhlmann, Walbert, 5n13
Bujo, Benezet, 148, 149n87

Cadiou, Rene, 152, 152n97
Calvin, J. P., 151n93
Chapp, Carmina, 109n46
Chauvet, Louis-Marie, 52n19, 53, 53n25, 53nn27–28, 54, 54n30, 55n33, 56, 56n38, 121, 121nn86–87, 127, 127n17, 128n18, 175
Chibuko, Patrick, 104, 104n37
Chike, Chigor, 63n13
Childs, Brevard, 127nn15–16, 128–29, 128n20, 129n21
Christ. *See* Jesus Christ
Chrysostom. *See* John Chrysostom
Chupungco, Anscar, 145n73
Clifford, Catherine, 67, 67nn30–31, 119n81, 124n1, 124n3
Congar, Yves, 65, 65nn21–22, 66n26, 144, 144n67, 155, 155n107
Conway, Pierre, 28, 28n65
Crichton, J. D., 48n1, 51n15

INDEX

Crim, Keith, 50n9
Cyprian, Saint, 5n11, 67, 77, 141
Cyril, Saint, 24n51

D'Costa, Gavin, 5n11
Descartes, Rene, 84n91, 190
Dickson, Kwesi, 111, 111n54, 149, 149n90
Dix, Gregory, 60, 187
Donders, Joseph, 90, 90n110
Douglas, Mary, 120n83
Dufour-Leon, Xavier, 155n109
Dulles, Avery, 34n80, 143, 143n64, 144n66
Dych, William, 39n97

Echema, Austin, 126n7, 126, 126n9, 129
Edwards, Paul, 52nn21–22
Ela, Jean Marc, 149, 149nn88–89
Eliade, Mircea, 51, 51n17, 102n27
Elijah, 89n106, 90
Emedolu, Christian, 133n37
Enoch, 17n24
Enochic-Metatron, 17
Eri, 106
Espin, Orlando, 97n4
Eze Nri, 107
Ezeanya, Stephen, 191

Fabella, Virginia, 180n2
Faggioli, Massimo, 34n81, 174, 174n2
Farley, Michael, 151n93
Ferrara, Dennis, 34n80, 110n49
Fiorenza, F. S., 151n93
Flannery, Austin, 11n1, 103n31
Fourez, Gérard, 48, 48nn2–3
Francis, Pope, 87, 87n100, 145, 145n72, 166, 166n149
Franke, John, 43nn109–111

Gailladertz, Richard, 4n7, 67, 67n27, 67nn30–31, 68n34, 69n35, 108, 119n81, 124n1, 124n3
Gavin, F., 16n18
Gennep, Arnold van, 50, 50n9, 50nn10–13, 99, 99n10, 103
George, Professor, 199

Gibellini, Rosino, 165n148
Gingrich, F. W., 20n37, 155n109
Gonzalez, Justo, 23n50
Gorman, Clem, 99, 99n11
Grainger, Roger, 52, 52n18, 101–2, 101n22, 101n25, 102n26, 103n30
Gray, Richard, 3n5, 70n37
Grenz, Stanley, 43nn109–11
Gros, Jeffrey, 71nn40–41
Guarino, Thomas, 27, 27n62, 30, 30n72, 37n89

Haight, Roger, 66, 66n24, 80n71, 81n74, 82n81
Hamori, 157
Hastings, Adrian, 196
Healey, Joseph, 131n30
Hearne, Brian, 76, 76n58
Hector, Kevin, 52n24
Heidegger, Martin, 43, 45, 46, 52n20, 53, 54, 54n29
Heijne, Camilla, 157, 157nn116–17, 158n118
Hengel, Martin, 16–17, 17nn23–28
Hillman, Eugene, 148n85
Hippolytus, 187
Hitchcock, James, 9, 9n26, 23n50
Hollervard, Tipot, 199, 200
Horton, Robin, 63n12
Hugo of Saint Victor, 112, 113n62
Hurtardo, Larry, 17, 18, 18n30, 18n32

Idowu, Bolaji, 2n1
Ignatius of Antioch, 23n49, 25, 25n57, 67, 68n32
Igwegbe, Isidore, 141n59
Irenaeus of Lyons, 23n49, 24, 24n54, 25n56
Isichei, Elizabeth, 4, 4n9
Iwuchukwu, Marinus, 71n40, 183

Jacob, 18n33, 21n41, 24n54, 157
Jacob, Louis, 17n29, 18n31
Jenkins, Philip, 4, 159, 159n124
Jeremiah, 21n39
Jeremias, Joachim, 20, 20n38, 21, 21n39, 21n40, 116, 116n73

INDEX

Jesus Christ, 1, 2, 16–19, 21–25, 21n39, 28–29, 31–32, 33n80, 35–39, 35n82, 37n90, 39n97, 42, 65–66, 68, 73, 77, 82, 91, 93, 94, 101, 102n27, 109–10, 112, 116, 119, 119n81, 120, 122, 124, 127, 129n24, 130, 134, 138, 140, 143, 145, 148, 150, 156, 158, 161–65, 166n148, 169, 175
Jethro, 21n41
John, John St., 16n18
John Chrysostom, 14, 14n14, 67
John Paul II, Pope, 2n4, 6, 6n16, 7, 7n20, 8, 9, 33n80, 74, 74n49, 87, 129n24, 130n23, 145n74, 148n85, 158n119
John XXIII, Pope, 71, 71n39
Jurgens, William, 26n59, 68n32, 153n99
Justin Martyr, 24, 24nn52–53
Juwer, Joann, 189

Kant, Immanuel, 43, 190
Karbitha, 197
Karkkainen, Veli-Matti, 144, 144n68
Keller, Catherine, 64, 64n19
Kilmartin, Edward, 25n58, 32, 32nn78–79, 33n80, 45, 45nn114–15, 109, 110n50
Kung, Hans, 106n38, 145, 145n71

Laban, 21n41
Lane, Dermot, 84–85, 84n91, 85n92
Lash, Nicholas, 69–70
Lombard, Peter, 29
Lonergan, Bernard, 80, 80n72, 82n80
Lubac, Henri de, 152n96, 152n97
Lussier, Ernest, 21, 21n42
Luther, Martin, 32
Luzebetak, Louis, 143, 143n65

MacNaughton, Edwin George, 49n7
Macquarrie, 82n80
Madathumuriyil. Sebastian, 130, 130nn26–28, 163, 163nn141–142
Magesa, Laurenti, 6, 6n17, 111–12, 111n53, 150, 150n91, 167n151
Maldonado, Luis, 124n5, 133, 133n39

Malula, Joseph, Cardinal, 191, 192, 195, 196
Marion, Jean-Luc, 56, 56nn36–37, 102, 175
Martey, Emmanuel, 131nn31–32
Martos, Joseph, 13, 13nn4–8, 14n14, 14n16, 15n17, 24n55, 26nn60–61, 137, 137nn50–51
Mary (Virgin Mary), 129n24, 144
Mbiti, John, 63n16, 136
McBrien, Richard, 39, 39n100
McDonnell, Kilian, 67nn28–29
McKenna, John, 161–62, 161n136, 162nn137–38
Mckeon, Richard, 28n64
Meland, 82n80
Messori, Vittorio, 84nn88–90
Metatron, 17n24
Saint Methodius, 24n51
Metuh, Ikenga, 4, 4n8, 133, 133n38, 190
Mignolo, Walter, 5n12
Mitloshazzi, Professor, 188
Monika, Hellwig, 16n18, 22, 22n45
Montague, George T., 67nn28–29
Moses, 18n33, 22n47, 24n54, 65
Mueller, J. J., 82nn80–81
Mulago, Sese, 191
Mulago, Vincent, 191
Mumba, Patrick, 196
Mushete, Ngindu, 191

Njoku, Francis, 147, 148nn80–81
Nwanegbo, Monsignor, 196
Nwigwe, Boniface, 134n37
Nwodo, Christopher, 154, 154n103
Nyamiti, Charles, 80n70, 143, 143n62, 148, 148n85, 148n86

Obiefuna, Albert, 186, 190
Odoemene, F. N., 155n108
Odozor, Paulinus, 2nn2–3, 7, 7n19
Ogwu, 198
Okoh, I. E., 141–42, 142n60
Okolo, Banabas, 189
Olikenyi, Gregory, 6n15, 147, 147nn82–83, 148n84

INDEX

O'Malley, William, 55, 55nn31–32, 55nn34–35, 115nn68–70, 116nn71–72
Onwubiko, Oliver, 167n151
Origen of Alexandria, 151, 152, 153, 153n99, 154, 164
Orobator, Agbonkhianmeghe, 146, 146n75
Osborne, Kenan, 35nn83–84, 37, 37n93, 38n94, 40, 40n101
Osigwe, Emmanuel, 100n18, 182–201

Paterson, James, 49n7
Paul, 18, 69, 75, 102n27, 119n81, 121, 145, 160n129, 164
Paul VI, Pope, 1, 2n4, 7, 7n20, 8, 9, 87, 122, 131, 131n30
Peter, 69, 77
Pius XI, Pope, 71, 129, 129n22
Pius XII, Pope, 124n4
Plato, 52, 52nn21–22
Plotinus, 63
Power, David, 99n9, 111nn56–58, 113n62, 118, 118nn76–77, 120, 120nn82–84, 174, 174n3

Rahner, Karl, 29, 29n69, 31n73, 35, 38, 38n96, 39, 39nn97–99, 77, 77n62, 82n80, 177, 201
Rasing, Thera, 49n6
Ratzinger, Joseph, 19n33, 21, 21n39, 22, 22n44, 22n47, 23, 23n48, 71. *See also* Pope Benedict XVI
Rausch, Thomas, 65n23, 66, 66n23, 66n25, 87n98
Rordorf, Willy, 16n18, 25n56, 25n57, 68n32

Bishop Sarpong, 191
Saul (Paul), 56
Schillebeeckx, Edward, 33n80, 35, 36, 36nn86–88, 37n91, 82n80
Schreiter, Robert, 86n95, 159n125, 179n1
Sedmak, Clemens, 73, 73n47, 74n51
Segundo, Juan, 176, 176nn6–8
Semmelroth, Otto, 35
Shorter, Aylward, 6n18

Sluga, Hans, 53n26
Smith, Linda, 159n122
Sobrino, Jon, 82n80, 83, 83n82
Sommer, Benjamin, 88nn101–4, 156–57, 156nn111–13, 157n113
Soyinka, Wole, 173
Sugirtharajah, R. S., 158n122, 159n122
Sybertz, Donald, 131n30

Terrien, Samuel, 19, 19nn34–35
Tertullian, 13, 16n18, 67, 67n28
Theisen, Jerome, 5n11
Theresa of Avila, 195
Thiel, John, 103, 103n32, 177n9
Thion'o, 161n128
Thomas (Apostle), 68
Tilley, Terrence, 103, 103n33, 104n34
Tillich, Paul, 82n80, 83, 176, 200
Torres, Sergio, 158n121, 180n2
Tracy, David, 82n80, 97n5
Turner, Victor, 49, 49n8, 99, 100, 100nn15–17, 100nn19–20

Ukpong, Justin, 165n148
Uzukwu, Elochukwu, 2–3, 3n6, 4n8, 7–9, 8nn21–22, 9n25, 16n18, 35, 47, 51, 51n16, 56–57, 56n39, 58–61, 58n1, 59nn2–6, 62, 63n17, 64, 64n18, 64n20, 68n33, 72, 74, 74n50, 77, 77n63, 78, 78n64, 79, 79nn65–69, 80–84, 80n73, 81n75, 82nn76–79, 83n83, 84nn84–87, 87–91, 89n108, 90n109, 90n111, 91nn112–13, 92–93, 92nn114–16, 93nn117–118, 93n120, 95, 98, 101–3, 101nn23–24, 103n29, 104–10, 104n35, 105n39, 106n40, 107nn41–44, 108n45, 109nn47–48, 110nn51–52, 111n55, 112nn59–61, 113n65, 114–19, 114nn66–67, 116n74, 117n75, 118n78, 119n79, 121–22, 123, 125, 126, 126n11, 129, 129n23, 131–34, 132nn33–34, 134nn40–41, 135nn42–43, 135nn45–46, 136–44, 136n47, 137nn48–49, 138nn53–54, 139n55, 145–47,

218

INDEX

146nn77–79, 150–56, 151nn94–95, 152n98, 153nn100–102, 154n106, 156n110, 158–60, 158n120, 159n123, 160n126, 164–67, 164nn142–44, 165nn145–47, 166n150, 168–77, 176n5, 178–80, 182–201

Vanderwilt, Jeffrey, 99nn12–13
Vorgrimler, Herbert, 12–13, 12n2, 13n3, 14nn11–12, 21n43, 28n67, 29n68, 31n74, 126n10, 127, 127n14, 177, 177n10

Waliggo, John, 148
Wangbu, John, 150, 150n92
White, James, 18n33, 20n36, 22, 22n46, 69n36
Wickeri, Philip, 4n10
Wicks, Jared, 50n14
Wittgenstein, Ludwig, 43–44, 44nn112–13, 52, 52n23
Worgul, George, 41nn103–4, 41n106, 49n4, 96, 96n3
Wright, Ernest, 89n105, 89n107

Zizioulas, John, 108, 132, 132nn35–36, 142, 142n61

www.ingramcontent.com/pod-product-compliance
Lightning Source LLC
Chambersburg PA
CBHW051641230426
43669CB00013B/2389